D0301490

Taking Archaeology out of Heritage

Taking Archaeology out of Heritage

Edited by

Emma Waterton and Laurajane Smith

CAMBRIDGE
SCHOLARS
PUBLISHING

Taking Archaeology out of Heritage, Edited by Emma Waterton and Laurajane Smith

This book first published 2009

Cambridge Scholars Publishing

12 Back Chapman Street, Newcastle upon Tyne, NE6 2XX, UK

British Library Cataloguing in Publication Data
A catalogue record for this book is available from the British Library

ISBN (10): 1-4438-1442-3, ISBN (13): 978-1-4438-1442-3

CONTENTS

LIST OF ILLUSTRATIONS

LIST OF ABBREVIATIONS

AHD	Authorized Heritage Discourse
AKI	Archaeological Knowledge Inventory
ALGAO	Association of Local Government Archaeological Officers UK
ASB	Accounting Standards Board
BBO	Bodemarchief in Behoud en Ontwikkeling
CAC	Central Archaeological Council, Greece
CBA	Council for British Archaeology
CCGG	Cawood Castle Garth Group
CIDOC	ICOM's International Committee for Documentation
CP	Conservation Plan
CRM	Cultural Resource Management
DCLG	Department for Communities and Local Government, United Kingdom
DCMS	Department for Culture, Media and Sport, United Kingdom
DIVA	Documentaire Informatievoorziening en Archief
GEM	Group for Education in Museums
GOY and H	Government Office of Yorkshire and the Humber, United Kingdom
HEEP	Historic Environment Enabling Programme
HER	Historic Environment Record
HLF	Heritage Lottery Fund, United Kingdom
HMSO	Her Majesty's Stationery Office
HSC	Historic Seascape Characterization
ICOM	International Council of Museums
ICOMOS	International Council on Monuments and Sites
IfA	Institute for Archaeologists, United Kingdom
IHBC	Institute for Historic Building Conservation, United Kingdom
LDCS	Learning Direct Classification System
LHI	Local Heritage Initiative
MAP2	Management of Archaeological Projects
MoRPHE	Management of Research Projects in the Historic Environment

NCM	National Contact Monument
NMR	National Monuments Record
NVM	Nederlandse Museum Vereniging
PoP	Power of Place
QAA	Quality Assurance Agency UK
QCA	Qualifications and Curriculum Authority
RAE	Research Assessment Exercise
RACM	Rijksdienst voor Archeologie Cultuurlandschap en Monumenten
RCAHMS	Royal Commission on the Ancient and Historical Monuments of Scotland
RCAHMW	Royal Commission on the Ancient and Historical Monuments of Wales
RCHME	Royal Commission on the Historic Monuments of England
SMR	Scheduled Monuments Record
SNA	Stichting Nederlandse Archeologie
STOP	Stop Taking our Past
TAG	Theoretical Archaeology Group
UNESCO	United Nations Educational, Scientific and Cultural Organization
YAF	York Archaeological Forum

CHAPTER ONE

INTRODUCTION:
HERITAGE AND ARCHAEOLOGY

LAURAJANE SMITH AND EMMA WATERTON

The impetus behind this volume emerged from a session organized at the Theoretical Archaeological Group (TAG) Conference hosted by the University of York in 2007. The aims of the session, and subsequently this volume, were to examine the conflation of heritage with archaeology and ask whether archaeology could usefully contribute to critical understandings of heritage. Any critical understanding of heritage, we suggested, must consider heritage both in terms of what it *is* and the cultural, social and political work it *does* in contemporary societies. Our rationale for proposing such a session arose from the observation that archaeology has, on the whole, tended to dominate the development of public policies and practices applicable to what is often referred to as "heritage", but what some might also call "the historic environment" or "cultural resources", amongst other terms. As a consequence, archaeologists have been very successful in protecting what they perceive to be their database—a success that owes much to the development and maintenance of a suite of heritage management practices that work to legitimize their privileged access to, and control of, that database. However, is archaeological data actually heritage? Moreover, does archaeological knowledge offer a meaningful reflection of "the historic environment", in terms of the uses, values and associations it carries for the various and different communities or publics that engage with that environment/heritage?

In examining the historically complicated relationship between archaeological knowledge and heritage, and the bearing this has on how heritage is understood and managed in the present, this volume aims to explore a range of issues, including:

I. the current theoretical limitations of archaeology knowledge about heritage;

II. the reasons for these limitations;
III. the ways in which archaeological theory and practice work to exclude
or include other forms of knowledge and experiences centred on heritage;
and,
IV. theorizations of heritage that aim to extend our understanding of
heritage beyond the purely "archaeological".

At the crux of these issues lies the pricklier question of whether or not
archaeology and heritage are the same thing. Our contention is that they
are not, although they are often argued to be; the debates that arose around
this question during the TAG session proved to be something of a catalyst
and are explored in more depth here. Some of the contributors to this
volume, notably Kenny and Newman, have argued that they are, indeed,
the same. In response, we contend that this conflation tends to maintain the
legitimacy of archaeological knowledge and values, affording them a
position from which to identify and define what is or is not "heritage",
thus ensuring archaeological employment in the heritage sector. So much
is gained by archaeology in this relationship that it becomes difficult for
the collective discipline to mull over and accept the many different notions
and definitions of heritage that sit outside of archaeological frameworks.
We thereby suggested to the contributors of this volume that a useful
theoretical exercise would be to "take archaeology out" of definitions of
heritage so as to see not only what is left, but to consider what possibilities
might be revealed if a concern for materiality was deemphasized.

    This was not a purely abstract exercise. Indeed, it was one we believed
to be particularly important given the quantity and nature of the challenges
currently confronting material-based definitions of heritage favoured by
archaeologists. This is witnessed, for example, by the adoption of the
Convention for the Safeguarding of Intangible Cultural Heritage in 2003
by UNESCO as a response to non-Western lobbing against the World
Heritage Convention (and it's associated World Heritage List), which was
seen as unrepresentative of the concept of "heritage" (Munjeri 2004;
Aikawa-Faure 2009; Skounti 2009). To combat these criticisms, UNESCO
adopted the notion of "intangible cultural heritage", a concept that is
starting to influence Western heritage debates and practices. Material-
based notions of heritage have also been challenged by increasing public
assertions of community ideas of history and heritage. Explicit agitation
has come from Indigenous communities (see for instance Langford 1983;
Falch and Skandfer 2004; chapters in Smith and Wobst 2005; Beach 2007),
who have not only questioned the legitimacy of archaeological knowledge
in studying and controlling their past and heritage, but also the rights of
archaeologists to assume that they could in the first place. Implicit, but no

less powerful, challenges have also emerged from community groups in Europe, who assert their own sense of heritage, along with the links to community identity and well-being they draw from it, which simply extend or disregard archaeological definitions (see for instance Dicks 2000; Graham et al. 2000; Jones 2004; Riley and Harvey 2005; McClanahan 2007; Waterton 2008; Smith and Waterton 2009). As these challenges combine with the growing recognition of the dissonant and contested nature of heritage (Tunbridge and Ashworth 1996; Graham et al. 2000), comfortable and unproblematised archaeological definitions are no longer tenable or useful.

Our challenge to "take archaeology out of heritage" was met with a range of papers. To supplement these papers, which predominantly draw from academics or practitioners working within the heritage sector, we sought out community representatives and activists, asking them a series of questions that revolved around their own thoughts and experiences in working with archaeologists in collaborative archaeology and/or heritage projects. The views of four people are contained within three interviews interspersed between the more formally structured chapters.

For a topic so broad in scope, background and experience, structuring the contributions to this volume was no easy task. As such, the ten papers included here have been loosely grouped by theme and divided into three parts. Part I collects together those papers attempting to re-negotiate the meaning of heritage, Part II is themed around the limits of archaeology and Part III presents arguments for a continued and deliberate conflation of archaeology with heritage. The volume begins with our own chapter (Chapter Two), which sets out the arguments underpinning our call for "taking archaeology out of heritage", whilst also offering some new ways of examining and considering heritage. The position we take is no different to that alluded to in this Introduction, and argues that archaeological definitions of heritage are limited and highly self-referential. Through the course of the chapter, we build a case for greater engagement by archaeologists with the extensive and interdisciplinary literature that now exists under the rubric of "heritage studies". Unless archaeologists connect with this literature—and with what communities and other groups are doing with their heritage—they will be left behind, or left out of, the theoretical and policy developments that are happening within the heritage sector. These arguments are continued and developed in the chapters offered by Steve Watson (Chapter Three) and Kalliopi Fouseki (Chapter Four), who explore the possibilities and realities of heritage outside of archaeological definitions. Watson investigates the varied ways in which heritage and archaeology are visually negotiated and expressed, skilfully illustrating his argument that the two necessarily have different modalities and objectives with reference to Yearving Bell, an Iron Age fort in Northumberland, and the emerging tourism industry on the island of Rhodes. Adding to the Greek focus, Fouseki explores the concrete conflation of heritage and archaeology in Greek public policy, identifying the consequences this has had both for the discipline and for expressions of national identity.

The chapters in Part II explore both the limitations and possibilities of archaeology and its relationship with heritage. Ross Wilson (Chapter Five) explores the interrelationship of archaeology, collective memory and public consumption in relation to the Great War and its memorialisation in the United Kingdom. In Chapter Six, Keith Emerick maps the boundaries of both archaeology and heritage as they play out in community projects, using as an example the experiences of the Cawood Castle Garth Group in Cawood, North Yorkshire. For his part, Don Henson (Chapter Seven) interrogates the idea of archaeology, asking, in particular, what archaeology has become as a subject of enquiry. In doing so, he illustrates the ways in which concepts of "the past", archaeology and "heritage" have become intertwined. In the final paper of this section, Marjolijn Kok (Chapter Eight) outlines what appears to be a standard community archaeological endeavour in the Netherlands, but reveals the difficulties and tensions that arose when archaeologists assumed their sense of heritage was universal. In this case, archaeologists were placed in a difficult political position through their assumptions about the agendas, expectations and understandings of the values of the past held by all parties in the project. Consequently, Kok advocates the advisability of open and critical dialogue. What collectively emerges from the chapters in Part II is a sense that archaeology *does* have an ongoing and important relationship with aspects of heritage, but this is limited by two issues. The first is that although archaeological sites, artefacts and even knowledge may be heritage, not *all* heritage is archaeological, nor is it subject to archaeological frameworks. Second, archaeology's relationship with heritage inevitably thrusts archaeological knowledge into play with a range of complex social and cultural issues—whether that is the memories of the Great War and their cultural consequences, the aspirations of community groups in Cawood, or the agendas of social integration versus social diversity in the Netherlands.

The chapters in Part III are united by their response to our deliberately provocative challenge, which is underpinned by their belief in the legitimacy and necessity of archaeological involvement in heritage. "Take archaeology out of heritage? Why would archaeology want to leave?" asks

Martin Newman (Chapter Nine, page 83), who makes a passionate and considered plea for maintaining archaeological input into heritage management practices and policies. He notes how much archaeology has gained as a consequences of its ability to align itself with heritage—a point we cannot dispute!—and while we would acknowledge that archaeology has indeed gained, it has done so at the cost of recognizing the legitimacy of other perceptions of heritage. Consequently, this has, we argue, stifled intellectual growth within the discipline (see also Smith 2004). John Carman (Chapter Ten) develops a measured argument about the utility of archaeological notions of materiality. While acknowledging other forms of heritage, he notes that most Western concepts of heritage *are* places, sites and artefacts and as such, an understanding of their materiality is vital. The final paper (Chapter Eleven), by Jonathan Kenny, draws upon practitioner experience of an archaeologist working closely with a range of community groups around Yorkshire and outlines various models of archaeological work with communities that, he suggests, illustrate the interrelationship of archaeology and heritage. Collectively, these papers provide a strong thread of dissonance that reacts against our general call for papers, demonstrating the complexity of the issues at hand and challenging us to continue pushing for both a definition and practice that "takes archaeology out of heritage".

It would be disingenuous of us to pretend that we, as editors, are editorially neutral about the papers presented in Part III. The arguments we set out in Chapter Two must indicate that we are fundamentally and irrevocably in disagreement with them, and some more than others. Indeed, we would suggest that the papers by Kenny and Newman in particular actually illustrate some of the points we make in Chapter Two—but then, we would say that! While the exercise of "taking archaeology out of heritage" has produced some interesting and provocative debates, what has proved ultimately revelatory are the interviews presented throughout the volume. Those interviewed report useful and constructive engagements with archaeologists, supporting some of the contentions and assumptions made by Kenny. It needs to be noted, however, that those positive engagements occur in association with community *archaeological* projects. When asked about heritage, those interviewed revealed that heritage and archaeology were not the same—that heritage was much more than simply "archaeology". For some, such as Janet Hobson at Poppleton, this was a simple observation of fact. For Alison Drake at Castleford, however, this observation was more problematic, leading as it did to a range of tensions for the Castleford community. What emerges from these interviews is that we can celebrate the successes of community archaeology, but we cannot assume that such projects are *necessarily* about, or to do with, "heritage". The arguments and experiences presented in this volume suggest that while concepts and definitions of heritage and archaeology may in certain contexts overlap, they are not inherently the same. This is not meant to threaten archaeological authority or the relevance of archaeology to public debates about the meaning of the past; rather, it is an observation that a re-theorization of the relationship between the two is required. One of us made a similar plea for re-theorizing heritage practice and its relationship to archaeology more than a decade ago (Smith 1994). Since then, Heritage Studies has become a recognizable and interdisciplinary field of inquiry in its own right. In that time, quite how far the debate on heritage in archaeology has advanced remains open to deliberation.

Works Cited

Aikawa-Faure, Noriko. 2009. From the Proclamation of Masterpieces to the *Convention for the Safeguarding of Intangible Cultural Heritage.* In *Intangible heritage* ed. Laurajane Smith and Natsuko Akagawa, 13–44. London: Routledge.

Beach, Hugh. 2007. Self-determining the self: Aspects of Sámi identity management in Sweden. *Acta Borealia: A Nordic Journal of Circumpolar Societies* 24 (1): 1–25.

Dicks, Bella. 2000. *Heritage, place and community.* Cardiff: University of Wales Press.

Falch, Torvald and Marianne Skandfer. 2004. "Sámi cultural heritage in Norway: Between local knowledge and the power of the state". In *Northern Ethnographic Landscapes: Perspectives from Circumpolar Nations,* ed. Igor Krupnik, Rachel Mason and Tonia Horton, 356–375. Washington DC: Smithsonian Institute.

Graham, Brian, Gregory Ashworth and John Tunbridge 2000. *A geography of heritage: Power, culture and economy.* London: Arnold.

Jones, Sian. 2004. *Early medieval sculpture and the production of meaning, value and place: The case of Hilton of Cadboll.* Edinburgh: Historic Scotland.

Langford, Ros. 1983. Our heritage—Your playground. *Australian Archaeology* 16:1–6.

McClanahan, Angela. 2007. The cult of community: Defining the 'local' in public archaeology and heritage discourse. In *Which Past, Whose Future? The Past at the Start of the 21st Century,* ed. Sven Grabow, Daniel Hull and Emma Waterton, 51–57. Oxford: Archaeopress.

Munjeri, Dawson. 2004. Tangible and intangible heritage: From difference to convergence. *Museum International* 56 (1–2): 12–20.

Riley, Mark and David Harvey. 2005. Landscape archaeology, heritage and the community in Devon: An oral history approach, *International Journal of Heritage Studies* 11 (4): 269–288.

Skounti, Ahmed. 2009. The authentic illusion: Humanity's intangible cultural heritage, the Moroccan experience. In *Intangible heritage* eds Laurajane Smith and Natsuko Akagawa, 74–92. London: Routledge.

Smith, Claire and Martin Wobst (eds) 2005. *Indigenous archaeologies: Decolonizing theory and practice*, Routledge: London.

Smith, Laurajane. 1994. Heritage management as postprocessual archaeology? *Antiquity* 68: 300-309.

—. 2004. Archaeological theory and the politics of cultural heritage. London: Routledge.

Smith, Laurajane and Emma Waterton. 2009. *Heritage, communities and archaeology*. London: Duckworth.

Tunbridge, John and Gregory Ashworth. 1996. *Dissonant heritage: The management of the past as a resource in conflict*. Chichester: Wiley.

Waterton, Emma. 2008. Invisible identities: Destroying the heritage of Cawood Castle. In *An Archaeology of Destruction* ed. Lila Rakoczy, 107–127. Newcastle-upon-Tyne: Cambridge Scholars Press.

PART I:

NEGOTIATING HERITAGE

CHAPTER TWO

THERE IS NO SUCH *THING* AS HERITAGE

EMMA WATERTON AND LAURAJANE SMITH

Introduction

Archaeology in the UK, and indeed in many Western countries, has had a long association with heritage and its management. Historically, it was archaeologists who lobbied for legislation and public policy to protect sites and places of heritage, and who now work in heritage agencies, museums and amenity societies protecting what they define and understand as "heritage". This chapter explores the degree to which this historical association between the two concepts—"archaeology" and "heritage"—has confined and constrained the nature and meaning of heritage, particularly in policy and practice. Is, for example, the idea of heritage as established by archaeologists and now enshrined in heritage public policy and management processes sufficiently developed to be inclusive of non-archaeological views of heritage? Does it adequately encompass developing trends in heritage studies about the multivocality and dissonant nature of heritage? Can it be inclusive of the multilayered nature of community senses of heritage and place? Moreover, can it accommodate intangible heritage, non-Western ideas of heritage, or *any* conceptualization of heritage that stands outside of the dominantly understood notion of heritage as sites, monuments and buildings? More importantly, we also question whether archaeology has the intellectual and theoretical capacity to (re)develop its definitions and responses to engage adequately and productively with competing notions of heritage.

In asking these questions, our overarching aim is not to summarily dismiss the practices and philosophies of archaeology. What we do want to suggest is that archaeology, *as a discipline*, can no longer assume to hold all the answers when it comes to issues of heritage. Indeed, as heritage continues to come under sustained critique over issues of identity, memory and sense of place, and is increasingly challenged by a range of Western and non-Western interest groups, the more traditional assumptions regarding "monumental", "tangible", "great" and "authentic" heritage ceases to make sense. This growing number of scholars and interested parties engaged in a renegotiation of heritage draw from a diversification of informal, as well as formal, networks operating within the field, which collectively question European and Anglophone assumptions about heritage and attempt to de-privilege expert knowledge. As a consequence, a broader understanding of heritage has emerged, taking account of the relationships, experiences, uses and interplays between social and cultural encounters with "heritage", be they tangible or intangible. More recently, claims for multiculturalism, diversity and cultural tolerance—occurring at both national and international levels—are also intersecting with debates about the nature and meaning of heritage. What this interest has sponsored is an idea of "heritage" that is hotly contest, drawing responses from sociologists, anthropologists, cultural geographers, cultural studies, tourism studies, public analysts and museologists, *in addition* to the more traditional disciplines of archaeology, art history and architecture.

Despite the growing visibility of debates centred on the nature, meaning and uses of heritage, the ability of archaeology to engage with such debates appears stultified. In this chapter, we suggest that this inability to "move with the times", so to speak, is a symptom of more insidious, systemic issues, borne out of the discipline's own historical engagement with the legitimization of heritage as a concept and unit of management. As Smith (1994, 2004) has argued elsewhere, archaeology owes too much to a certain understanding of the nature of not only archaeology, but also "heritage", to allow any movement in its definition. To this end, archaeologists have been highly successful in protecting their database. This success, however, has been achieved through the development and maintenance of a range of heritage management practices, legal statutes and policy documents that work to legitimize their privileged access to, and control of, the database. Any serious shift in the definition of heritage, particularly any shift that lends legitimacy to non-archaeological values and cultural meanings, jeopardizes the authority of archaeological access to its database. What we hope to draw attention to in this chapter, then, are the legal and institutional positions of archaeology that ensure that archaeology is heritage and heritage is archaeology in a public policy sense at least. This, of course, does not mean to say that archaeological knowledge is all-powerful and does not lose out frequently to more powerful—say, economic—values and land management concerns. However, it is nonetheless archaeological concepts of heritage that underlie the policy process, and it is the embedding of this conceptualization within public policy that helps to solidify archaeological responses to competing notions of heritage.

To explore this argument, the chapter is structured around three parts. In the first part of this chapter, we explore the distinct formulation of heritage that underlies public policy and management practices in England, a concept that both archaeologists and architects helped to construct, and continue to maintain. It is a concept that has become so successful within the public policy process that it has obtained the status of a "commonsense" definition, or appears as the *natural* way of thinking about heritage. This naturalized understanding of heritage equates to what Smith (2006) has referred to previously as the authorized heritage discourse (henceforth AHD). We will then present a re-theorization of heritage, based on an understanding of heritage as a cultural process, or, as David Harvey (2001) suggests, a verb rather than a noun. From this re-theorization, we suggest that there is no such *thing* as heritage. Rather, it exists as a range of competing discourses that have significant and powerful cultural and political consequences and uses. In the final section, we will document the re-occurrence of the AHD in a range of policy contexts, and illustrate the ways in which archaeological knowledge is implicitly (and sometimes explicitly) drawn upon to close down broader understandings of what heritage might mean for different interest groups. Of particular interest here are the strategies deployed to facilitate and maintain archaeological expertise over heritage through the conflation of heritage and archaeology.

The Authorized Heritage Discourse

While the authorized heritage discourse developed in Western Europe in the nineteenth century, many of its core characteristics were solidified, or directly flowed out of, agitations by archaeologists and architects for the protection of material culture deemed to be of innate and inheritable value in the 1960s and 1970s. This could not be just *any* innate value, however, as it was required to represent distinct aspects of a country's national identity, and champion, in the case of England, a sense of Englishness, for example, to the rest of the world. In addition to a focus on nationally representative material culture, the AHD also places acute attention upon the "aesthetically pleasing", or artistic, picturesque or beautiful, notions that are themselves linked with concepts of "honesty" and "authenticity". As such, the AHD has come to define heritage as positive examples of *stuff* from the past in the form of material objects, sites, places and/or landscapes that current generations must care for and protect so that they may be passed to nebulous future generations. This collective sense of a nation's past is secured and revered for both its educational qualities, and its ability to forge a sense of common identity. Here, the idea of inheritance is stressed, thereby ensuring that current generations are disengaged from an active use of heritage. The idea that the value of material culture is innate, rather than associate, is securely embedded in this discourse, which consequently defines heritage is as fragile, finite and non-renewable. It is thus placed, as this discourse asserts, rightly within the care of those experts best positioned to stand in as stewards for the past, and understand and communicate that value of heritage to the nation— principally, archaeologists, architects and historians. Although Smith (2006) has developed this characterization of the AHD elsewhere, it is worth considering how this discourse emerged in more detail here. First, however, we need to expand a little on what we mean by the term "discourse" and why Smith's characterization is a useful framework for our discussion.

Discourse is, as Richardson (2007, 237; see also Bloor and Bloor 2007) points out, an endlessly debated concept. In this chapter, however, we adopt a particular usage of the term, drawing from a critical discourse analytic perspective that sees discourse as "language in use" (Fairclough 2001, 2003; Richardson 2007). Not only, then, is discourse a particular way of speaking, thinking or writing about an issue, it also *does* things. Thus, at the same time that discourses represent elements of social life and the world around us in a number of different, and often competing, ways, they also (re)create, constitute and condition these different ways of seeing social life and the world. A useful way of understanding the term "discourse" in the context of this chapter is to think about ideas of regulation, as discussed by van Leeuwen (2008). Here, the AHD forms part of a wider social practice that has been specifically developed to regulate the management of heritage, often with reference to strict laws and prescriptive procedures. However, the AHD is itself implicitly regulatory as a consequence of its near naturalization. What we mean here is that the AHD has assumed the face of "commonsense", and thereby has become an effective mechanism of social regulation, or a socially regulated way of doing things (Leeuwen 2008, 6). It does this by virtue of the fact that it is difficult to approach heritage in ways that sit outside the parameters of the AHD, and have those alternative approaches *legitimized*. In short, the social practices of heritage management are regulated not only by the formal legislative texts we recognize as Acts or documents of public policy, but also by a discursive pressure to conform to what appears to be normalcy.

With this understanding of discourse in mind, we now turn to a consideration of the AHD's historical development in an attempt to denaturalize, or reveal, its regulatory processes. One of the guiding principles of the AHD derives from John Ruskin's and William Morris's notion of "conserve as found", which was originally developed for architectural and landscape conservation practices. As Cosgrove (2003, 121) points out, this conservation ethic encapsulates the belief that "the material remains of the past possessed an integrity that demanded their protection as sacred relics, to be revered but not violated by any modern intervention". Clearly articulated within this ethic, then, are notions of inherent value and inheritance. Moreover, such a degree of importance was placed on the materiality of Western culture and its expressions of romantic nationalism, and so much was simply "understood" by the aesthetics of such objects and landscapes, that the material has since come to stand in for the social and cultural values it symbolizes. Subsequently within the AHD, heritage *is* the monument, archaeological site or other material thing or place, rather than cultural values or meanings. Ultimately, these assumptions about the innate value of heritage and its materiality work to reinforce the idea that heritage represents all that is good and important about the past that has contributed to the development of the cultural character of the present.

An important characteristic of this discourse is the assumptions it makes about "identity". Here, heritage is about the construction of a range of identities and, more specifically, *national* identity. This, however, is an assumption that is rarely scrutinized within the management process, and as a consequence, little work has been done that offers a clear sense of *how* identity is actually constructed by, or from, heritage sites or places. This lack of understanding helps to facilitate the acceptance of established and legitimized cultural and social values, and thus identity, which becomes an immutable given somehow inherently embedded within heritage/archaeological monuments, sites and buildings.

As our earlier introduction to discourse suggests, the AHD constructs not only a particular definition of heritage, it also provides the parameters within which authorized discussions about heritage can take place. As such, the AHD also becomes a sort of social mentality, deployed to understand and deal with certain social problems centred on claims to identity. Tangled up with this social mentality is the idea of expertise, which has allowed particular forms of knowledge to create and maintain those parameters for thinking about heritage, which simultaneously work to exclude other forms of knowledge, skill and experience. The particular forms of knowledge identified within the AHD are those associated with archaeology, architecture and art history, as it is these disciplines that are presumed to hold the intellectual and cultural tools necessary for acting as stewards or caretakers of the nation's heritage.

The AHD, however, is not monolithic. The above characterization is open to variation and contestation—to some degree. However, it is also very "real" in the sense that an authorized understanding of heritage exists and has consequences. One of the most important consequences of this mentality is that it excludes those understandings of heritage that sit outside of, or are oppositional to, it. As such, it tends to exclude understandings of heritage that are felt and promoted by a) non-expert interest groups and stakeholders; b) Non-Western interest groups and stakeholders; and c) those who find meaning and value in non-middle- and upper-class cultural symbols and experiences. This is because the AHD is very much influenced by elite values and experiences, which derive from both the cultural sense of importance afforded to this class in England, and the ability of these classes to *be heard* within the management and public policy processes. This adherence to the cultural symbols of the elite may also be understood in terms of "hegemony", through which subordinate classes and interest groups acquiesce to the dominance of the ruling classes' institutions and values (Richardson 2007, 35). Despite claims to represent a "common" or "universal" heritage, then, the naturalization of the AHD in no way interrupts the implicit dominance of a distinct and exclusive set of cultural values and symbols.

A central reason for this is that the AHD continually validates those forms of knowledge and values that contributed to it—in particular archaeological and architectural knowledge and understanding. The AHD is itself part of the heritage process of value and meaning creation, arbitration and negotiation—it is a mentality or gaze that continually legitimizes and de-legitimizes a range of cultural and social values. However, where does this observation leave us with understanding and defining the idea of heritage? If heritage is more than just historic monuments, archaeological sites and landscapes, what is it?

A Re-theorization of Heritage

Heritage is a subjective and political negotiation of identity, place and memory. Smith (2006) offers a re-theorization of heritage that we adopt here, which stresses the idea that heritage is a cultural process or a performance (Smith in press) that is concerned with the regulation, mediation and negotiation of cultural and historical values and narratives. Heritage becomes not so much the thing or place identified by the AHD as "heritage", but instead the values and meanings that are constructed at and around them—heritage is what is *done* and not what is conserved, preserved or managed. Heritage becomes an act of communication (Dicks 2000) and a process of emotional and cultural engagement (Byrne 2009; Bendix 2009) that is about the assertion and mediation of historical narratives and collective memories, and the cultural and social values that underpin these. Indeed, within this definition, the AHD and the management and conservation practices it frames, are themselves part of the process of heritage. In this definition, all heritage is intangible, as it is redefined as a cultural process in which the values and cultural and social meanings that help us make sense of the present are identified and negotiated. These negotiations may occur around the decisions we make to preserve, or not, certain physical places or objects and the way these are then managed and interpreted. They also occur in the way visitors engage or disengage with them. However, what is important is that heritage is *not* the archaeological site or historic monument, but is the cultural tools that societies use to remember and, in that process of remembering, construct meanings that have relevance and utility to the present. These places are given value by the act of naming them heritage and by the processes of heritage negotiations and re/creations that may occur at them. Some of these acts of meaning creation may be archaeological—the archaeological excavation, for example, is a performance of meaning and heritage creation—but it is important to understand this is only one act among many of meaning construction, albeit an authorized one. The act of naming something "heritage" gives the place or artefact so named an authority to represent, stand in for and thus give solidity to amorphous social and cultural values that we associate with "identity", "belonging" or "sense of place". The heritage place then becomes a space—both physically and conceptually—around which particular social problems, debates or issues are (re)negotiated.

What this theorization does is open up the conceptual space so that we are less obsessed with the object or site and are able to consider the "work" that heritage as a cultural process does in society. The negotiations that are entered into about how, or if, we should manage and conserve certain places or objects can be seen as occurring within the context of ongoing social and public debate about what it means "to be" a member of a particular collective, and the values that underpin this sense of belonging. Heritage sites and places becomes resources of power, based on their ability to give a sense of "objectivity", solidity or reality to formless values and cultural meanings, which are used to assert and validate claims to social status and social "place" that appeal to historical and other measures of "time depth". In England, the AHD works to maintain the legitimacy of elite history and the social hierarchies that flow from this, while warding off challenges from subaltern groups who offer a different sense of historical and social experience. Within this process, certain forms of knowledge become privileged in maintaining authorized historical and cultural narratives—archaeological knowledge is one such example. Indeed, so embedded is archaeological knowledge within the authorized cultural processes of heritage, that disciplinary identity has become inextricably linked to the processes of heritage management in the UK. As Lahn (1996) points out, the possession of certain high status artefacts or sites by individual archaeologists becomes representative of their status and identity within the discipline. The ability of archaeologists collectively to possess and control that which others call "heritage" provides the discipline with both a collective identity and a certain degree of power to influence particular cultural and social debates and meanings. Thus, archaeologists often become central players in disputes between communities and other collectives whose sense of heritage stands in opposition to the AHD.

Heritage Policy: An Historical Overview

In the second half of this chapter, we want to document the occurrence of Smith's notion of the AHD, both in historical debates and in those more subtle guises in contemporary current cultural policy. The type of commentary we want to present in this part of the chapter rests on the idea of intertextuality, which suggests that elements of one text will surface, implicitly or explicitly, in elements of other texts. This notion of intertextuality is a core component of critical discourse analysis and is defined by Fairclough (2003, 218) as such:

> The intertextuality of a text is the presence within it of elements of other texts (and therefore potentially other voices than the author's own) which may be related to (dialogued with, assumed, rejected, etc.) in various ways.

At its most basic, then, intertextuality refers to snatches of texts within texts (Fairclough 1992). In conjunction with intertextuality, the analytical category of assumption will also be used to perform important work, as the aim of this chapter is to reveal the background against which archaeology became synonymous with heritage. The term "assumption" is employed here to mean assessing the implicit meanings of a text, or the implicitness regarding what may exist, what can (or cannot) be the case and what is good or desirable (Fairclough 2003, 55). One of the arguments we are attempting to build in this volume is that the particular idea of heritage that animates policy and management in England *does not appear to dominate, it appears as natural*: it is uncritically accepted as the "commonsense" definition of heritage that underpins management processes in England (see Waterton 2007 for a fuller discussion). This section therefore aims to substantiate this argument and reveal a series of instances within which the practice of archaeology is not only *equated* with heritage, but is granted a position from which to dominate and mediate the heritage management process.

In a sense, this section could begin with Sir John Lubbock's "tireless advocacy" that archaeological remains should be used to underwrite the history and identity of Britain, a position he promoted in the nineteenth century when lobbying for the *Ancient Monuments Protection Act* of 1882 (Murray 1989, 56). Likewise, the *Ancient Monuments and Archaeological Areas Act of 1979* could be seen to be key to the argument we are developing here, as it signalled a renewed interest in the idea of heritage as a discursive topic. However, rather than trace a fine-grained picture of the history of heritage legislation, we want to talk more generally about a series of specific arguments that surfaced in the 1970s and 80s, a period that saw "heritage" quite suddenly become a political issue. It is these decades that are most commonly associated with the emergence of heritage management as a set of principles and the resultant enactment or emendation of legislative codes (Walsh 1992; Graham et al. 2000; Wainwright 2000). As Cleere (1989, 2) notes, the formal materialization of a conservation ethic at this time was no coincidence, nor was it confined to the national level. Indeed, from this point, heritage became, as Samuel (1994, 25) notes, "…one of the major…social movements of our time". This social movement spanned policy, academic and popular discourses, and produced a list of readily identifiable heritage initiatives, both nationally and internationally.

It is important to note that these decades were characterized more generally by expansion, warnings of global shortages, spectacular nuclear accidents, huge growth in both urban and rural development, and thousands of miles of new motorways, all of which provided the urgency for reassessing the state of the natural and cultural worlds (Cleere 1989; Hajer 1996; Wainwright 2000). Operating in conjunction with the environmental rhetoric of "the fragile earth" and the "ecowarrior", the prevailing image of heritage—both politically and popularly—became that of a "fragile, finite and non-renewable resource". Simultaneously, a privileged place for the archaeological profession was discursively and socially mapped, as the:

... rescuers, as the saviours, because they were the one's who stopped development and got in there...they are the environmental crusaders ... fighting the good fight (Interviewee, English Heritage, 10th November 2004).

Not only, then, were archaeologists, and to some degree architects and art historians, heavily associated with the lobbying process underpinning the arrival of legislative texts in the 1970s, they were also seen as the collection of people actively responding to development, particularly in the context of what is remembered as rescue, or salvage, archaeology. A natural consequence of this "crisis" was the assumption of universal relevance. The joint discourses of a "threatened" and "universal" heritage thereby combined to offer an apparently consensual view, prompting the need for action:

The preservation of our heritage for future generations is a duty *that we are all agreed upon* (Lord Mowbray and Stourton, House of Lords, HANSARD, Ancient Monuments and Archaeological Areas Bill [H.L.], 5th February 1979: 463, emphasis added).

In this extract, we can see assumptions regarding "common ground" being made that make the rest of the debate regarding the enactment of the 1979 Bill *appear* necessary. For example, the necessity to preserve heritage is distinguished by the existential assumption that it *is our duty*. Further, a particular value assumption is being made by virtue of the participial adjective "agreed", which suggests that it is something that is desired by all. As well, this statement reflects wider appeals to consensual heritage, with the legitimizing technique of appealing to conformity—or, what is proposed is legitimate because "everybody says so"—also recognizable (van Leeuwen and Wodak 1999, 105). There is no sense of uncertainty surrounding this statement; rather it is simply the case that the preservation of heritage for future generations *is* a duty. In taking the continuation of this statement, the extent of that vision becomes apparent:

Thus from our distant past we have the Iron Age fort at Figsbury, Wiltshire, the famous Broch of Mousa in Shetland; Wideford Hill – that famous cairn – in Orkney, and the Roman theatre at Verulam, and hundreds of other ancient monuments (Lord Mowbray and Stourton, House of Lords, HANSARD, Ancient Monuments and Archaeological Areas Bill [H.L.], 5th February 1979: 563, emphasis added).

Of particular relevance is the discursive work undertaken by the utterances *our heritage, we are all agreed upon* and *thus from our distant past*. The grammatical and semantic relationships between these statements are elaborative, such that a list of ancient monuments is put forward in order to define *our heritage*. In this timeframe, we see a high level of commitment to an idea of "heritage" confined to the distant past in the guise of tangible and monumental remains. Here, we see the beginnings of the notion that *our heritage* is synonymous with a strictly archaeological sense of the past.

Reviewing Heritage Policy Today

While this initial overview is admittedly brief, we nonetheless want to shift focus and begin to examine how this discourse—the AHD—has been operationalised intertextually in the more recent policy context. In the past eight years, the heritage sector has undertaken two significant reviews of heritage policy, once in 1999–2001, and again in 2002–present. Throughout this period, little has changed in terms of the primacy afforded to the archaeological discipline. Rather, through an implicit re-working of the archaeology/heritage dyad highlighted in earlier sections of the chapter, the position of archaeological practice has been sustained. In addition to assumptions embedded in a range of policy documents, this view is also intertextually reworked in speech acts used in interview:

> I sometimes feel that they think archaeology is the only heritage (Interviewee, English Heritage, 10th November 2005)

> As an evidence-based discipline, it [archaeology] provides the understanding upon which all decisions would have to be taken about change…we would say that if you don't understand what it is that you are managing then you can't possibly make intelligent decisions about how you are going to change it and manage it and make, er, release the public potential, benefit that is in it…so we would say that archaeology has that primacy in the sense that it is the process for understanding that has to underpin conservation (Interviewee, Council for British Archaeology, 8th June 2005).

The primacy of archaeology and archaeological knowledge is also rehearsed in various policy documents, and usually resemblance the following utterance:

> English Heritage believes it is essential that statutory criteria of architectural, archaeological and historic importance should continue to be the sole basis of what parts of the historic environment should be added to the new list (English Heritage 2003, 5).

Not only is archaeological importance highlighted as essential for considering, identifying and managing heritage, an implicit hierarchy is implied *within* and *between* those types of heritage presumed worthy of protection and conservation. So, in addition to creating parameters that see heritage as sites, monuments, buildings or landscapes, a distinct hierarchy in terms of significance is also evident. Such is the degree of naturalization regarding this understanding of heritage that the addition of wider cultural debates concerned with social inclusion, multiculturalism and the recent concept of "public value" has done little to unsettle the hierarchical approach to "heritage" developed in the 1970s. This discrepancy between established values and public value is elaborated in the extract below (see also Figure 2.1)

> In a sense, the way the legislation … er, in the 20th century... [we are] starting to create a sort of pyramid of heritage and this [public value] is just another layer of that …(Interviewee, English Heritage, 3rd August 2005).

The pyramid of heritage the extract above refers to looks like this:

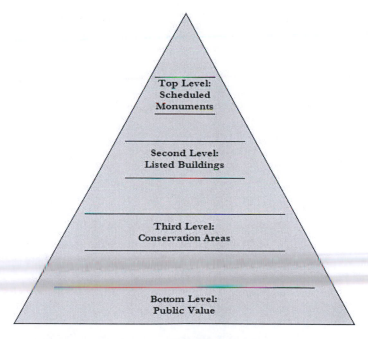

Figure 2.1: The Heritage Pyramid as Illustrated by Interviewee, English Heritage, 3rd August 2005

The "heritage pyramid" was explained thus:

> ... at one level you have at the beginning of the twentieth century scheduled ancient monuments, which are the best of the best in the land ...
>
> ... After the Second World War, and the swathe of interest in private rights and public rights, you had the developing notion of listed buildings ...
>
> ... In the 1960s you got conservation areas, which was of a lower order ...
>
> ... This [public value] has come to a head over the pathfinder schemes ... these are not of particularly any special architectural merit, and yet the local population like to live there ... (Interviewee, English Heritage 3rd August 2005).

The addition of "public value" to the above pyramid is more of a concession made by heritage professionals on behalf of "the public", and thus non-archaeological notions of heritage are seen to exist at the lowest order, with professional values (read here archaeological) invested in monuments, buildings and, to a lesser degree, conservation areas privileged. Non-archaeological understandings of heritage are further constrained by carefully guarded tropes of responsibility and knowledge:

> There are conflicts around that [community-led approaches to heritage], there inevitably are, about what is saved and what is deemed as important, and if we hand over responsibility we will lose things that are valuable (Interviewee, Institute for Public Policy Research, 26th August 2005).

The value assumption here is evident. There are things that are valuable, which are recognizable by experts, and then there are those things valued and argued for by non-expert groups. Particularly telling here is the use of the participial adjective *deemed*, which adds a degree of modality to the statement, which stands in comparison to the non-modalised statement that *are valuable*—things valued by community groups, for example, are characterized by a median commitment to truth, whereas those things valued by experts are distinguished by a very high commitment to truth. In other words, the latter simply *are* valuable, whereas the former are open to question.

The most recent series of policy to emerge from the heritage sector has been created in association with the Heritage Protection Review (see also Smith and Waterton, in press). This review is a collection of genres and texts comprising of policy documents, press releases, internal reports and consultation documents, each of which is intertextually related to others within the collection. With a focus upon statutory protection, the review process seeks to modernize the processes of designation, listing and registering various "parts" of the historic environment, which will be combined within the proposed heritage "Register" for England (cf. DCMS 2003, 10, 11). At the outset, the review process was set up with the intentions of maximizing "opportunities for inclusion and involvement" and supporting "sustainable communities". It is through the disjunction between these laudable aims and the policy rhetoric that eventually emerged that we really start to see the limited capacity for the development of a productive and engaged sense of heritage. The following statements, for example, are indicative—and typical—of this:

> The List[1] would include the most important sites and items from the past, according to certain broad statutory criteria, including sites valued for their archaeological importance [evidential], their architectural significance [evidential and aesthetic], their association with major historical events [historical] or because they represent a type of building or social use from a particular period (DCMS 2003, 12, inclusions added).

> The Departments rely on English Heritage to employ archaeologists to give expert input into the formulation of heritage policy and decision making…

What this focus suggests, particularly with emphasis on the types of value privileged here (evidential, aesthetic and historical), is the continued acknowledgement that the debates regarding "public" value stand apart from debates underpinning the review process. Once again, there is a continued, yet unspoken, distinction implied between the stage at which "expertise" is accepted within the management process and the stage at which non-expertise is accepted. Of particular importance is the apparent need for expertise to confer authority, and the insipidness of the power relations that work to maintain this cultural logic. In arguing that heritage is discursively constructed, we must also look upon the *actual* work undertaken by the construction of heritage that has come to dominate. Here, the concept of "inalienable possessions", as developed by Weiner (1992) and Lahn (1996), offers a useful reminder of the underlying specifics of that logic. Three assumptions are central here: (1) the assumed finite nature of "heritage"; (2) the resultant sense of "crisis"; and (3) the need for expertise to moderate and regulate that crisis. Operating in and around these assumptions is an inflection of power that allows a select few to clip,

---

[1] "The List" is the proposed replacement regime for Scheduling and Listing, which will see a simplification of the current systems into one List (DCMS 2003, 10).

shape, define and label this collective idea of heritage, and make it *matter*; and, moreover, make it matter in terms of *possession*. This overview also finds synergy with Weiner's (1992) notion of "keeping-while-giving", and what we want to suggest here is that this very careful structuring of heritage is itself an inalienable possession, and thus subject to the intricacies of keeping-while-giving. This is particularly visible in recent contexts of social inclusion, cultural diversity and multiculturalism. "Heritage" as assumed equivalent with sites, monuments and buildings of a defined time-frame, is used to regulate the flow of discursive exchanges in policy, academic and popular contexts. Simultaneously, the authority of expertise is exhorted, with only specific collections of knowledge considered capable of extending "proper" care to the past. What this offers, however, is an approach to heritage that is deaf to the discursive struggles and tensions ongoing between different interest groups and stakeholders attempting to define meaning.

Conclusion

What we hope to have indicated in this chapter is the emergence of a series of assumptions that have remained crucial in structuring the relationship between heritage and archaeology. Indeed, "archaeology" has often become synonymous with "heritage" within this process—or at least been placed in a position of control and possession. This has not been a casual or inadvertent development. The archaeological discipline has gained considerable authority and sense of purpose from this process. So much, indeed, is owed to this conflation of archaeology and heritage that the archaeological discipline has too much at stake to recognize that what it may regard as its "archaeological heritage" is not necessary everyone else's idea of heritage. Archaeology operates within the confines of the AHD and, as such, lacks both the will and conceptual apparatus to engage with and comprehend the range of heritage expressions and performances that sit outside or in opposition to the AHD and the heritage management practices it defines.

This chapter also argues that the conflation of heritage with archaeology—and indeed, for that matter, with architecture and art history—that occurs with the AHD has meant that not only are other forms and expressions of heritage are obscured or denied, but that the work heritage does in society is also concealed. Understanding that heritage—regardless of whether or not it is perceived as a 'thing' or as a cultural process—has a consequence for how nations, communities and other collectives are recognized, understood and relegated. Social "place", power and/or privilege is a vital conceptual first step in recognizing the legitimacy of non-archaeological forms of heritage. However, such recognition immediately exposes the work that the AHD, and archaeological knowledge within that, does in maintaining existing social values and hierarchies—a recognition that by implication jeopardizes archaeological identity, access to data and sense of purpose.

Works Cited

Bloor, Meriel and Thomas Bloor. 2007. *The practice of critical discourse analysis*. London: Hodder Arnold.

Bendix, Regina. 2009 "Heritage between economy and politics: An assessment from the perspective of cultural anthropology". In *Intangible heritage*, eds Laurajane Smith and Natsuko Akagawa, 253–269. London: Routledge.

Byrne, Denis. 2009. "A critique of unfeeling heritage". In *Intangible heritage*, eds Laurajane Smith and Natsuko Akagawa, 229–252. London: Routledge.

Cleere, Henry. 1989. "Introduction: The rationale of archaeological heritage management". In *Archaeological heritage management in the modern world* ed. Henry Cleere, 1–19. London: Routledge.

Cosgrove, Dennis. 2003. "Heritage and history: A Venetian geography lesson". In *Rethinking Heritage: Cultures and Politics in Europe* ed Robert Shannon Peckham, 113–123. London: I.B. Tauris.

DCMS 2003. *Protecting our historic environment: Making the system work better*. London: Department for Culture, Media and Sport, Architecture and Historic Environment Division.

Dicks, Bella. 2000. *Heritage, place and community*. Cardiff: University of Wales Press.

English Heritage 2003. *DCMS consultation paper: Protecting the historic environment—making the system work better—The English Heritage response*. London: English Heritage.

Fairclough, Norman. 1992. *Discourse and social change*. Cambridge: Polity Press.

—. 2001. "The discourse of New Labour: Critical discourse analysis". In *Discourse as data: A guide for analysis*, eds Margaret Wetherell, Stephanie Taylor and Simeon J. Yates, 229–266. London: SAGE Publications.

—. 2003. *Analyzing discourse: Textual analysis for social research*. London: Routledge.

Graham, Brian, Gregory Ashworth and John Tunbridge 2000. *A geography of heritage: Power, culture and economy*. London: Arnold.

Hajer, Maarten. 1996. "Discourse coalitions and the institutionalization of practice: The case of acid rain in Britain". In *The argumentative turn in policy analysis and planning,* eds Frank Fischer and John Forester, 43–76. Durham: Duke University Press.

Harvey, David. 2001. "Heritage pasts and heritage presents: Temporality, meaning and the scope of heritage studies". *International Journal of Heritage Studies* 7 (4): 319–338.

Lahn, Julie. 1996. "Finders keepers, losers weepers: A 'social history' of the Kow Swamp remains". *Ngulaig* 15: 1–61.

Murray, Tim. 1989. "The history, philosophy and sociology of archaeology: The case of the Ancient Monuments Protection Act (1882)". In *Critical traditions in contemporary archaeology,* eds Valerie Pinsky and Annette Wylie, 55–67. Cambridge: Cambridge University Press.

Richardson, John. 2007. *Analyzing newspapers: An approach from critical discourse analysis*. London: Routledge.

Samuel, Raphael. 1994. *Theatres of memory. Volume 1: Past and present in contemporary culture*. London: Verso.

Smith, Laurajane. 1994. Heritage management as postprocessual archaeology? *Antiquity* 68: 300–309.

—. 2004. *Archaeological theory and the politics of cultural heritage*. London: Routledge.

—. 2006. *Uses of heritage*. London: Routledge.

—. In press. The "doing" of heritage: Heritage as performance. In *Performing Heritage: Research, practice and development in museum theatre and live interpretation*, eds Anthony Jackson and Jenny Kidd. Manchester: Manchester University Press.

Smith, Laurajane and Emma Waterton. In press. Constrained by commonsense: The authorized heritage discourse in contemporary debates. In *The Oxford handbook of public archaeology*, eds John Carman, Robin Skeates and Carol McDavid. Oxford: Oxford University Press.

van Leeuwen, Theo and Ruth Wodak. 1999. Legitimizing immigration control: A discourse-historical analysis. *Discourse Studies* 1 (1): 83–118.

Van Leeuwen, Theo. 2008. *Discourse and practice: New tools for critical discourse analysis*. Oxford: Oxford University Press.

Wainwright, Geoffrey. 2000. Time please, *Antiquity*, 74 (286), 909–43.

Walsh, Kevin. 1992. *The representation of the past: Museums and heritage in the post-modern world.* London: Routledge.

Waterton, Emma. 2007. Rhetoric and "reality": Politics, policy and the discourses of heritage in England, PhD diss., University of York.

Weiner, Annette. 1992. *Inalienable possessions—The paradox of keeping-while giving.* Berkley: University of California Press.

CHAPTER THREE

ARCHAEOLOGY, VISUALITY
AND THE NEGOTIATION OF HERITAGE

STEVE WATSON

Introduction

This chapter examines the relationship between archaeology and heritage as a negotiated process of cultural production. It argues that whilst archaeology and heritage are linked, they are necessarily distinct and separate discourses. This distinction, however, tends to be obscured in both archaeological and popular usage. The chapter also explores visuality as a significant factor in the negotiations that link archaeology with the production-consumption nexus of heritage. Visuality, in its broadest sense as *visibility with social depth*, is both a condition for, and an outcome of, these processes of negotiation and transformation. This argument is based, and indeed dependent, on the proposition that archaeology and heritage have different objectives and modalities, both conceptually and in practice. That archaeology has its own discursive domain has been long established. Shanks and Tilley (1987a), for example, have argued that archaeology has its own distinct discourse: "a structured system of rules, conventions and meanings for the production of knowledge, texts". Whilst heritage is often conflated with this discourse in phrases such as "archaeological heritage", as well as in common usage, the critical heritage debates of the last twenty years would suggest, more than anything else, a separation in terms of scope, content and mode of address.

This discursive separation of archaeology and heritage is first apparent in their different purposes, and Lowenthal (1998, 102) has made a similar distinction between heritage and history. It is also evident in their different range and scope, with archaeology centred on material culture as data and evidence, and heritage referring—in an ill-defined way—to a wider range of objects and practices, including some which are intangible. So, while heritage might refer, in some cases, to the same material culture as archaeology, it is clearly larger in its range of both material and intangible referents. It is different in other, and perhaps more significant ways, however, and it is these that concern us here. The heritage debate, as it emerged in the 1980s, was essentially a critique of the way that the heritage *industry* acted on material culture, the impression being that it did *bad things* to the objects of the "real" past by presenting them within a new nexus of consumption (Hewison 1987, 1991; MacCrone et al. 1995; Lowenthal 1998). These bad things were mainly concerned with the production of heritage as a commodity:

> History is the remembered record of the past: heritage is a contemporary commodity purposively created to satisfy contemporary consumption. One becomes the other through a process of commodification (Ashworth 1994, 16).

This was a broad debate, however, and heritage was accused of inciting other forms of wickedness such as elitism, trivialization and eclecticism, to the extent that Lowenthal (1998, 100) identified within it an "anti-heritage animus". In addition, there was a view that heritage represented a glossing of the past, particularly of social conflict and thus, the deracination of the past in the present (Walsh 1992).

This varied analysis inevitably generated a plethora of views and perspectives about what heritage is, which Skeates (2000) attempted to reconcile by asserting, simply, that heritage has two meanings: one is merely shorthand for the bricolage of physical objects to which the word heritage, in common parlance, refers; whilst the other refers to the processes described above, and through which these same materials are re-evaluated and re-used in the present. It is pointless, he says, to argue over which of these definitions is correct, since both are established usages (2000, 9–10). The problem with this analysis, apart from its simplistic convenience, is that it overestimates the significance of archaeology in heritage as a whole, and it still treats the material components of heritage as given, rather than a construction based on the social and cultural significance that heritage actively represents. It also ignores the critical theorization of heritage that is essential to any understanding of its role in the economy, culture and society. For this we must turn to Laurajane Smith (2006), who has convincingly argued that heritage, in this sense, is concerned with the production of a special kind of discourse, formed from the narratives of national and elite class experiences that refer, in turn, to a range of supporting values involving continuity, time and tradition, expert knowledge and monumentality (2006, 4). While Smith leaves room to consider the nuances, specific moments and mechanisms of the heritage process, her concept of an authorized heritage discourse (henceforth AHD) has provided a powerful framework within which such analyses can take place.

What we are left with after this consideration is evidence of two separate and distinct discourses, separate in their contents and referents, separate in their scope and objectives, and separate in their mode of address: discourses that are *necessarily* distinct. Yet both common sense and experience suggest a link between the two, so that material culture, including archaeological material is *one* of the objects of heritage and that heritage acts on material culture in a transformative way to assign, absorb, and assimilate its meanings into its own discursive processes. If the relationship between heritage and archaeology is defined in this way, then a form of negotiation is implied, however unequal it is in its engagements, where only a small proportion of what constitutes archaeology, or the archaeological record, actually enters the wider realm of heritage, where it is noticed, selected, displayed and invested with social, cultural and often commercial value. Philip Duke (2007, 22) has voiced something of this two stage process in describing the engagement of tourists with archaeological sites in Crete:

> A tourist who enters an archaeological site enters—literally and metaphorically—an intersection of contemporary forces that have already begun to filter the information the tourist receives. The filter is composed of two sieves. The first is made by archaeologists whose selective interest in the past is contextualised within their own individual intellectual paradigms and ideologies ... The second sieve is constructed by site managers over what is presented to the public in terms of site access and presentation, and by the tourist industry, both state and private sector, which uses particular archaeological sites, museums and artefacts—and thereby a particular past—to entice tourists to Crete.

The distinction between the archaeological record and what is done with it is well established (Michell 1982; Carman 2005; Ascherson 2004; Holtorf 2005), but the precise mechanisms by which these transformations take place have only begun to be explored. As Bruner has put it, "[c]onstruct, produce, invent, and market are verbs that highlight the processual, active nature of culture, history, tradition and heritage" (2005, 127). It is argued here, that this process is based on forms of negotiation in which certain conditions must be satisfied in order for archaeological objects to be selected and transformed into heritage. Further, it is argued that a refined concept of visuality can be associated with this transformation as a way of understanding both its preconditions and its outcomes. The term visuality is thus used to denote not only the literally visible, but also a metaphorical social visibility that is culturally constructed. Moreover, in attaching a social and cultural dimension to the visual, the negotiation of heritage, with its attendant processes of identity and nation-making, social change, ideology and performative interaction, is critically revealed and elucidated. Visuality is thus more than what is physically displayed. It is about the way that heritage is signified, understood and valued, and about what is important in the cultural and political landscape as well as the physical one. Applying Adorno's (2001) analysis would place heritage within the *Culture Industry,* where not only are its objects, such as sport and music, subject to mechanisms of production, standardization and commodification, but also where individuals and audiences might variously interact with some kind of authoritative narrative. The important mechanisms here, I would argue, are those associated with visuality; the narrative is the AHD identified by Smith (2006).

Negotiating Heritage

If all archaeology is heritage, then what does the word "heritage" confer that the word archaeology does not? If the broader concept of heritage discussed above is applied, some additional values come into play—a process that is acting on archaeology to transform some aspects of its materiality into something else: a display of some kind, or a monument, or another kind of text. As such, it gains or is affected by a range of values that effectively separate it from archaeological discourse. The archaeological heritage is what results when these processes have acted upon archaeological objects: artefacts, buildings, sites and even archaeological ideas and concepts, such as the Bronze or Iron Ages or the Medieval, and the texts that describe them.

The conflation of archaeology with heritage, either intentionally or unwittingly, tends to treat archaeological objects as "resources" (as in "cultural resource management"), and in this *resource-based* model there is an implicit assumption that objects already have value of some kind. Typically, however, it is archaeologists who have ascribed this value through their own discourse, a discourse that generally involves recognition, investigation, description, taxonomy and occasionally aesthetic judgement. Despite the clear existence of such a process, these values come to be considered as inherent within the object rather than the process. Here they wait to be unlocked and released by the authority of the very experts from which they are derived in the first place. Within this can also be detected the role of the state in attaching significance, and therefore value, to selected sites and objects (Thomas 2004, 192–3). Another reason, as Merriman (2004, 87) has stated, may be the tendency for archaeological curators to focus on archaeology rather than communication, together with the amassing of archaeological collections and archives that are hardly used by archaeologists, let alone a wider public. These authorized, expert-defined and essentially fetishized concepts of heritage and its objects have a tendency to stifle debate about the processes and discourses that create it. Inherent value is thus naturalized as indeed is the object itself, as a valued object, whilst obscuring the fact that to be so requires something more than an archaeological record number or a report; it requires reference to values outside the realm of archaeology, which are consonant with other cultural practices such as tourism, market imperatives and identity.

As an alternative to this resource-based model, the *discourse* model proposed by Smith (2006) acknowledges the essential separation of heritage from archaeology, so that heritage is a process that is susceptible to critical interrogation and analysis. Archaeology can be the National Monuments Record, research that might be published or as yet unpublished, it might be the mysterious activities of some people in a trench, and it might be the humps and bumps in a field as yet un-surveyed, but until heritage as a process has acted upon it, it remains un-esteemed as such.

Archaeological heritage is therefore necessarily separate from the archaeological objects and data from which it is derived, but subject to the transformative and negotiated processes of heritage, archaeology enters the same consumption nexus as any other part of the culture industry. It becomes something that people go to see; read about in a guidebook; purchase a ticket for; something they experience; something that they feel, perhaps when they are in the presence of an object or a place; or something that they complain about because it has become commercialized or trivialized. Through this process it enters the world of all other heritage, and so it moves from the "sacred" knowledge of the scholar and professional to the quotidian realm of the profane; from the purity of the archaeological object with the archaeologist as the discoverer of truth through modern science, to the heritage of the tourist, the genealogist, the enthusiast, the viewer, the *Modern Antiquarian* and the discovery of personal heritage on the Web. The epistemological distinction between archaeology and heritage is deepened when archaeological objects enter these additional representational spaces and when other imperatives come into play. It seems unlikely, for example, that a local authority tourism officer imbued with the modalities of destination management would place an archaeological site at the top of any list of heritage attractions, unless it was Stonehenge or something of similar existing significance. Such official designations will tend to direct the gaze of the tourist to objects that connect, or can be connected, to the AHD, because it is a system of meaning that ascribes heritage value to the archaeological object (Smith 2006, 299–300).

Social networking sites on the Internet enable people to construct their own past and indeed their own concept of archaeological significance. Every phase of new technology in representation increases both the quantity and the quality of images, texts and meanings that are projected into public space. Again, archaeology has little to do with this as process and significance do not derive from the archaeological data or sites as such, but rather, the actions and intentions of the individual in the moment, influenced by the social and cultural forces that affect them, not least, the AHD. Archaeology is not, therefore, seen as central to heritage in the way that archaeologists might perceive it.

As a construction of place, the representation and symbolism of landscape also provide powerful evidence of the schism between an object and its heritage value and cultural status. Cosgrove and Daniels (1989, 8), for example, have described the "conservative picture of a 'deep' England with its stable layers of historical accretion profoundly threatened by modernization". It is also a deep and abiding cultural construction that symbolizes—and in itself represents—the social structures that created it. A landscape is, as Cosgrove and Daniels suggest, "… a cultural image, a pictorial way of representing, structuring or symbolizing surroundings" (1989, 1). For Aitcheson et al. (2000, 4), the cultural value of landscape has been revealed by the growth of leisure and tourism as activities that are characteristically located within the countryside where "regimes of signification in which the production, representation and consumption of landscape are mediated by sites and processes of leisure and tourism". Palmer (1999, 2003, 2005) associates these processes with symbols of national identity that are revealed and celebrated in tourism, which has become an important means for providing such signifiers. The result has been an accumulation of meaning around the countryside that refers to its display as a cultural construction. Thus, its tranquillity, beauty and, not least, the attribution of permanence, and the linkage of these values with concepts of nationhood that modulate perceptions of the nation as a social structure, are key to its meaning as displayed through tourism. As Palmer (2005, 8) states, "[i]t is a discourse where nationness is presented as unifying and where tourists are invited to celebrate and commune with the core characteristics of Englishness". Such themes are also instruments of domination, however, particularly in colonial situations where, as Mitchell (2002, 22) puts it, visual conventions are used to absorb "alien lands" into a kind of pictorial imperialism.

Similar observations are made by Deborah Cherry (2003, 41) in her account of what she refers to as "pictorializing" and "framing" in the representation of French Algeria within European visual conventions. The point here is that visuality and its processes are expressions of discourses that serve distinct purposes—are, indeed, *expressions* of these purposes—and they can exist independently of the object of their apparent interest. The same dynamic can be seen in relation to the separation between archaeological objects and their representation as heritage. What part does visuality play in the process of negotiation and how is this expressed in terms of representational practice and the consequent transformations of heritage materiality?

Negotiation, Visuality and Heritage Transformations

Visual culture has an established place in the understanding of heritage largely because of the centrality of artefacts, monuments, architecture and their associated modalities of display. Interpretation is a key process here, in providing the media through which the archaeological object is transformed into the object of heritage, because it depends mainly (though not exclusively) on visual display. Brett (1996, 61), for example, has described progress in the technology of image reproduction and distribution and its place in the exhibition and display of heritage under the twin headings of visualization and simulation. Likewise, Hooper-Greenhill (2000) has suggested that the visual is at the core of interpretive practice, closely aligned with modalities of display, design and the museum as a medium of communication. According to Merriman (2004, 87), this is associated with advances in the technology of presentation and part of what he describes as the "turn towards the public". Thus for Merriman, the growth in the visual is inevitably associated with the need to make museums more attractive to visitors and to service the requirements of contemporary marketing. This is apparent in the way that reconstruction, re-enactment, models and the very latest in audio-visual and interactive display have become mainstays of the heritage industry, and, as such, represent a further remove from archaeological discourse. As long ago as 1987, Shanks and Tilley (1987b, 87) made the point that such activities have a tendency to suppress conflictual aspects of the past and to fix it in a way that seems unconnected to the social conditions of the present. Wright (1985) had already made this point in examining the cultural significance of heritage as it emerged in the 1980s. The past through display was thus "purged of political tension ..." and "a unifying spectacle" (1985, 69), a point later developed by Walsh (1992) in describing a past effectively sealed or frozen over and thus isolated from the present.

Once the cultural significance of visuality is recognized it can be seen in relation to the processes of negotiation by which archaeology is transformed into heritage. Various competing rights, claims and interests that modulate the negotiation of heritage between representational forces associated with agencies and individuals can be detected within these processes, which are variously and differentially empowered in this transformation. The result of these negotiations and the mechanisms of visuality associated with them is the heritage displayed and signified within a given cultural context. Having been established thus, they become valued as heritage within the consumption nexus of tourism, for example, and the AHD, which in turn determines what else might be absorbed and assimilated.

As noted earlier, however, none of these values are intrinsic to the object. Rather, they are all ascribed in relation to external social and cultural values. What we are concerned with then, following Smith (2006, 56), are the processes that are associated with the selection of objects and their inscription with these values. Once selected, however, it seems to be necessary for additional visual value to be attached to these same objects, as if in emphasizing their visuality they are further marked out as culturally significant. Additional visuality, of course, facilitates presentation, interpretation and touristic interest, all of which are also in the service of cultural signification. Whilst these enhancements can be virtually limitless in their content and means of transmission, they can be seen to begin with on-site and embedded interpretation, and extend through the various manifestations of the visitor experience and into cyberspace. Whilst this process broadly reflects MacCannell's (1999) schema for sight sacralisation, it also responds to, and contains, the significant social and cultural values of the society within which it takes place. The conditions and processes associated with negotiation and visuality might now be tentatively proposed.

The first condition for the negotiation of heritage is that there must be a visible *beginning object*. Characteristically, in archaeology, this could be a building, a site or an artefact, and officially recognized in some way as part of an archaeological corpus. Thus authorized as an archaeological object and embedded within archaeological discourse, the negotiation at this stage is largely between archaeologists, and may have taken place over long periods of time. Such negotiations have charted the development of archaeological knowledge and practice in relation to such sites as Stonehenge and Avebury, for example, where variously "Ancient Britons", druids and Romans are invoked before eventually an authorized provenance is fixed upon (Piggot 1989). Less famously, some of the linear earthworks on the Yorkshire Wolds were once thought to be Roman and are now believed to be late Bronze Age land divisions. The nearby Dane's Dyke at Flamborough Head remains, however, of uncertain provenance and is still the subject of discussion within archaeological discourse.

The second condition is that there needs to be a reason to *do something* with the object, either in order to preserve it or to include it within a required representational process or discourse, although these are likely to be related. In other words, there must be a purpose, or logic in display: a museum that infers identity values from its objects, or a tourism initiative, or an exhibition (Kirshenblatt-Gimblett 1998). In other words, there has to be a need for representation beyond the purely archaeological context and the archaeological record. In tourism, such processes are often motivated by commercial imperatives, but even here there has to be a suitable narrative. As Smith (2006) has shown, an authorized discourse confers heritage value on certain objects. This infers a cultural context for representation, an urge to complete or support some narrative about identity, social structure or social change.

Within that broader discourse, the object should contain or refer to a third condition, which is that there should be some narrative related to the object that makes sense to a wider audience, or which can be *made* to make sense to a wider audience if additional visual values are attached to it. The resulting narrative might even be more important than the beginning object to the extent that physical space and activity are organized around it. A hint of this is evident in MacCannell's (1999, 111) concept of marker involvement. His observations at the Bonnie and Clyde ambush site showed that whilst there was nothing there but a sign, visitors would engage with this as a signifier of a narrative with which they were familiar and which they might experience through the physical space that Bonnie and Clyde had once fatefully occupied. So whilst some objects might be very visible, others might hardly exist in physical space. To become heritage, however, they must be connected to an active and appropriate narrative within which they must be socially and culturally visible.

In an archaeological context, the Northumberland hillforts in the United Kingdom illustrate something of this problem. Yeavering Bell is an Iron Age hillfort, the significance of which, in archaeological terms, is well established. It is, literally, a matter of record. Accordingly, it is well-known to archaeologists and it has been extensively surveyed as part of a recent English Heritage project (Oswald et al. 2007). The Northumberland National Park, however, charged with the responsibility to encourage tourism in the area, has attempted to represent it as an object of archaeological heritage. In so doing, it has addressed the second problem outlined above: a significant physical object with a visible presence in the landscape but which lacks a well established heritage narrative. The next question is whether the object is susceptible to the addition of heritage value through some display medium, in this case a leaflet that accentuates the visuality of the monument, referring to it as "Northumberland's most *spectacular* Iron Age hillfort".[1] It is also interesting that access to the fort is by a so-called "permissive path"[2], which indicates a fourth condition for visuality—that the object has to be accessible or made accessible. A site with no access has little visuality beyond whatever images of it are reproduced. Here, access is literally negotiated: the National Park Authority negotiates permissive paths and access agreements with landowners. Along the path, the visitor is reminded of this negotiation by notices nailed to posts indicating that this access has been agreed under the terms of the relevant legislation.

So for Yeavering Bell, the first four conditions for the negotiation of heritage are satisfied: the remains of the fort are quite substantial and thus present a beginning object, there is an official touristic agenda for the site, a promotional leaflet is available and access has been negotiated. However, there is still something missing: the fifth condition. What the hillfort does not possess, I would argue, is cultural visibility, or visuality, expressed in a coherent narrative that links it with the AHD. What is a hillfort? Why is it important? Where does it fit with what we know about the national past? What does it say about us? In areas of the British Isles where there is an appeal to Celtic or non-English identities, the representation of such a monument as part of a nation-building narrative would be unproblematic, but in England it means little because it does not connect properly with an appropriate national narrative. The risk, then, is that it remains resolutely archaeological, at best a curiosity, and struggles to assume the mantle of heritage because it fails to meet this essential, final condition.

At the base of Yeavering Bell is a flat and apparently featureless field. It is the site of Gefrin, the royal capital of the early Anglo-Saxon Kingdom of Northumbria, and a site with an archaeological and cultural significance that is belied by its lack of physical presence and visibility. It has also been excavated, and it is associated with known historical events, namely the attempts of St Paulinus to convert the Saxon King Edwin and his court, and the local community, to Christianity. Whilst this narrative satisfies the fifth condition that was missing at the hillfort overlooking it, the site presents little by way of a visible beginning object, and visual enhancement is required in order to compensate for this. Every opportunity has been taken to achieve this additional visuality, with embedded interpretation boards rich with images and conjectural reconstructions. Even the fence posts are carved with Anglo-Saxon-looking designs. In the absence of a visible object, the narrative struggles to fill the void with text and visible textual objects. At the edge of the field is a substantial monument with a plaque. The monument is built in dry stone and visually reflects both the ruggedness of the surrounding landscape and a sense of primitive pastness (Figure 3.1). The language of the plaque is solemnly performative: "AT THIS PLACE WAS GEFRIN..." and the visitor is invited to participate in a moment of emotional engagement with an identity-forming commemoration (see Smith 2006 66–74, for a discussion of performativity at heritage sites).

Even if the problem of the beginning object is mitigated by the modern monument and the interpretation boards, the problem at Gefrin is the negotiation of physical access. The field can be entered but to what extent? There are signifiers of access but all the material of interpretation is crowded around the edge, and whilst one of the interpretation boards is located in the field, implying that access exists, there is a feeling of uncertainty about how far into the field the visitor can venture without trespassing on private property. There is actually a kerb of stones around the immediately accessible area: kerbing or curbing?

The question remains, however, as to whether such a framework for analysis can be transferred to other contexts despite the obvious situational factors in the examples quoted above. The Greek island of Rhodes provides an opportunity to evaluate the possibility of generalizing the analysis outlined above by applying it to an emerging heritage tourism industry. The island exhibits the polarities of contemporary tourism. It is, in parts, a highly developed, "packaged" destination based on beach holidays and notoriously associated with the commercial excesses of the north eastern resort of Falaraki. The inland parts of the island, however, particularly in the centre and south, are less developed, and allow an analysis of the way that heritage is being negotiated as a driver of alternative, more "up-market" forms of tourism. It also provides an opportunity to interpret the processes of negotiation and visuality that are at work and the way that these are related to contemporary cultural and political imperatives.

Figure 3.1: Birth of a nation: The visual enhancement of an apparently empty but significant field at Yeavering, Northumberland

Given its proximity to the Turkish coast and its history of Italian and Turkish occupation, it is hardly surprising to discover that what is significant about the heritage narrative on Rhodes is its Greekness, and an authorized Christian heritage that represents its difference from Turkishness. This effectively constitutes a *logic of display*, as Kirshenblatt-Gimblett (1998, 6, 78) has referred to it, which in turn orders and organizes what constitutes "hereness" in a very systematic way. Thus the Neolithic archaeology of the island, which is significant in archaeological terms, has neither the visibility nor the visuality to enter the heritage sphere. Clearly marked (with new brown signs) are virtually any sites with Mycenaean or classical Greek connections and the fragmentary remains of Byzantium, the "Empire of the Greeks". The small monastic churches, which are widely distributed throughout the island, are similarly prized and many are marked on the tourist maps. They also have brown signs—sometimes it appears there are more brown signs than churches and it is often difficult to work out which church is which.

The small church of St George Vardas near Appokalia demonstrates the key ingredients that are necessary for it to enter the sphere of archaeological heritage in Rhodes. The original object is authorized as such: it is part of a narrative of nationhood and identity; it contains early Christian wall paintings, so that these buildings are sometimes known as "painted churches"—in other words they have a category name that in itself suggests significance. The church is also accessible and marked as such. It is curious and perhaps revealing however, that whilst clearly some investment has been made on marking these objects there is little evidence of preservation and conservation. Marking them for scopic purposes, their visuality in other words, seems to be more a priority than their conservation, at least for the time being.

These churches are also part of a continuing practice of church building and memorializing that goes on to this day. The old churches therefore provide an authorized Greek Orthodox Christian heritage that in turn authorizes its continuity as an identity-making cultural practice. New frescoes can even be provided by a small number of well known painters dedicated to the task, and, more significantly, newly built churches are marked by the same brown signs that mark out the old ones. Narratives of the Christian heritage are also provided by the castles of the Knights Hospitallar, and there is a similar urge to represent these as touristic, but there is a degree of negotiation around access. Some of the ruins are inaccessible or structurally dangerous, and these remain outside the authorized spaces of heritage tourism. A structure that is physically dangerous is not negotiable as heritage until it has been selected for some intervention involving safe access and visitor management, although there are clearly borderline cases: whilst the castle at Monolithos is represented as a valid touristic space with good access paths and a café for refreshments at its base, the precipitous cliffs upon which it is perched would be considered a source of unacceptable risk in more litigious jurisdictions.

On Rhodes, then, we find the same impulses and issues that exist at Yeavering: beginning objects, a desire to attract tourists, promotional activity, access, and a clear narrative—in this case Greekness as opposed to Turkishness—and the visual enhancement of the chosen places, thus propelled into touristic space. It seems almost as if official representational practices are rooting out the symbols of Greekness in a way that relied on an audience being receptive and responsive, however vaguely, to the appropriate narratives and discourse. This reflects the findings of Macdonald and Shaw's (2004) research on perceptions of what constitutes Ancient Egypt at the Petrie Museum in London. Thus amongst the "mythic themes" and resonant images were the size and splendour of Ancient Egyptian architecture, its relationship with an exotic landscape and the association with historic mythic individuals such as Cleopatra and Tutankhamen (2004, 120). In other words, a kind of symbolic lexicon was already available that was both essentially visible and susceptible to visual representation. The task is then to negotiate these objects into touristic space, through official recognition, marking, access, presentation, interpretation and the enhanced visuality associated with heritage management. In some cases, this is simply not possible, not so much because the object is on private property, but because access is dangerous or difficult to manage.

At Kritinia Castle in the west of the island, an attempt has been made to consolidate the ruins and create public access (Figure 3.2). It seems likely, given the installation of a kiosk in 2007, that an admission charge will be made. At Lindos almost every element of the Greek narrative is present. It is an ancient site with its own goddess Athene. It has a classical acropolis, the remains of a byzantine church and a crusader castle. Even the path to the summit has a signifier of Greekness to remind the visitor of the site's significance—a relief carving of a trireme ship dating to the second century BC. Together with the town itself, the site presents an ensemble that represents and emphasizes a clear identity-bearing narrative, "the most unified, classically Greek expression in the Dodecanese", according to one guide book.[3] The acropolis itself has received the ultimate visual enhancement: partial reconstruction. It should be added that Lindos is one of the most visited destinations on the island.

Figure 3.2: Building the past: Restoration, access and visitor management at
Kritinia Castle, Rhodes

Clearly, in these different contexts archaeology has been used as a
basis for the social construction of a culturally relevant past. In each case
visuality in its different forms has been both a condition and an outcome
of a negotiated process of selection and representation. This process
operates at the interfaces of archaeology and heritage as two distinct and
separate discourses in the locations concerned. In neither case has the
negotiation been without difficulties, either in terms of the representation
of archaeological space in tourism, or in terms of the relationship between
archaeology and heritage. In the case of the Northumberland hillforts, an
agency whose brief it was to capitalize on these apparent assets, has
sought to project them into public, touristic space. This has required
negotiation with archaeologists—in relation to their archaeological
significance—with landowners—crucially, because of access—and the
local state, whose interests in economic development are inscribed in the
process. At each of these interfaces the negotiation has been largely
successful, but in the end these objects fail as heritage because one
condition has not been met, a coherent relationship with an authorized
discourse. The latter is concerned primarily with signifiers of Englishness
and the attainment of the cultural capital associated with it (Smith 2006,
144), and, as Palmer has indicated, the experiencing of Englishness through

symbols that are projected by tourism (1999, 2003, 2005). Ultimately, the object is visible, but its cultural significance is not, and the enhanced visibility afforded by the negotiation of access and the promotional leaflet is insufficient to compensate for this *invisuality*. At Gefrin, the opposite applies. The narrative is freely available: the first Christian king of Northumbria is baptized in the river, an historical event and one of the founding narratives of Anglo-Saxon England. The negotiation with history works, and the visuality lies in the cultural significance of the story, but the object is not visible in the space that it occupies. Access is not fully negotiated and the field is devoid of visible structures. The negotiation with archaeological discourse provides a conjectural reconstruction which crowds, like the rest of the interpretation and signage, around the margins of an empty inaccessible space.

The situation in Rhodes is, inevitably, different, but similar processes are at work. Here, the motive is to make visible the cultural significance of Greek archaeology and objects. Their existing and long-standing cultural significance already confers a degree of visuality on the objects. They are, in a sense, *expected to be seen*, even though the remains are often fragmentary and difficult to interpret. However, the logic of display requires additional visual enhancements to be made. Brown signs point the hapless and often confused traveller into a landscape with barely the infrastructure to support such extravagant pursuits; the fragmentary remains of Byzantine churches are marked out and interpreted and the castles, to the extent that public safety allows, are opened as tourist attractions. There is also another level of negotiation at work in Rhodes, a negotiation between its authorized heritage discourse and its recorded history and archaeology. The Turkish history of the island, to use Landzelius' (2003) terminology, is actively disremembered or erased in this discourse, despite the fact that the island was under Turkish rule for four hundred years. In the Old Town of Rhodes, the Turkish Quarter is largely neglected and the Mosques are either closed or semi-derelict, with only a few basic interpretation signs. Only the Muslim Library seems to attract the curious, although it's uncertain status in touristic terms appears to leave visitors confused about its significance as an attraction.

Conclusion

I have argued throughout this chapter that not only are archaeology and heritage separate discourses, but that they are *necessarily* separate. They do different things, have different objectives and address their objects in fundamentally different ways. When the two are conflated it only serves to obscure them both, and in particular the processes associated with the formation of heritage. At the same time they are very obviously linked. Archaeology provides objects, places and texts that enter a process of negotiation that is culturally determined and politically active, a process that leads to the cultural and representational practices that we associate with heritage, amongst which tourism is a powerful agent. Yet in a sense it is the link between that marks their separation. The link and its attendant processes of negotiation and transformation represent the difference between them and enables one to become the other under certain conditions.

In order to further define the relationship between archaeology and heritage I have attempted to describe one such set of conditions, for which I have used the term visuality, which I believe is central to the way heritage is negotiated from the materiality of archaeology. Visuality is a key dynamic in the process of representation. It is both a condition and an outcome of the negotiation of heritage. Objects require visuality in the form of social and cultural significance, but they also require visual enhancements to make them objects of representation and consumption. Mere visibility is not enough for the process to work effectively. For example, Yeavering Bell is spectacularly visible, but its *invisuality* is guaranteed by its lack of cultural significance. Gefrin, on the other hand, though invisible, is highly visual because of its links with a recognizable narrative, part of the identity-making AHD. Its visuality is strained, however, because of equivocation about access that makes it an uncomfortable space for visitors. Similar display imperatives are at work on the Island of Rhodes, where an authorized heritage is built around markers of Greekness as an oppositional identity to Turkishness. Here, minor fragments are visualized with brown signage and interpretation, and crumbling castles are invested with visitor management, wherever access and safety allow.

The link between archaeology and heritage is not accidental or happenchance. It is a function of cultural and political dynamics that situate a version of the past in relation to the imperatives of the present. The processes involved are thus conditioned by what is significant in social and political terms in a particular place at a particular time. Given the dynamism and functionality of the relationship itself, how could archaeology and heritage ever be conflated except in the broadest terms and most common usage? The point has been made by Lowenthal (1998, 121): "Heritage is thus no usurper of the past after all, but simply another use of it, neither plausible nor testable, but a declaration of faith, not susceptible to the validations of the historical method". Not historical method, but perhaps critical social study holds the key. Archaeology is not heritage. It simply contributes something to it, through processes that I have described in terms of visuality, or social visibility. These are processes that at once seek to engage with archaeology, but at the same time create distance with it, because the discourse of visuality in heritage relates not to archaeology, but to the wider forms of consumption that are defined and articulated by the hegemonic and representational modalities of contemporary cultural production.

In the end, heritage has its own agenda and it leaves a great deal by the wayside—most of the archaeological record, in fact; all those humps and bumps in the ground that remain resolutely archaeological, even when the agencies of tourism attempt to project them into more public spaces. Heritage toys with the archaeology of the Northumberland hill forts, but the story is a difficult one to tell, whilst the empty field of Gefrin receives more attention because of its nation-building visuality. In Rhodes, the heritage sweeps up native Christianity and the hospitallar's futile castles, whilst in both—and in nation-founding monuments—it signifies, displays and performs a Greek identity. The conflation of archaeology with heritage leaves too much unexamined and too much assumed. Archaeology is not heritage until it is used as such, and then it becomes another, bigger, issue.

Acknowledgements

I would like to thank the Research and Enterprise Office at York St John University for providing the necessary project funding for the research to be carried out on the Island of Rhodes, and colleagues in CEEMED (Culture and Environment in the Eastern Mediterranean) for their help and advice throughout and in the drafting of this chapter.

Notes

[1] The National Park issued a free leaflet "Yeavering Bell, the Hill of the Goats" from which this quotation is taken.

[2] A permissive path is not a public right of way, but a path that can be used by the public with the permission of the landowner. This permission may be withdrawn at any time.

[3] Frommer's Guide, 4th edition, 416-439.

Works Cited

Adorno, Theodore. 2001. *The culture industry*. London: Routledge.

Aitcheson, Cara, Nicola E. MacCleod, and Stephen J. Shaw, ed. 2000. *Leisure and tourism landscapes: Social and cultural geographies*. London: Routledge.

Ascherson, Neal. 2004. Archaeology and the British media. In *Public archaeology*, ed. Nick Merriman, 145–158. London: Routledge.

Ashworth, Gregory. 1994. *Building a new heritage: Tourism, culture and identity in the new Europe*. London: Routledge.

Brett, David. 1996. *The construction of heritage*. Cork: Cork University Press.

Bruner, Edward M. 2005. *Culture on tour, Ethnographies of travel*. Chicago: Chicago University Press

Carman, John. 2005. *Against cultural property: Archaeology, heritage and ownership*. London: Gerald Duckworth.

Cherry, Deborah. 2003. Algeria in and out of the frame: Visuality and cultural tourism in the nineteenth century. In *Visual culture and tourism*, ed. David Crouch and Nina Lübbren, 41–58. Oxford: Berg.

Cosgrove, Daniel and Stephen Daniels, ed. 1989. *The iconography of landscape*. Cambridge: Cambridge University Press.

Duke, Philip. 2007. *The tourists gaze, the Cretans glance, archaeology and tourism on a Greek island*. Walnut Creek, CA: Left Coast Press

Hewison, Robert. 1987. *The heritage industry*. Methuen: London.

—. 1991. Commerce and culture. In *Enterprise and heritage: Crosscurrents of national culture*, ed. John Corner and Sylvia Harvey, 162–177. London: Routledge.

Holtorf, Cornelius. 2005. *From Stonehenge to Las Vegas: Archaeology as popular culture*, Lanham, MD: Altamira Press.

Hooper-Greenhill, Eileen. 2000. *Museums and the interpretation of visual culture*. London: Routledge.

Kirshenblatt-Gimblett, Barbara. 1998. *Destination culture, tourism, museums and heritage*. Berkeley: University of California Press.

Landzelius, Michael. 2003. Commemorative dis(re)membering: Heritage, spatializing disinheritance. *Environment and Planning D: Society and Space* 21: 195–221.

Lowenthal, David. 1998. *The heritage crusade and the spoils of history*. Cambridge: Cambridge University Press.

MacCannell, Dean. 1999. *The tourist: A new theory of the leisure class*. Berkeley: University Of California Press.

MacCrone, David, Angela Morris, and Richard Kiely. 1995. *Scotland—the brand: The making of Scottish heritage.* Edinburgh: Edinburgh University Press.

Macdonald, Sally and Catherine Shaw. 2004. Uncovering Ancient Egypt: The Petrie Museum and its public. In *Public archaeology*, ed. Nick Merriman, 109–131. London: Routledge.

Merriman, Nick. 2004. Involving the public in museum archaeology. In *Public archaeology*, ed. Nick Merriman, 85–108. London: Routledge.

Michell, John. 1982. *Megalithomania: Artists, antiquarians and archaeologists at the old stone monuments.* London: Thames and Hudson.

Mitchell, W.T.J. 2002. Imperial landscapes. In *Landscape and power*, ed. W.T.J. Mitchell, 5–34. Chicago: Chicago University Press.

Oswald, Al, Stewart Ainsworth, and Trevor Pearson. 2007. *Hillforts, prehistoric strongholds of Northumberland National Park.* London: English Heritage.

Palmer, Catherine. 1999. Tourism and the symbols of identity. *Tourism Management*, 20 (3): 313–321.

—. 2003. Touring Churchill's England, rituals of kinship and belonging. *Annals of Tourism Research*, 30 (2): 426–445.

—. 2005. An ethnography of Englishness: Experiencing identity through tourism. *Annals of Tourism Research*, 32 (11): 7–27.

Piggott, Stuart. 1989. *Ancient Britons and the antiquarian imagination.* London: Thames and Hudson.

Shanks, Michael and Christopher Tilley. 1987a. *Social theory and archaeology.* London: Polity Press.

Shanks, Michael and Christopher Tilley. 1987b. *Reconstructing archaeology.* Cambridge: Cambridge University Press.

Skeates, Robin. 2000. *Debating the archaeological heritage.* London: Gerald Duckworth.

Smith, Laurajane. 2006. *Uses of heritage.* London: Routledge.

Thomas, Roger M. 2004. Archaeology and authority in the twenty–first century. In *Public archaeology*, ed. Nick Merriman, 191–201. London: Routledge.

Walsh, Kevin. 1992. *The representation of the past, museums and heritage in the post-modern world.* London: Routledge.

Wright, Patrick. 1985. *On living in an old country.* Verso: London.

CHAPTER FOUR

"I OWN, THEREFORE I AM":
CONFLATING ARCHAEOLOGY
WITH HERITAGE IN GREECE –
A *POSSESSIVE INDIVIDUALISM* APPROACH

KALLIOPI FOUSEKI

Introduction

The concept of "possessive individualism", developed by Macpherson in 1962, stresses that an individual is imbued with a dual and internally contradictory ontology; the ontology of the infinite consumer coupled with the ontology of the individual as developer of his/her own self. The core principle of this theory, "I own, therefore I am", constitutes a powerful mechanism for understanding a range of power relations within any given society, thereby rendering it an idea that is applicable and adjustable in various historic, political, social, temporal and geographical contexts. I use Macpherson's theory as a basis for understanding the conflation of archaeology with heritage, and examine this within the particular social and political contexts offered by Greece. I argue that this conflation overwhelmingly derives from—and leads to—"possessive individualist" attitudes inherent in the archaeological profession; a point also made by Lahn (2007) regarding the struggle for disciplinary identity in the field of archaeology. In her work, Lahn suggests that the possession of certain objects, particularly high status objects, becomes a symbolic statement of individual or collective identity. Lahn, in examining the Kow Swamp repatriation case in Australia, argues that possession and control over those things deemed "archaeological" is a significant aspect or statement of disciplinary identity. The need to "own", control or possess to confirm individual professional and disciplinary identity is thus a significant factor in the conflation of archaeology with heritage in Greece. This conflation reinforces "possessive individualist" attitudes inherent in the archaeological profession and simultaneously reinforces archaeological power and authoritarianism. As a result, archaeologists in Greece play a significant and regulatory role in the management of heritage. This is in part a consequence of the narrowly constructed understanding of heritage that dominates the management process, and links the term with "antiquities" and other "cultural objects". It is also a consequence of implicit and underlying power structures. It is this dominance of archaeological knowledge and thought over the management of heritage that constitutes one of the main sources of conflict and tension between archaeological authorities and local communities in Greece.

The Power of Authority and Possession
in the Archaeological Profession

Macpherson's concept of "possessive individualism" is often seen as the basis for society in liberal democracies, based as it is on the principles of being "anti-monarchical, anti-authoritarian, anti-hierarchical" (Leone 2005, 37). However, the application of Macpherson's ideas within a capitalist context is somewhat conservative, "because it equated property with success and the right to govern...defining those who were capable of governing as those owning real property" (Leone 2005, 35). This is why Mark Leone defines "possessive individualism" as a "mask that hides something far from real: the steep hierarchy of wealth, power, slavery, poverty, oppression, and exploitation" (Leone 2005, 35). Similarly, "possessive individualism" in Greek archaeology hides and reveals conservatism and authoritarianism, which unavoidably cultivates potential tensions and conflicts.

One of the first applications of this concept in museum anthropology was provided by Richard Handler, who used "possessive individualism" as a theoretical means to interpret possessive, curatorial attitudes towards museum collections and cultural objects (Handler 1992). Handler argued that the focus of curators on "the intrinsic value" of an object of "museum quality" is characteristic of modern "possessive individualism" (Handler 1992, 23). According to Handler, curators value an object for its "museum quality" on the basis of its material condition. The better the condition of an object, the closer they feel to the "moment that the craftsman [sic] finished it and use began" (Handler 1992). Here, Handler parallels "possessive individualism" with Locke's ideas on labour value, according to which human beings appropriate an object as a discrete entity into themselves when they mix labour with a piece of the natural world (Locke

1965, 327–44). In this rendering, then, "possessive individualism" works to privilege "isolable individuals and defines them with respect to the material objects they may be said to detach from the world around them and thereby possess" (Handler 1992, 23). In his study, Handler draws upon the example of repatriation, and makes the claim that the repatriation of objects, in extreme cases at least, may reproduce the "positivistic hegemony" of things (Handler 1992, 27), since minority or oppositional groups may replicate the cultural politics of the nation-states whose legitimacy in other respects they challenge (Handler 1988; 1991). In the case of heritage management, these "possessive individualist" attitudes have been reinforced through the regulatory nature of the Authorized Heritage Discourse (AHD).

The AHD, as Smith (2006, 29) points out:

> ... focuses on aesthetically pleasing material objects, sites, places and/or landscapes that current generations "must" care for, protect and revere, so that they may be passed to nebulous future generations for their "education", and to forge a sense of common identity based on the past.

Within this rendering, heritage is saved for future generations by the current generation of experts, who are seen as stewards or caretakers of the past (Smith 2006, 29). A particular suite of experts are perceived to be the only ones who have the ability, knowledge and understanding to identify the intrinsic significance of heritage (Smith 2006). The AHD explicitly promotes the experiences and values of elite social classes and national identities, thereby excluding sub-national forms of identity. This, Smith (2006) argues, is a significant consequence of its provenance, as this discourse developed in, and was influenced by, nineteenth-century ideas of nationalism and romanticism. Heritage has also been conceived within the AHD as a discrete site, object, building or other structure with identifiable boundaries, which has led to a separation of landscape and culture (Waterton 2005). In addition, the heritage user or visitor within the AHD is often conceptualized as a passive consumer of the heritage message (Mason 2004).

Similarly, archaeologists in Greece were—and are—seen not only as experts, but those best placed to protect archaeological heritage for future generations. This assumption of expertise emerged during the first half of the nineteenth century, when heritage was used for shaping national identities and forming a new independent state (Yalouri 2001, 34–6; see also Hamilakis 2007; Hamilakis and Yalouri 1996, 1999; Voudouri 2003). The Greek Archaeological Service was established in 1835 with the aim to conserve and manage the restoration of archaeological works (Kokkou

1977, 72). Classical antiquities became the emblems of national identity (Yalouri 2001, 35) and, therefore, their preservation was prioritized. Within this context, archaeologists were viewed as the main protectors of the "glorious, national past" (Yalouri 2001, 186) and they were ultimately empowered to define and speak for this past. This empowerment encouraged the development of "possessive individualist" attitudes towards the archaeological record, which inevitably led to the development of an authorized heritage discourse in Greece that dominated, and often still dominates, archaeological practice, as will be exemplified below.

Forms of Conflating Archaeology with Heritage in Greece

The conflation of archaeology with heritage in Greece will first be exemplified through the analysis of the "criteria of significance" that archaeologists use to justify their decisions on *in situ* conservation of archaeological remains discovered on rescue excavations. The argument is illustrated by a study of current archaeological law as well as the dominant Central Archaeological Council (CAC), which is the dominant decision-making body in heritage management issues at the Ministry of Culture.

Understanding the Conflation:
A "Possessive Individualist" Approach

One of the clearest examples of "possessive individualist" archaeological attitudes is the issue of intellectual ownership of archaeological data derived from systematic or rescue excavations. In these instances, archaeologists are seen to hold the legal right to "possess" the archaeological data for publication. Current legislation limits intellectual possession to five years, whereas in the past, archaeological data may have been stored for several years. This arrangement has been rightly described by self-described "activist archaeologists" who work for the Greek state but nonetheless criticize the legislation as providing "the most provocative forms of looting … an attempt to exploit antiquities for the personal interest" [author's translation] (Papakonstantinou 2003, 95). In addition to the five-year parameters of possession of data, another paradoxical phenomenon occurred—and occasionally still occurs, the right of the archaeologist-excavator to pass intellectual ownership rights of archaeological data to members of their family in those cases where a family member is a "protégée archaeologist" (Zoes 1990, 27). This authoritarian possession and privatization of what in Greece is often called

common, national heritage is indicative of the "possessive individualist"
attitudes of archaeologists in Greece.

This attitude is further indicated by the type of archaeological data that
is selected for preservation and conservation, and the criteria upon which
such preservation and protection is based. For example, the criteria of
"cultural significance" in Greece, which justifies the *in situ* preservation of
a site or an object, are strictly defined by archaeologists and relate to their
narrow personal, academic interests without taking into consideration any
social values that may exist for associated communities and interest
groups. A thorough examination of the Greek annual archaeological
newsletters from the 1880s demonstrates that preservation criteria for
archaeological remains discovered on rescue excavations are based on
either (a) scientific values, including the topographical significance of the
remains, uniqueness or rarity of a monument; (b) aesthetic criteria
interrelated with the monumentality and state of preservation; or (c)
criteria that will provide archaeologists with further potential research,
such as the continuation of the site to an adjoining plot or extensiveness
(Figure 4.1) (Fouseki 2008a;b). As the list of criteria in Figure 4.1
illustrates, any reference to the social and/or public value of the *in situ*
material conserved remains absent.

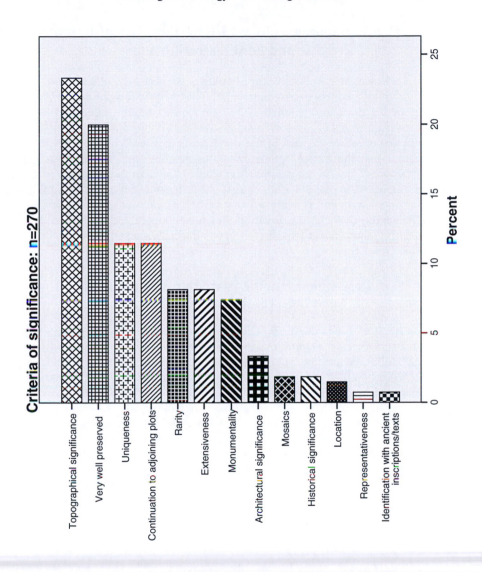

Figure 4.1: Criteria of "cultural significance" for justifying in situ conservation

Conflating archaeology with heritage in legislation and administration

This section analyses how heritage is narrowly understood as "antiquities" and "modern monuments". The analysis focuses on a current legislative document entitled *"On the Protection of Antiquities and Cultural Heritage in General"*, and also reflects upon the CAC. A cursory examination of the content of the law reveals that the broader concept of cultural heritage is predominantly represented by, and corresponds to, "antiquities" and, to a much lesser extent, to "modern monuments" (with an emphasis on buildings/structures). This narrow definition is further illustrated through a study of the CAC, which is responsible for adjudicating over the conservation and protection of archaeological and modern monuments in Greece (for more information on CAC see Loukaki 2008, 168–72).

Legislation: "On the Protection of Antiquities and Cultural Heritage in General"

The title of the current law designed to protect heritage in Greece, *On the Protection of Antiquities and Cultural Heritage in General* (Law 3028/2002), echoes the inferior position that "cultural heritage" holds in Greece, as well as the authoritarian voice of the "expert" that underpins heritage management. Attempts to revise the former Greek archaeological law that dated back to 1932 took place after the 1980s. After long-term discussions with archaeologists, local authorities, architects and the Church (Rozos 2004, 20) the current archaeological legislation was finally formulated in 2002. The current law reflects the principle of the revised Constitutional Law in 2001 according to which cultural heritage is a "public good" preserved for the "common benefit" (Rozos 2004, 20). In addition, the current legislation echoes a series of international legislative documents including the Hague Convention (1954), the 1970 *Convention on the Means of Prohibiting and Preventing the Illicit Import, Export and Transfer of Ownership of Cultural Property*, the 1972 World Heritage Convention, the 1992 Valetta Convention and the 1995 UNIDROIT convention (see Voudouri 2004, 25–7).

Authorization, and its resultant appeals to "possessive individualism", is indicated by a commitment to inheritance, patrimony and by the "objectification" of heritage. The first article of the legislation, for example, states the aim to protect cultural heritage for the preservation of historical memory for "present and future generations" (Article 1.1). This statement not only echoes similar statements of international documents such as the Venice Charter, which has influenced the practice of anastylosis in Greece (Vacharopoulou 2005, 2006), but also makes "reference to the cognitive validity of conservation professionals" (Waterton et al. 2006, 348). This, in effect, works to legitimize archaeologists and other experts as the most appropriate professionals for "safeguarding" heritage. This "ethical professional responsibility" (Hamilakis 2007, 22) pre-assumes the role of archaeologists as appropriate professionals for the conservation and protection of archaeological record and is, according to Hamilakis, an expression of capitalist modernity (Hamilakis 2007). Moreover, if we accept that "possessive individualism" is a distinctive expression of capitalism (Leone 2005), then it can also be argued that professional archaeologists represent "individual capital", which does not necessarily have economic connotations (Hamilakis and Yalouri 1999), but relates to their own personal, individual possession of knowledge, skills, and access to the archaeological record (Smith 2004; Lahn 2007).

"Possessive individualism" is further indicated by the "objectification" of cultural heritage in this text which, contradicts the implicit suggestion of encompassing "intangible heritage" within the scope of cultural heritage, as implied by the initial statement to preserve "historic memory for present and future generations and for *enhancing the cultural environment*" (Article 1, my emphasis). Likewise, Article 1.2. offers a typical example of cultural objectification. The article reads: "The cultural heritage of the country consists of *cultural objects* found within the boundaries of Greek territory". In this standard definition, cultural heritage is narrowly confined to cultural objects; this objectification unavoidably leads to the materialization of heritage. The logic underpinning this definition establishes archaeologists, as experts on material culture, as the primary stewards of the past. The objectification of cultural heritage subordinates and undermines the importance of cultural environments, implying that the significance of environment is dependant on the significance of the cultural objects rather than vice-versa.

The only instance in the legislation document under examination which absoluteness or certainty are not imparted occurs within Article 9.3, which reads:

If it is decided to preserve the antiquity, the owner of the immovable [antiquities] may be obliged to allow its visit under conditions to be determined by decision of the Minister of Culture, following an opinion of the Council (Law 3028/2002, my emphasis).

The use of "if" and "may", in this case, reveals a governmental willing to relinquish some control over the ownership of ancient remains that occur within private property. However, the relinquishing of control does not happen to any serious degree, since the Ministry of Culture and the CAC are the only governmental bodies that determine the conditions of any visit.

Administrative Framework: The Example of the Central Archaeological Council (CAC)

The previous section showed why and how antiquities are narrowly conflated with heritage. I argued that this conflation is a reflection of "possessive individualist" attitudes of experts who function authoritatively to "safeguard" heritage for future generations. This section will analyse this argument further by considering one of the main, governmental councils responsible for making decisions over major archaeological matters and issues. Before this analysis, however, a brief introduction to the basic structure of the Hellenic Ministry of Culture is required, particularly in relations to its management of "antiquities" and "cultural heritage".

The protection of cultural heritage in Greece reflects the narrow definition of heritage as antiquities and modern monuments. There are three central governmental councils: CAC, the Central Council for Modern Monuments and the Council for Museums (Figure 4.2) involved in heritage management. In addition, the Council for Museums deals with museological matters. At this stage, it is worth noting that the employment of museologists, a profession that was officially recognized in Greece in 2004, pre-requires a degree in archaeology (FEK 3K/2008).

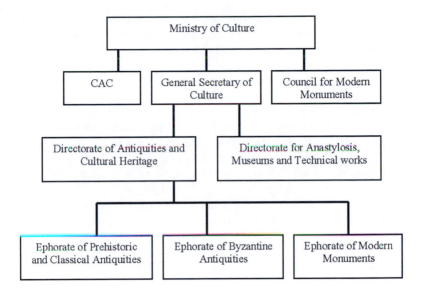

Figure 4.2: Schematic representation of the core, administrative bodies responsible for the management of cultural heritage in Greece

The *Directorate of Antiquities and Cultural Heritage* further divides the "objects" of archaeology into *antiquities* and *modern monuments*. Accordingly, the Ephorates of Prehistoric, Classical and Byzantine antiquities are responsible for the management of antiquities and the Ephorates of Modern Monuments are responsible for the Modern Monuments. Other forms of heritage, such as archives and oral traditions hold an inferior position in the Hellenic Ministry of Culture, despite the existence of some non-governmental significant organizations and research institutions that are responsible for the study and management of other, excluded forms of heritage and sit outside of the schema represented by Figure 4.2. The limitations that result from this are clearly reflected in the philosophy of CAC, which is also characterized by an internal contradiction inherent in its "philosophy": its official website reveals a tension between democratization and authoritarian dominance and between interdisciplinarity and the dominance of "experts".

CAC in Greece claims to be an interdisciplinary advisory council belonging to the Hellenic Ministry of Culture (Hellenic Ministry of Culture). The current "interdisciplinary" committee consists of the General Secretary of the Hellenic Ministry of Culture, a legal advisor, the director of the *General Directorate of Antiquities and Cultural Heritage*, the director of the *Directorate for Anastylosis, Museums and Technical Works*, four directors from the Ephorates of Antiquities, the director of Numismatic Museum, five academic archaeologists, one academic architect, a geologist and the director of the Town Planning department for the *Ministry of the Environment and Public Works*. The nature of this committee reveals two main things: First, a tendency to bridge theory with practice through inviting both academics and practitioners to participate together. Second, interdisciplinarity is still perceived narrowly, as only architects, archaeologists, and one geologist are included in the committee, thereby neglecting the significance of other disciplines such as sociology, anthropology and psychology. Here, the dominance of archaeologists and architects as the appropriate experts for dealing with cultural heritage again becomes apparent. Since the majority of issues with which the CAC deals relates to conflict situations, psychologists, sociologists, communication theorists and negotiators *should* be involved in the committee. The role of the CAC as "negotiator" is highlighted on the official website of the Ministry of Culture[1] which states that:

> It is natural that trends reflecting different approaches regarding the protection of cultural heritage are expressed in terms of the extent of interventions, the absolute or relative protection in relation to other public, social rights (as the right of employment, ownership, transportation, energy, disability access and other public facilities) acknowledged by the constitutional law. Our answer to the dividing and absolute 'either this or the other' is *the compromise statement 'both this and the other through seeking solutions that are accepted by both parties'*. Our care for our cultural heritage is the common ground on which our approaches are based [author's translation and emphasis)] (Hellenic Ministry of Culture).

According to this statement, the CAC is the protector not only of antiquities but also of "cultural heritage"; it acknowledges the dissonance of heritage and aims to function as a mediator and negotiator by encouraging compromise. On this basis, the CAC allows interested parties to participate in meetings where, with the advice and guidance of lawyers, they can support their claims and arguments (Hellenic Ministry of Culture). However, the compromising style that the CAC claims to adopt becomes clouded when reading the next paragraphs of the website, which state that among the interested parties that participate in the meetings there

---

[1] The website was accessed on 13 July 2007, when the General Secretary of the Hellenic Ministry of Culture was Mr Christos Zachopoulos. The website cannot currently be accessed since, according to the link, viewers "are not authorised to view this page".

are some individuals and groups of people who are "strong-minded (in a negative way), aggressive, rude, uneducated and fanatical" (Hellenic Ministry of Culture). These characterizations clearly depict a lack of democratization and dialogicality in cultural heritage management in Greece. I argue that this lack of democratization derives from the inherent possessive individualist approaches of archaeologists who have been empowered by the state to safeguard the *cultural heritage in general*. The following example reveals these attitudes.

Conflating Heritage Management with the Science of Archaeology

In 2005, three years after the passing of the current legislation *"On the Protection of Antiquities and Cultural Heritage In General"* (Law 3028/2002), the government, represented by the right-wing party Nea Democratia, suggested a revised scheme for the structure of the Hellenic Ministry of Culture regarding the management of heritage in Greece (ASA 2005). The suggested scheme aimed at limiting the managerial responsibilities of archaeologists and the Ephorates (Directorates) of Antiquities by developing regional committees that would include a substantial number of people from local authorities, thereby empowering private enterprises to play an active part in heritage management (ASA 2005). The suggested scheme, which has several weak points that are outside the scope of this article, was perceived by the majority of archaeologists as a governmental attempt to de-centralize their power. This is clearly reflected in a statement published by the "Committee for the Environment and its Sustainability" (In Greek: Epimeleterion Perivallontos and Viosimotitos, 2005) in collaboration with the Association of Greek Archaeologists (Committee for the Environment and its Sustainability), which reads:

> The *Ministry of Culture* has the responsibility for the administration of Greek *cultural heritage*. For states with limited material power and rich historical past, like Greece, *this jurisdiction* [the management of cultural heritage] *is, indeed, the most important public policy*. [This is] because it is not about the management of material resources, but about the safeguarding of the symbols of Hellenism which define our national identity [author's translation] (Committee for the Environment and its Sustainability 2005, original emphasis).

The concept asserted here is that archaeologists are the protectors of national identity since all material culture (mostly archaeological) is the symbol of "Greekness" and Greece. The statement continues:

> To the jurisdiction of the Ministry of Culture lies also the support towards
> contemporary folk culture (contemporary art, folklore etc.). *These two*
> *public policies differ substantially with regard to the nature of the object*
> [original emphasis]. The first one [management of cultural heritage] is
> administered according to the *strict principles of archaeological science*
> [my emphasis], while the second one [management of contemporary art] is
> clearly an empirical policy that aims at facilitating contemporary artistic
> expression and, simultaneously, at ensuring the creative autonomy of the
> supported artists.

In this statement, it is not only archaeology that is immixed with cultural
heritage, but so too is heritage management conflated with archaeological
site management. The implication that the management of cultural heritage
should be based "on the principles of archaeological science" is revealing
of the misconception of what heritage management is, and endangers the
nature of heritage management as a social practice. This narrow conflation
is legitimized not only by the role of archaeologists as "safe guarders" of
national heritage, but by the fact that archaeologists have also been defined
by the state as the most *appropriate* experts who can deal with its
management in a statement that reads:

> There is no room in the public administration of cultural heritage *for*
> *individuals who are not experts* [my emphasis] since both the aims and the
> means of this policy are dictated by *the familiar science of archaeology*
> [original emphasis]. Therefore, no political and public councils, social
> stakeholders, companies etc should be part of it ...The management of
> cultural heritage ...should not be confused with the recent science of
> cultural management, that is based on financial criteria and principles
> shaped according to the practices imposed by the industry of public
> spectacle. The management of cultural heritage is held by *the specialist*
> *body of archaeologists of the central administration* [my emphasis], who
> have the status of the *public servant* [original emphasis]. The rest of
> scientific specialities are simply contributing to the activities of
> archaeologists [author's translation] (Committee for the Environment and
> its Sustainability 2005, original emphasis).

From this statement, it becomes apparent that archaeologists, and the
broader practices of archaeology, are identified as *the* key players in the
management of heritage. This unavoidably leads to a "selective" process
of heritage management, in which archaeologists are considered the only
ones capable of choosing which parts of heritage will be preserved,
conserved and presented, how they will be preserved and for whom.

Archaeologists traditionally favour those things considered "aesthetically pleasing" and "monumental", materiality, as Smith (2006) has argued, and as illustrated above, tends to mean that the protection and preservation of heritage will unavoidably include only tangible heritage with an emphasis on the "glorious", "elite" and/or "aesthetic" sites and objects.

Consequences of the Conflation of Archaeology with Heritage

The authoritarian, possessive, individualist ethos that has been analysed not only excludes several forms of heritage that are at risk of loss, it also causes constant tensions and conflicts with individuals or groups of people who do not necessarily feel that "antiquities" and "cultural objects" are preserved for the common benefit of the nation and, more importantly, for their own benefit. Examples of "violent" attacks towards archaeological remains are not rare. In Crete, for example, the decision by the local Ephorate of Antiquities to integrate *in situ* conserved mosaics into the new hospital building—resulting in the reduction of the size of the hospital—led the local inhabitants to violently respond, attacking the remains with axes (AD 1987, 558–63). Open-air archaeological sites have often been characterized as "walls and holes that simply attract mice and snakes", occupying open-air spaces that could have a social function for the common benefit of the community (Apostolakis 2004; Fouseki 2008b). In other cases, massive expropriations of plots valued by experts for their archaeological potential or significance are legitimized by law, despite the massive dislocations of local communities that result, as in the case of the building of the New Acropolis Museum (Fouseki 2006, 2007, 2008a,b). It is therefore imperative that archaeologists, as with any group of experts, transform their possessive, individualist attitudes into collective attitudes that holistically, rather than partially and selectively, support the "common good" and "common benefit" by adopting a holistic approach to the management of heritage.

Conclusion

This chapter endeavoured to address the various ways in which archaeology is objectified and conflated with heritage. The objectification of archaeology and its conflation with heritage leads unavoidably to the objectification of cultural heritage, as indicated by the use of the term "cultural objects". The objectification of "antiquities" and "cultural objects" can be interpreted as an expression of the "possessive individualist" attitudes of "experts". Here, experts are perceived as ethically and professionally responsible for the protection and management of the archaeological record and cultural heritage. In Greece, these are mostly archaeologists and architects. "Possessive individualism", as an expression of modern capitalism, empowers archaeologists and transforms them, often, into authoritative "public servants" who care for heritage for the common benefit of present and future generations.

Archaeologists in Greece view themselves as the most appropriate "guardians" of emblematic, national heritage and *cultural heritage in general* and, thus, they perceive that heritage management relies within their own territory exclusively. This conflation of archaeology and the archaeological profession with heritage and heritage management respectively excludes broader forms of heritage, for example intangible heritage. Cultural heritage instead of constituting "social heritage" and reflecting social values for wider local communities refers narrowly to cultural objects. This approach in turn accounts for a lack of multivocality that leads unavoidably to constant tensions and conflicts between the Greek Archaeological Service and citizens. The latter, according to the Constitutional and current archaeological law, ironically and contradictory, are the main beneficiaries of the heritage that is being preserved.

Acknowledgements

First, I would like to thank Kathy Tubb for supervising my PhD thesis, as well as the Greek State Scholarship Foundation and the British Federation of Women Graduates that funded my postgraduate research studies. Furthermore, I would like to express my gratitude to Georgios Alexopoulos for his constructive comments on an early draft of this paper. Last but not least I would like to thank Dr Laurajane Smith and Dr Emma Waterton for their hard and excellent editing work.

Works Cited

AD (Archaeologikon Deltion). 1987. *Archaeological newsletter* (Αρχαιολογικόν Δελτίον) (In Greek)
Apostolakis, Sakis. 2004. *Valuable or "useless walls"?* (Αξιόλογα ή «παλιοντούβαρα;), Eleftherotypia, September 29, Arts section.
ASA (Association of Greek Archaeologists), 2005. *The Protection of our monuments is non-negotiable–Proceedings of a one-day conference*

under the subject: The protection of cultural heritage and the new scheme for the Organization of the Ministry of Culture (Η Προστασία των Μνημείων μας είναι Αδιαπραγμάτευτη—Πρακτικα ημερίδας με θέμα: Η προστασία της πολιτιστικής κληρονομιας και το νέο σχέδιο Οργανισμού του υπουργειου Πολιτισμου), Byzantine and Christian Museum, Thursday 14 April. Athens: Association of Greek Archaeologists (in Greek)

Committee for the Environment and its Sustainability. 2005. Epimeleterion perivallontos kai biosimotitos. Arxaia. http://www.environ-sustain.gr/main.htm (In Greek).

FEK (Φύλλο ελληνικής κυβερνήσεως). 2008. *Governmental newsletters* (In Greek).

Fouseki, Kalliopi. 2006. Conflicting discourses on the construction of the New Acropolis Museum: Past and present. *European Review of History* 3 (4): 533–48.

—. 2007. Developing and integrating a conflict management model into the heritage management process: The case of the New Acropolis Museum. In *Which past, whose future: Treatments of the past at the start of the 21st century*, ed. Sven Grabow, Dan Hull and Emma Waterton, 127–136. Oxford: Archaeopress.

—. 2008a. Discerning the origins of "in-situ museums" in Greece, *SOMA 2005: Symposium on Mediterranean archaeology. Proceedings of the ninth Annual Meeting of Postgraduate Researchers, University of Chieti, Department of Archaeology, 23–26 February 2005*, eds. Oliva Menozzi, Maria Luigia L. Di Marzio, and Domenico Fossataro, 447–454. Oxford: Archaeopress.

—. 2008b. Conflict resolution in the management of in-situ museums. PhD diss., University College London.

Hamilakis, Yannis. 2007. From ethics to politics. In *Archaeology and capitalism: From ethics to politics*. Ed. Yannis Hamilakis and Philip Duke, 15–40. Walnut Creek, CA: Left Coast Press.

Hamilakis, Yannis, and Eleana Yalouri. 1996. Antiquities as symbolic capital in modern Greece. *Antiquity* 70: 117–129.

Hamilakis, Yannis, and Eleana Yalouri. 1999. Sacralising the past: Cults of archaeology in modern Greece. *Archaeological Dialogues* 6 (2): 115–159.

Handler, Richard. 1988. *Nationalism and the politics of culture in Quebec.* Madison: University of Wisconsin Press.

—. 1991. Who owns the past? History, cultural properly, and the logic of possessive individualism. In *The politics of culture*, ed. Brett Williams, 63–74. Washington, DC: Smithsonian Institution Press.

—. 1992. On the valuing of museum objects. *Museum Anthropology* 16 (1): 21–28.

Hellenic Ministry of Culture. "Central Archaeological Council". http://www.yppo.gr/0/kas.

Kokkou, Ageliki. 1977. *The care for antiquities and the first museums* (Η Μέριμνα για τις αρχαιότητες και τα πρώτα μουσεία). Athens: Hermes (In Greek).

Lahn, J. 2007. Finders keepers, losers weepers: A social history of the Kow Swamp remains. In *Cultural heritage: Critical concepts in media and cultural studies*, ed. Laurajane Smith, 361–410. London: Routledge.

Leone, Mark P. 2005. *The archaeology of liberty in an American capital: Excavations in Annapolis*. Berkeley; Los Angeles; London: University of California Press.

Locke, John. 1965. *Two treatises of government*. Ed. Peter Laslett. New York: Mentor.

Loukaki, A. 2008. *Living ruins, value conflicts*. Aldershot: Ashgate Publishing.

Macpherson, Crawford Brough. 1962. *The political theory of possessive individualism: Hobbes to Locke*. Oxford: Clarendon Press.

Mason, Rhiannon. 2004. Conflict and complement: an exploration of the discourses informing the concept of the socially inclusive museum in contemporary Britain. *International Journal of Heritage Studies* 10 (1): 49–73.

Papakonstantinou, Vasilios, 2003. *Manual of archaeological looting, official and unofficial* (Εγχειρίδιο Αρχαιοκαπηλίας, επίσημης και ανεπίσημης). Periplous publications: Athens (in Greek)

Rozos, Nikolaos. 2004. *General presentation of the Law 3028/2002 "On antiquities and the cultural heritage in general"* (Γενική παρουσίαση του Ν. 3028/2002 «Για την προστασία των αρχαιοτήτων και την πολιτιστική κληρονομιά εν γένει». In *Cultural heritage and the law* (Η πολιτιστική κληρονομιά και το δίκαιο) ed. Eleni Trova. 19–24. Athens & Thessaloniki: Sakkoula (In Greek)

Smith, Laurajane. 2004. The repatriation of human remains-problem or opportunity? *Antiquity* 78: 404–413.

—. 2006. *Uses of heritage*. London: Routledge.

Vacharopoulou, Kalliopi. 2005. Conservation and management of archaeological monuments and sites in Greece and Turkey: a value-based approach to anastylosis. *Papers from the Institute of Archaeology* 16: 72–87.

—. 2006 Conservation of classical monuments: A study of anastylosis with case studies from Greece and Turkey. PhD diss., University College London

Voudouri, Dafni. 2003. *State and museums: The statutory framework of the archaeological museums* (Κράτος και Μουσεία: Το θεσμικό πλαίσιο των αρχαιολογικών μουσείων). Athens & Thessaloniki: Sakkoula publications (in Greek)

—. 2004. *The new legislative text 3028/2202 in the light of the international and European regulations for the protection of cultural heritage (Ο νέος νόμος 3028/2002 υπό το φως των διεθνών και ευρωπαϊκών κανόνων για την προστασία της πολιτιστικής κληρονομιάς). In Cultural heritage and the law* (Η πολιτιστική κληρονομιά και το δίκαιο) ed. Eleni Trova. 25–41. Athens & Thessaloniki: Sakkoula (In Greek)

Waterton, Emma. 2005. Whose sense of place? Reconciling archaeological perspectives with community values: Cultural landscapes in England. *International Journal of Heritage Studies* 11 (4): 309–326.

Waterton, Emma, Laurajane Smith and Gary Campbell, 2006, The utility of discourse analysis to heritage studies: The Burra Charter and social inclusion. *International Journal of Heritage Studies* 12 (4): 339–355.

World Heritage Convention 1972. *Convention concerning the protection of the world cultural and natural heritage.*

Yalouri, Eleana. 2001. *The Acropolis: global fame, local claim.* Oxford and New York: Berg.

Zoes, Antonis., 1990. *Archaeology in Greece: Realities and prospects* (Η Αρχαιολογία στην Ελλάδα: πραγματικότητες και προοπτικές). Athens: Polytypon (In Greek)

An Interview with Alison Drake
(Chair, Castleford Heritage Trust)[*]

Can you give some examples of how communities and archaeologists have worked together, both successfully and unsuccessfully?

AD: Well, I'd like to talk about the successful things first, because there are some local and regional archaeologists who have been absolutely fantastic with us, they have encouraged us every step of the way. They have really backed us. The first meeting we had at Castleford, we had 400 people there. I rang, don't know where I got the numbers from, really, as I didn't know anybody at that time, but I rang the ancient monuments inspector for our area because we have a Roman Bath House site in the town, and I asked if he would come to our meeting. He came to the meeting, and he was affected by the power and the response coming from the community in terms of how they honoured and respected their own heritage. The older people knew about their heritage and wanted to reclaim it. They wanted to celebrate it and they wanted to use it for education and leisure and to share it with our children and young people.

Right from the start there have been a number of archaeologists who have actually worked with us, and yet, I think, behind these people there seems to be a sense that they are side-stepping to work with us. This is sometimes, not all the time, but sometimes they have had to find ways of working with us that works around the organizations that they work for or works around the expectations of their discipline, and that is a shame. We have been successful by chance sometimes. We got *Time Team* to come and make a programme in Castleford at just the right time, when we needed that type of publicity, to publicize what the Castleford Heritage Trust (CHT) and people in Castleford were trying to do. *Time Team* and Tony Robinson and archaeologists in the region did us a lot of good. People are proud of their Roman heritage and extremely interested in what goes on with it. In the last couple of years, the Mott of Castleford's Castle at Whitwood was found and the local district archaeologist included the community in digging the Mott and it was determined that it was an early

---

[*] Interviewer: Gary Campbell

Norman Mott—so Castleford did have a Castle after all. That was interesting and exciting for the community. Museum professionals have also helped us do work with schools and the local community and that has been useful.

Some tensions occur though, because the local community see all these things, and when I say "things" I mean the stories and the meanings and the background to the objects, as *ours*. You know, when archaeologists dig up things in Castleford from the Roman period, when they dug up the Iron Age Chariot Burial on the edge of town, Castleford people think that all these things belong to them. The collection of pottery and glass that our community made[1], and that the town collected, and the things that were acquired by local firms and by local communities who gave these things to the local borough, when it became a borough in 1955, represents a good collection—the town's silver, if you like. People of Castleford regard this as theirs—they belong to our family, our community and Castleford people. However, when archaeologists take things away we think that they are just doing a professional job with them, but that they don't own them. I think that is where we have come a cropper because archaeologists think that they have a right to do what they like and decide themselves what will happen to these things, and how they will be used, and how they will be presented. Castleford people don't agree with that, they don't like that, they just laugh at that—it's a ludicrous idea. For instance, last night there was a talk by the local conservator of the district about conserving things and getting them ready to put in the new Forum Museum [a new community museum], and she said they have a list of the things they are going to put in the museum; a list of the things they are going to conserve. Coming out of the talk one of the old ladies said to me: "I wanted to ask her how on earth she is making this list of things they are going to conserve as a priority to put in the museum. Until they have asked us what it is we want in that museum, which things out of the collection we actually want in order to tell our story, how can they make this list? I wanted to ask her that. We must make sure we ask her how she is doing that and they come back to talk to us. Until we told them what we want in that museum then their list is useless!" It is often taken for granted by archaeologists that they are going to be the ones deciding what's going into that museum because they see it as their project. They see it as their museum, they see them as their artefacts, and I think archaeologists are just carrying on doing their professional job thinking that they know what they are doing and that they are the ones that know what should be done. Therefore, they will only tell us bits about what they are doing. Yet local people want to tell them what they should be doing. That is where I think we have been unsuccessful in working with archaeologists: when they haven't actually understood where the community is coming from and the community certainly doesn't understand where the archaeologists are coming from, and they certainly don't agree with them.

To what extent can heritage and archaeology be said to be the same?

AD: If you talk about archaeology to local people they immediately start thinking of the Roman and Iron Age artefact collections and sites, and I think archaeologists have tended to concentrate on the distant past. However, what local people think when they talk about heritage can be different. They mostly mean the recent history and heritage of the town, and what we actually have had passed onto us, and what we are actually passing on to the next generations, and you don't always mean in terms of collections, sites and artefacts. Archaeologists control heritage and have a different view from the community of what we are dealing with because they are concentrating on the collections, the things that they have been excavated from the distant past. Moreover, archaeologists want them kept safe from contamination and the dangers posed by their use by local people. However, local people think that heritage is what we are using and passing on and showing to our young people and telling them stories about. Those things are valuable and we do want them to be kept safe too, but on the other hand, they are not valuable to us unless we are using them and can benefit from them.

How would you define heritage, and is archaeology relevant to that definition?

AD: I think heritage is the things in our community, and I don't mean always tangible things. Heritage can be stories and the values that we have and they are just as important as tangible things. The characteristics of the local community, and the way they go about things, as well as those experiences and skills that we have and have developed and have from the past—these are also heritage. These things from the past are heritage as well as the tangible collections and objects and buildings that we think as a community are worthy of passing on to future generations and use today to inspire, to motivate, to educate and to enjoy with our young people and our children. That's what heritage is and using that—the use of it and the things we do, the things that we share, that's heritage. One old lady put on our heritage quilt recently—we are making this out of embroidered squares sewn together that name people or name aspects of the town—she put on one of the embroidered squares that "our heritage is the people of Castleford" and that's absolutely true. Passing on stories, achievements and those values of local people that are useful for us today and for future generations, that's what heritage is.

Who should manage heritage?

AD: Well, when you say "manage" I think there are certain levels of management. I think if you are thinking of the decisions of how heritage should be used, that, I think, is the responsibility of the local community. Some people in the community couldn't give a damn. They are just getting on with their own lives, going out to work every day and they're not interested. However, people can come to periods in their lives when they think, well yes, I do want to pass something on to my children. Also such people may become concerned if there was a fight over something or an argument over heritage then they may join in. Then there are the local people who are thoughtful and are involved, and have an understanding of their own community and do take the trouble to have a say. Those groups, families and individuals really work hard and can see the vision of how local heritage could and should be used; I think they ought to be the dominant voice in managing heritage.

However, I also think we need the professionals to help us see the possibilities. Sometimes communities, like ours, can't always see the possibilities of how to care for objects, how to collect stories, how to use them in the most successful ways. There are innovative ideas in other communities that professionals may know about and that can be brought and shared across communities. That is what professional heritage managers ought to be doing. They ought to be seeing what's happing across communities and sharing and developing some of the best practices with us, but letting local people decide.

For instance, our group has hold of two local pit banners, which we won't let go, because we know if the managers, conservators and people like that get their hands on them they won't let us use them. We use them by hanging them and displaying them in actives, workshops, celebrations, and festivals that we organize. If they are just shoved away, as most of them are in various museums, we will never see them and they become worthless to us as a community. The one's we have are probably being damaged each time we hang them, because we don't hang them in the best places or in the best situations. However, to me, and to our group, it is more important that we use them in order to pass on that heritage, the heritage of the messages and meanings within those banners—the mottos on those banners and the pictures on them. It is more important that our young people in our community see them, enjoy them, celebrate them and learn from them than that they are put away, even if they are damaged in the process.

Notes

[1] Castleford's past industry included not only mining, but also potteries, glass making and a chemical works, while current industries include Tailoring, confectionary and flour milling, amongst others.

Further Reading

Castleford Heritage Trust. n.d. Castleford Heritage Trust: Welcome. http://www.castlefordheritagetrust.org.uk/

Drake, Alison. 2008. The use of community heritage in pursuit of social inclusion: A case study of Castleford, West Yorkshire, unpublished MA dissertation, University of York.

Smith, Laurajane. 2006. *Uses of heritage*. London: Routledge.

Smith, Laurajane and Emma Waterton. 2009. *Heritage, communities and archaeology*. London: Duckworth.

PART II:

THE LIMITS OF ARCHAEOLOGY

CHAPTER FIVE

ARCHAEOLOGY QUIET ON THE WESTERN FRONT

ROSS WILSON

Introduction

As archaeologists excavate the former battlefields of the Western Front in France and Belgium, the particular relationship between archaeology, heritage and memory is also exposed; the manner and the extent to which archaeology shapes and informs popular memory can thereby be examined and considered. The advent of archaeological projects on the Western Front, initiated by teams from Britain, France and Belgium, highlights how archaeology engages with popular memory and how concepts of heritage possess vivid and powerful emotive affect. This emotional hold derives in part from the hallowed place the Western Front still holds within Britain, France, Belgium, Germany, Australia, Canada and New Zealand. Even to speak of "the trenches" of the Western Front in Britain, for instance, is to call to mind a subject that still remains powerful within cultural life. After the passing of ninety years, the Western Front continues to haunt. The names of the former battlefields of France and Belgium still possess an evocative, poignant quality: the Somme, Ypres, Arras, Vimy (Winter 1995, 1). These names seem to conjure images of a devastated landscape, hideous industrialized war, and infinite pity for those who fought. As Dyer (1995, 7) has remarked, these perceptions and memories:

> ... seem ... to have pulsed into life in the nation's collective memory, to have been generated down the long passage of years, by the hypnotic spell of Remembrance they are used to induce.

The history and memory of the conflict can therefore be described as an ongoing trauma. This situation is best illustrated in Britain by the calls in 1998 for the pardon of soldiers executed by the British Army during 1914–1918 (Corn and Hughes-Wilson 2002). This campaign, recently brought to a successful conclusion, focused on using the popular image of the British "Tommies" in the trenches as victims of the war. The pardoned soldiers were placed alongside their comrades as a popular memory of the Western Front as an atrocious, pitiful waste of life was affirmed. This popular memory of the Western Front has recently been criticized by historians, who have labelled it a misguided creation born out of the images of the battlefields conveyed in popular television shows and film, such as *Blackadder* and *All Quiet on the Western Front* (Bond 2002; Sheffield 2002). Archaeological projects have implicitly or explicitly attempted to follow this example by also seeking to "debunk" the so-called myths and memories of the war (see Pollard and Banks 2007). This in effect mirrors a wider trend within studies of archaeology and "heritage", as expertise and institutional knowledge are regarded as defining principles of the constitution of "heritage" (Smith 2006). This avoids or neglects the significant issues of societal identity and memory latent within notions of heritage and the wider perceptions of the past (Harvey 2001). In contrast to this, studies of memory have highlighted how practices of remembrance within societies concern the affirmation of identity for individuals and groups, are significant in the struggle for representation and importantly form a means of resistance. What is constant in these studies is recognition that the remembrance of the past, in various forms, is always an activity or performance undertaken by groups for specific reasons (Wertsch 2002).

Rather than consider the popular memory of the Western Front as a passive consumption of media images, therefore, it can be examined as an informed, active choice (Wilson 2007). The popular memory in Britain of the Western Front should be acknowledged as a version of the past chosen and preferred above others. Investigating these "myths and memories", which have proven so powerful, enables a consideration of the ways in which archaeology is involved with the consumption of the past but is by no means its instigator. Placing the ongoing archaeological work on the battlefields in the context of the history and literature of the Western Front demonstrates the necessity of examining the wider implications of this popular memory and the implications it has for the formation of British identity. Attributions, negotiations, resistance and domination of cultural and social values form the terms "heritage" and "memory". Through the study of how archaeology and history are drawn upon by wider society to create rather than inform cultural memory themselves, the manner in which "heritage" is created and remade through cultural practice is reinforced. Heritage and memory are constitutive of more than disciplinary practice but are values created within a wider public discourse.

The Western Front in Memory

The Great War on the Western Front (1914–1918) is remembered in Britain as "the trenches" and "no man's land"; filled with mud, splattered in blood, covered in shell holes and infested by huge rats. Soldiers are thought of as plagued by a constant threat of death and suffering the horrors of industrialized war at the hands of incompetent generals. The vast scale of death amongst the British army is recalled poignantly as the "lost generation". The Western Front is remembered as the war poetry of Owen and Sassoon, of the "old lie" of *Dulce et Decorum Est* and through *Blackadder* and *Oh! What a Lovely War*. It is remembered through moments of peace such as the Christmas Truce of 1914 but ultimately it is remembered as a tragic, futile waste. This popular memory of the Western Front is also reiterated within the expressions, metaphors and similes which have shaped and continue to shape the memory of the Western Front (after Schudson 1992, 154). Frequent usage of terms such as "going over the top", describing argumentative positions as "entrenched", or respective parties being "in the trenches", speaking of "no man's land" as a dangerous and threatening area, using the "Somme" or "Passchendaele" to describe desolated areas, futile wastes, or tragic encounters, further shape and define the popular memory of the Western Front as one of horror, pity, and pointless attrition. It is these factors which have constituted a "dense and impenetrable insular mythology" concerning the battlefields, and has perhaps ensured that the British sections of the Western Front are seen not just as the only battlefield, but as the whole war; consequently, the front is often viewed as, "a private British sorrow" (Terraine 1980, 171). It is therefore remembered in contrast to World War Two, which is viewed as a "good war" or a "necessary war", whereas the Great War and the Western Front is remembered as a senseless tragedy.

A cursory examination of the dominance of the memory of the Western Front and its perception as "the definition" of the Great War in Britain would appear to be morally and historically unjustifiable (Corrigan 2003, 9). More than nine million soldiers, sailors and airmen of all nations were killed around the world during the Great War (Bond 1984, 100). A further five million civilians are also estimated to have perished under occupation, bombardment, hunger and disease. Additionally, the genocide of Armenians in Turkey, the worldwide influenza epidemic which began as hostilities were still ongoing, and the suffering of civilians in Belgium, Serbia and Germany, should place the Western Front and the British losses of over 700,000 in perspective (Gilbert 1995, xv). Yet despite this evidence to the contrary, it is the Western Front—and the British role in it—that is still assumed to be *the* Great War. The hold the Western Front has over British popular memory is undeniably derived from the fact that the majority of British troops served in this theatre of war. Nor had Britain ever witnessed such a mobilisation of civilians or scale of fatalities (Corrigan 2003, 54).

This popular memory has been subject to revision by military historians who point to the significant achievements of the British Army during the conflict, particularly the fact that it was eventually victorious (Sheffield 2002). They highlight the tactical and technological advancements during the war, the numerous memoirs and accounts of veterans who fondly recalled their days in the army with their comrades, the gross errors in accounts of the war by the war poets and the skewed perspective these provide (Todman 2005). Archaeologists working on the battlefields have largely followed this lead, seeking to establish the material and physical surroundings of the Western Front not as "Armageddon", but as a landscape which can be explained and comprehended through "phases" and "military activity" (Price 2004). Such is the hold of the Western Front as a national tragedy in popular memory that it has even been argued that this assessment has prevented and overshadowed attempts by historians to research the battlefields (Badsey 2001). Using Hobsbawm's (1983) work regarding "the invention of tradition", historians, such as Beckett (2001) have sought to undermine popular memory by highlighting how it has been constructed by media representations over the last ninety years. They have detailed how the memory of the conflict has changed since the Armistice, emphasizing how it is through the publication of certain memoirs and novels, television programs and film that the memory of the battlefields as a tragedy has been created. They highlight how the notion of "soldiers as victims", which rose to prominence during the campaign for the pardon of executed soldiers, is a relatively recent concern, pointing to the emergence of novels such as Barker's (1991) *Regeneration* trilogy and Faulk's *Birdsong* (1993), as reflecting and encouraging this trend (Bond, 2002). However these historians freely admit that they have yet to make any impact on revising the popular public memory of the Western Front, the sentiments of which are best encapsulated in Porter's (1983, 40) poem *Somme and Flanders*:

> One image haunts us who have read of death
> In Auschwitz in our time—it is just light,
> Shivering men breathing rum crouch beneath
> The sandbag parapet—left to right.
> The Line goes up and over the top,

Serious in gas masks, bayonet fixed,
Slowly forward—the swearing shells have stopped—
Somewhere ahead of them stop-watch ticks.

Their world was made of nerves and mud.
Reading about it now shocks me—Haig
Gets transfusions of their blood.

Drawing upon these works of literature, it is important to remember that the Western Front has never been preserved as a static, unalterable myth or memory. Military history is but one narrative amongst many, and is itself formed and constructed through the selection and filtering of evidence. Over the last ninety years, military history has been competing with and inevitably challenged not only by media representations, but other forms of historical discourse; oral history, family history and micro-history. Historical discourse has also been accompanied by literary and cultural studies, all of which have examined the battlefields through their own methodological and theoretical lenses. Studied—and thereby remembered—from a variety of perspectives, the Western Front represents a site of memory that has been constantly reconstructed since the Armistice (Korte 2001, 121). This (re)selection of memory is reflective not only of cultural, societal and generational differences, but also of the various needs and desires of those articulating and remembering the battlefields. Studies of the memory of the wars and conflicts of the twentieth century, an ever-growing field, have frequently reiterated this aspect of renegotiation in remembrance. This concept of memory denies the thesis famously stated by Nora (1989), which argues that these "renegotiations" of memory are anxious endeavours by a society dislocated from its history, to gather together remnants and prolong that which can no longer be possessed. Memory is, in this fashion, located within a continual cycle of negotiation and creation, as individuals, groups and societies seek to affirm a particular memory of the past congruent to their present context (Wertsch 2002, 8).

Popular Myth and Memory

By regarding memory and remembering as an active choice made by society, as a consideration of what should and what should not be recalled, the specific role of action and agency requires examination. What this study aims to draw attention to are the choices and tactics employed in consumption, how cultural forms such as literature, film, television but also archaeology and history, are consumed by society in the form of "mediated action" (Wertsch 2002, 12). The concept of "mediated action" refers to the subtle devices involved in the reception and consumption of cultural forms across society, where some meanings are preferred and others rejected. Whilst Gramsci (1971, 181–2) regarded hegemonic structures as self-perpetuating to an extent, reproducing the conditions of society, its social mores, beliefs and habits, this structure should not be regarded as a closed system. Indeed, de Certeau (1984) has highlighted the performance of "oppositional tactics", or "ways of operating" within the consumption of cultural forms, which occur within the conditions of everyday life. These are intended not to overturn the dominant element in society, but to alter the situation for the minority individuals or groups. As de Certeau (1984, xiv) points out:

> These "ways of operating" constitute … innumerable practices by means of which users reappropriate the space organized by techniques of sociocultural production.

It is this use of tactics through "mediated action" that will be used to understand the popular memory of the Western Front in Britain. This "mediated action" will inevitably be informed and shaped by the continually changing drives, desires and requirements in society, corresponding to generational and cultural changes. Nevertheless, this action provides an alternative means by which the popular memory of the Western Front can be examined. The lament by military historians and others within the professions, including archaeologists, that this popular memory is entirely informed by media representations, fails to take into account the way in which popular memory is constructed (Halbwachs 1992). The assumption behind these assertions is that the influence of media shapes popular perceptions because memory and remembering is regarded as an inactive habit. Individuals and the wider public in this interpretation are "passive dupes", accepting and vapidly consuming particular media-memories of the Western Front because they are "easier" to take hold of. Such a conclusion is insufficient as it takes a complacent response to the active processes of remembering and the undeniable power this popular memory holds over contemporary society. As such the memory of the Western Front in Britain should not be considered as merely submissively accepted by the public, but rather chosen for specific reasons. This should not be regarded as an admission of relativism as this fails to consider the veracity of this remembrance. It should rather be considered as an acknowledgement that "myths and memories" have real purpose for the society which uses them. As Samuel (1989, xxxvii) makes clear:

In dealing with the figures of national myth, one is confronted not by
realities which became fictions, but rather by fictions which by dint of their
popularity, became realities in their own right.

The figures, facts and intrigue gained from intense historical or
archaeological study in this manner are rendered insignificant, as they
cease to find social and cultural currency outside of academic institutions.
Instead, they gain greater meaning when considered alongside what these
facts and dates *mean* for the people who use them—in the choices they
make about the past and the stories they wish to tell about themselves
(Denning 1994, 340). This is the concept of mediated action, it is the
utilisation of cultural forms to shape and inform the remembrance of the
past (Wertsch 2002). This "selection" remains unaddressed within the
context of the memory of the Western Front in Britain; as military
historians and archaeologists have been quick to dismiss the popular
memory as regrettable "myths." Samuel and Thompson (1990, 8) have
indeed highlighted how historians may seek to undermine popular memory
without considering the "selection, ordering and simplifying" which takes
place in the creation of the popular perceptions of the past. Although
studies following Hobsbawm (1983) have sought to show the historical
development of the memory of the battlefields in Britain, such an approach
does not explain why this memory is chosen, the reasons behind its appeal,
and its development by those who use it (after Samuel 1989, xxix). The
memory of the Western Front in Britain should be considered therefore as
an active, cultural choice.

To demonstrate this we can observe how the recent novels from the
1990s, regarding the battlefields, reveal how the memory of the Western
Front is a vehicle for expression (Wilson 2008). The image of the soldiers
suffering in the trenches is an especially interesting feature of these novels
(after Korte 2001). Set in the immediate aftermath of the war in
Switzerland for example, Edric's (1997) novel *In Desolate Heaven*, the
Western Front becomes a nightmarish vision which haunts the soldiers
who were there and who survived it. Hartnett's (1999, 324) novel *Brother
to Dragons* also uses images of the trenches of the Western Front in a
shocking and disturbing manner. In a parody of a letter informing a
relative of a soldier's death, the death-scene in the trenches is recounted:

> … attempting, as part of his company's second wave, to climb out of a
> support trench he had not acted "bravely" but mechanically, his mind
> having already vacated a body anaesthetized on Navy issue rum; nor, being
> hit by a piece of shell casing that tore the face away from the skull could be
> said to have died "gallantly".

Korte (2001, 124) also describes how this theme is particularly prevalent in Barker's (1991) first novel in her *Regeneration* trilogy. The book is set mostly in the Craiglockhart Hospital, where soldiers received treatment for the effects of shellshock and the trauma they experienced in conflict. For Barker, shellshock is a literary device whereby the image of the victimized and brutalized soldier can be communicated. This use of the medical trauma of shellshock followed from its recent inclusion as a topic of interest for social historians, who have stressed the varied means of therapy and the wider acceptance of the condition in society (Leese 1999). Represented in the novels, however, it serves as a means whereby readers can attribute a powerful and distinct sense of pathos to the soldiers in the trenches (Korte 2001 124). As it has been asserted by some commentators that soldiers suffering from this condition were executed by the British army, "shellshock" itself has become a feature of public debate. This was particularly so during 1998, when many sought to gain pardons for those executed during the Great War. The weight of public opinion aroused by this claim intensified as the eightieth anniversary of the Armistice drew near. After much procrastination, the Government refused to grant such pardons, although it would later agreed to do so in 2006. The Government nevertheless recognized in 1998 that these soldiers should be considered alongside their comrades as "victims of the war" (Corns and Hughes-Wilson 2002, 352). It is this public appeal towards victim-hood and the status of soldiers as "victims" that provides a revealing glimpse of the nature of the mediated re-articulation of the memory of the trenches in the 1990s and its effect. The eightieth anniversary of the Armistice in 1998, and the debates concerning the pardons for executed soldiers, proved to be a platform for the wider expression of the notion of victim-hood, as a public voicing of pain and outrage concerning the war in the trenches of the Western Front emerged through and within the popular media (Stummer 1998, 12).

Although historical discourse had long represented the soldiers' perspective, especially since the advent of oral history in the 1960s, commentators noted that the eightieth anniversary of the cessation of hostilities was the first occasion when these feelings of victim-hood were expressed on such a wide scale (Smith et al. 2003, 87). Novick (1999, 5), through his work on the Holocaust, has suggested that this association with suffering reflects the wider cultural shifts which occurred in the late twentieth century, which has placed the notion of "passive suffering" and "vicarious victim-hood" as a desirable and advantageous quality. If the construction of identity is regarded as on ongoing discourse that utilizes the memory of the past to articulate current desires and needs, then the memory of the suffering soldiers of the Western Front can be seen as a resource around which to wrap a distinctive identity concurrent with the prevailing societal context (Hall 1996, 222). The catharsis witnessed with the commemoration of the eightieth anniversary of the Armistice, and the debates concerning the issue of shellshock, can be interpreted therefore as an expression of national identity. As Lyn MacDonald stated at the time, "people are interested because they *care*, people *care* about this ... People realize it is relevant to our country now" (quoted in Stummer 1998, 16).

Memory and Archaeology

As excavations continue to examine the remains of the world's first industrialized conflict, the role of archaeology and its relationship with the popular memory of the battlefields in Britain requires assessment. The archaeological projects on the Western Front provide a focus through which the construction and negotiation of memory can be examined. Rather than relying on the reports and findings of the archaeologists themselves, this memory can be regarded as being actively constructed using archaeology apart from archaeologists. The remembrance of the past is consequently constructed through cultural forms, by the choices made by knowledgeable agents, rather than by the cultural forms in themselves (after Wertsch 2002).

A number of archaeologists have attempted to understand the functioning of archaeology in this complex relationship between public use and consumption of archaeology and the role of the professional. The most prominent of these is Holtorf's (2005) work regarding the place of archaeology in popular culture. Holtorf expertly unravels how archaeology and archaeological concepts are prominent in popular culture, and how they have shaped popular consciousness. He suggests that this mode of thought should be used in developing an alternative practice of archaeology, which engages with how the past is comprehended in the present (Holtorf 2005, 158). This, Holtorf (2004) argues, will require archaeologists to open dialogue with alternative voices. Archaeologists, in this respect, are encouraged to relinquish the monopoly they possess in the interpretation of the past and allow wider public involvement in the process of understanding the lives of past peoples. This idea of facilitating public engagement is an argument also developed by Carman (2005) in his study regarding issues of heritage, "ownership" and illicit trade in antiquities. Carman (2005, 81) suggests that the key to finding solutions regarding these issues is to treat both the subject of archaeology—and the material it studies—as a "common resource". He states that rather than viewing archaeology as having sole access to "the past", public co-ownership of the past and its uses will engender a wider involvement with the process. If both the public and archaeologists have a share in the materials being studied, the interests of all parties can be satisfied.

Likewise, Hamilakis (1999) suggests that the relationship between archaeology and the public be re-considered along these lines. Regarding the archaeologist's role as an intellectual within society, Hamilakis maintains that far from alienating the practice of archaeology from public life, archaeologists as intellectuals should involve themselves in public discourse. This inevitably means renouncing the control archaeology as a discipline has enjoyed in the interpretation of the past, but it facilitates a more engaged and inclusive archaeology, which listens to the desires and needs the public possesses towards its past. Archaeologists are still in control of their own work, but now the way in which this work is fashioned is decided by a wider public consensus (Hamilakis 1999, 66). The intentions of this approach, bridging the divide between archaeological academia and its diverse public audience, should be applauded, but the idea that the discipline can ever be considered as provided "for" the public needs to be addressed. To state that archaeology can become open and accessible through the work of individuals connecting with the public is in actuality to maintain the boundaries between public and academia. Indeed, it neglects the multiform ways in which knowledge in social life is transmitted, used, manipulated and recreated in the public sphere. Popular memory, in this instance, is still treated as if it can be moulded by the work of archaeologists. Whilst these ideas might appear to consider the public body of knowledge as an active agent, in effect they still allow for archaeology to impact upon popular culture and knowledge as a primary instigator.

An archaeological study of the British sections of the Western Front cannot dismiss the ways in which its interpretations will be taken up and used. In so doing it must take into account the reasons for the persistence of certain memories of the battlefields, and their use and value within British society. Whilst a number of studies have considered the relationship between archaeology and memory there exists no comprehensive analysis of how archaeology forms the process of "mediated action". Shackel (2000), in his study of Harpers Ferry National Park, addresses some of these issues, recognizing the role of archaeology within dissonant histories of the site. The Ludlow Collective (2001), in their examination of the site of the Colorado Coal Fields Massacre of 1914, similarly locate their work within the wider history of the America Trade Union Movement. The manner in which archaeology reacts with ingrained responses to historical periods, episodes in history which affect not only national identity and character, but individuals and their families, is an issue rarely explored within Anglo-American, or indeed Western, archaeology. While these issues have arisen in the context of Indigenous or post-colonial archaeology, Western archaeologists have seldom faced up to similar situations occurring in their own cultures (Given 2004).

Archaeology on the Western Front

The excavation of trenches, battlefields and other wartime structures along the Western Front has expanded greatly since the early 1990s. The potential for the study is well attested. Archaeologists working in the region are often confronted with plentiful examples of the lives and deaths of the soldiers who fought in the world's first industrialized war (de Meyer and Pype 2004). As Saunders (2001, 48) has observed, excavations uncover "trenches, dugouts, material and human remains often perfectly preserved, just centimetres beneath the surface." Groups from Britain, France and Belgium, both professional and volunteer, have conducted work in the region (Saunders 2002). The research motivations of these groups' ranges from a desire to preserve the remains and inform the public of the war to more overt anti-war stances (see, for instance, the Great War Archaeology Group 2006; No Man's Land 2006). All these organisations, however, rely to an extent on a use of archaeology to "remember" the war on the Western Front. The role of the wider popular memory is not regarded as significant in these endeavours, as it is often viewed as a barrier to sober, objective study (Price 2004).

However, it has been the public reaction to excavations on the battlefields that has been one of the most significant factors but certainly one of the most understudied. The excavation of human remains in particular from the Western Front has focused attention on the way in which popular memory utilizes archaeology. For instance, with widespread public approval and support, the remains of "Unknown Soldiers", from the battlefields of the Western Front, were excavated and repatriated by Australia in 1993, Canada in 2000 and New Zealand in 2004. Within Britain there was also a great expression of emotional intensity which was aroused by the excavation of human remains. The furore surrounding a television programme featuring the Belgian volunteer archaeology group, "The Diggers", unearthing the remains of a British soldier was so passionate that it led to the formation of the British All-Party Parliamentary War Graves and Battlefield Heritage Group (Barton 2003). Saunders (2001, 49) has compared the sensitivities involved within these situations to the ongoing debates regarding the repatriation of Indigenous artefacts and human remains from Western museums. Examining the excavations from the battlefields therefore provides a means of highlighting the archaeological work that is undertaken but also the manner in which it is received (Boura 1997, 1998, 2000).

It is the excavation in 1991 of a mass grave at Saint-Rémy-la-Calonne, near Verdun, that has proven to be both the instigator of a wider archaeological study of the battlefields, as well as providing the first indication of how archaeology can impact on the memory of the soldiers of the First World War (Desfossés 1998, 38). The site had always attracted speculation due to its association with the writer Henri-Alban Fournier, known as Alain-Fournier, author of *Les Grand Meaulnes* (Hill and Cowley 1993). Twenty-one soldiers of the 288th French Infantry Regiment, led by Fournier, were known to have disappeared on the 22nd of September 1914, during an attack on a German medical unit, and were all believed to be buried at the site (Boura 1998). The bodies of the twenty-one soldiers were located during the excavation of a small pit measuring approximately five by two metres, and had been placed in two rows of ten bodies, each laid head-to-foot, with the twenty-first body placed in the middle, across five of the others (Hill and Cowley 1993, 99). It appeared that the bodies were not buried randomly by their German enemies, but were buried according to hierarchy, as excavations revealed that the Captain was the first to be buried at one end of the pit, followed by the Lieutenant, the Second Lieutenant, then officers and the other ranks (Adam 1998, 32). The study was also sought to dispel the widely-held belief in France that Fournier had been executed by the German soldiers; analysis of the remains showed that the men had died from wounds sustained in combat. Six men did, however, have single bullet wounds to the head, although these may have been mercy shots, as their skeletons showed signs of sustaining other injuries (Krumeich 1998, 85–87). The large scale public interest in this excavation however ensured that although excavations revealed the manner of Fournier's death, it is still the poignant image of Fournier which remains within wider popular memory in France (Desfossés 1998).

Similarly, the 2001 excavation of a mass grave at Le Pont du Jour, near Arras in northern France, has not only furthered the recognition of the archaeological study of the battlefields, but has provided an insight into how archaeology is used to remember. The excavations revealed the bodies of twenty British soldiers, who were carefully laid out presumably by those who had served with them. The grave was marked in the expectation that they would be recovered, and re-interred by a burial party (Desfossés et al. 2003). Some of the skeletons showed the extensive damage inflicted upon human bodies by the war. For instance, one of the soldiers in the burial was found to have been hit by three pieces of shrapnel, one piece cutting his larynx, the second entering his rib cage and possibly perforating his heart, and the last cutting into his right knee (Bura 2003, 93). This excavation at Le Pont du Jour drew attention for the first time to the way in which soldiers buried their comrades. It is this aspect that also served to act upon the popular memory of the conflict in Britain. The haunting images of a line of skeletons placed side-by-side by their comrades attracted speculation in the national press that it demonstrated the deep and affectionate bonds engendered between British soldiers during wartime. This seemed to link in with the memory of the noble, heroic, yet tragic British "Tommy", fighting in brutal conditions, but maintaining a sense of camaraderie (Bowcott 2001).

In 2003, at the Beaumont-Hamel Memorial Park on the Somme, archaeologists unearthed a variety of implements, food utensils, plates, cutlery, condiment bottles, empty cans of corned beef, as well as cattle bones complete with butchery marks from a stretch of communication trench held by the Allies. The excavation thereby detailed the various activities of the soldiers in the trenches, overwhelmingly the mundane and everyday, all of which had taken place for several years by troops from several different countries (Piedalue 2003). The excavation, however, did not make an impact upon the ingrained memory of this section of the battlefields. The site, owned by Parcs Canada, is where the Newfoundland Regiment launched their attack on the 1st July 1916, which left three-quarters of the 801-strong force dead or wounded. The battlefield site, which was left untouched after the Armistice to serve as a memorial ground, because of this scale of fatalities, is a significant site for Canadian and Newfoundland identity. The memorial ground is consequentially remembered for the events that took place on the first day of the Battle of the Somme rather than the various activities that the excavation revealed (see Gough 2004).

Similarly, the excavation at Auchonvillers, also on the Somme, provided another perspective of the trenches of the Western Front. The dugout and stretch of reserve trench were neatly lined with bricks from the ruined village it circumvented. Far from the mud-filled pits so often prominent when "the trenches" are spoken of, the excavation revealed a well-organized and well-structured space through which the soldiers moved to get to the front lines (Fraser 2003). Archaeological projects have provided a valuable insight into the battlefields of the Western Front. Groups such as No Man's Land (2006) have attempted to inform the public about the lives of the soldier on the Western Front, the reality of the routine, day-to-day life in the trenches, the boredom of long periods of inactivity as well as the violence and brutality of war. Significantly, however, it is not these excavations that have attracted the most public attention in the popular media. Rather newspaper and television programmes have drawn upon the tragic image of the British "Tommy" in the trenches, suffering as a victim of the war.

An indication of this public use of archaeology can be gathered from reactions in Britain to the physical remains of the trenches. On the 11th of November 2003, various news bulletins across Britain reported the details of an archaeological excavation on the former battlefields of the Western Front (Black 2001). Near the Belgian town of Ieper, these excavations had unearthed sections of the front line held by British as well as Allied and German soldiers, discovering human remains, the material of the war, and the trenches and dugouts of the battlefields. The poignancy of choosing Remembrance Day to report these excavations—which had been ongoing for several months—caused a widespread public response regarding the responsibility and necessity of maintaining the memory of the Great War on the Western Front. The most striking feature of these images was that they served only to "pluck the chords of memory" (after Denning 1994, 353). Their effect seemed to serve the purpose of reminding the public of what they already remembered about the war: affirming memories of the trenches; the shape of the corrugated iron supports still observable; the narrow confines traceable; the duckboards still intact; their retrieval from the Flanders soil even leaving traces of mud clinging to the remains.

The recent excavation at Serre, on the Somme, conducted by the archaeological group, No Man's Land, also demonstrates the way popular memory can shape interest in the archaeology of the battlefields. The site was chosen specifically by television producers for its associations with the poet Wilfred Owen. The program was reinforced with readings from his poem, *The Sentry*. It was this poem which was inspired by his experiences stationed in a dugout at Serre (Brown 2005). What is significant in this example is the raw emotion of visitors to the site which was noted visitors by the archaeologists working on the excavation. The association with Owen, and the presence of human remains on the site, was also observed to touch visitors deeply. Excavations were even disrupted, "as a visitor scattered geranium petals so that the wind carried them into the working area" (No Man's Land 2006). This scene has also been noted by other groups working in the region. At the excavations in advance of the construction of the A19 motorway outside Ieper, in Belgium a number of human remains were located. Again, the emotional impact of this for visitors was noted by excavators (AWA 2004):

The many tourists and visitors to the excavation site also expressed their
respect for the retrieved bodies of the soldiers. At two spots where soldiers
were found on the Cross Roads site, makeshift memorials of poppies and
remembrance crosses were made, thus indicating that the excavation site
itself became some sort of place of pilgrimage and a focus of great interest
for the public.

Conclusion

The memory of the Western Front in Britain and within former
combatant countries is an active choice. It is a remembrance of the past
mediated through cultural forms for specific social and cultural concerns,
rather than mediated by cultural forms and accepted by a wider public. In
this respect, the term "memory", in the same way as the term "heritage",
becomes an attribution of value by individuals, groups and societies: an
activity conducted in the present (Harvey 2001). This attribution is carried
out within wider concerns of identity, place and recognition. What is
required from archaeologists and historians, therefore, is an understanding
of the myriad factors that constitute memory, heritage and the practice of
remembering: that these are felt, they are active and they are a very real
experience for those who hold them. Stating a shared ownership of the
past with the public succeeds in misunderstanding the ways in which the
knowledge of the past is appropriated and used by its audience. It is only
through the understanding that popular memory will be formed, with or
without the historian or archaeologists' involvement, based upon a variety
of reasons associated with societal conditions, that institutional disciplines
can critically realize their contribution within society.

Works Cited

Adam, Frederic. 1998. L'archéologie et la grand guerre. *14–18,
    aujourd'hui. Today. Heute.* 2: 28–35.
AWA. 2004. "Association for World War Archaeology". http,//www.a-w-
    a.be/.
Badsey, Stephen. 2001. Blackadder goes forth and the "two Western
    Fronts" debate. In *The historian, television and television history,* ed.
    Graham Roberts and Phillip Taylor, 113–125. Luton: University of
    Luton Press.
Barker, Pat. 1991. *Regeneration.* London: Penguin.
Barton, Patrick. 2003. The corner of a foreign field that will no longer be
    forever England. *Battlefields Review* 23: 13–15.
Beckett, Ian. 2001. *The Great War 1914–1918.* Harlow: Longman.

Black, Ian. 2001. Row over fate of First World War trench unearthed on Belgian motorway route. *The Guardian*, November 11.

Bond, Brian. 1984. *War and society in Europe 1870–1970*. Fontana: London.

—. 2002. *The unquiet Western Front*. Cambridge: Cambridge University Press.

Boura, Frederic. 1997. Le Poids des Morts ou Comment s'en Débarrasser, Que faire de l'encombrant patrimoine de la Grande Guerre? *Les Nouvelles de l'Archéologie* 70: 15–17.

—. 1998. Une tombe de Soldats A Saint-Remy-la-calonne. *14–18, aujourd'hui. Today. Heute* 2: 70–83.

—. 2000 L'écrivain sa famille et les archéologues, Autour de la Tombe d'Alain-Fournier, *L'archéologie du XX¹ siéle* 29–31.

Bowcott, Owen. 2001. Arm in arm: soldiers lie in their grave. *The Guardian*, June 20.

Bura, Pierre. 2003. Étude anthropologique de la sépulture multiple. 54: 92–98.

Carman, John. 2005. *Against cultural property, archaeology, heritage and ownership*. London: Duckworth.

de Certeau, Michel. 1984. *The practise of everyday life*. Berkley. University of California Press.

Corns, Cathryn and John Hughes-Wilson. 2002. *Blindfolded and alone, British military executions in the Great War*. London: Cassell.

Corrigan, Gordon. 2003. *Mud, blood and poppycock, Britain and the First World War*. London: Cassell.

Denning, Greg. 1994. *Mr. Bligh's bad language, passion, power and theatre on the Bounty*. Cambridge: Cambridge University Press.

Desfossés, Pierre-Yves. 1998. Préserver les Traces. *14–18, aujourd'hui. Today. Heute* 2: 36–51.

Desfossés, Pierre-Yves, Alain Jacques and Giles Prilaux. 2003. Arras "Actiparc" les oubiliés du "Pont du Jour". *Sucellus* 54: 84–91.

Dyer, Geoff. 1995. *The missing of the Somme*. London: Penguin.

Edric, Robert. 1997. *In desolate heaven*. London: Transworld.

Fraser, Alastair. 2003. The ocean villas, project-update, World War One battlefield archaeology on the Somme. *Battlefields Review* 28: 10–11.

Gilbert, Mark. 1995. *First World War*. London: Harper Collins.

Given, Mark. 2004. *The archaeology of the colonized*. London and New York: Routledge.

Gough, Paul. 2004. Sites in the imagination, the Beaumont Hamel Newfoundland Memorial on the Somme. *Cultural Geographies* 11: 235–258.

Gramsci, Antonio. 1971. *Selections from the prison notebooks of Antonio Gramsci*. London: Lawrence and Wishart.

Great War Archaeology Group. 2006. http.//www.gwag.org/.

Halbwachs, Michel. 1992. *On collective memory*. Chicago and London: University of Chicago Press.

Hall, Stuart. 1996. Introduction, who needs identity. In *Questions of cultural identity*, ed. Stuart Hall and Paul du Gay, 1–17. London: Sage Publications.

Hamilakis, Yannis. 1999. La trahison des archéologues? Archaeological Practice as Intellectual Activity in Postmodernity. *Journal of Mediterranean Archaeology* 12(1): 60–79.

Hartnett, David. 1999. *Brother to Dragons*. London: Vintage.

Harvey, David. 2001. Heritage pasts and heritage presents. *International Journal of Heritage Studies* 7(4): 319–338.

Hill, Derek and Dennis Cowley. 1993. A bundle of presumptions, military archaeology solves a literary mystery. *Quarterly Journal of Military History* 6 (1): 410–434.

Hobsbawm, Eric. 1983. Introduction, inventing tradition. In *The invention of tradition*, ed. Eric Hobsbawm and Tony Ranger, 1–14. Cambridge: Cambridge University Press.

Holtorf, Cornelius. 2004. Beyond crusades, how (not) to engage with alternative archaeologies. *World Archaeology* 37(4): 544–551.

—. 2005. *From Stonehenge to Las Vegas, archaeology as popular culture*. Walnut Creek, CA: Altamira Press.

Korte, Barbara. 2001. The grandfathers' war: Re-imagining world war one in British novels and films of the 1990s. In *Reinventing the past in film and fiction*, ed. Deborah Cartmell, I.Q. Hunter, and Imelda Whelhan, 120–131. London and Sterling: Pluto Press.

Krumeich, Gerard. 1998. L'Archeologie des Sources Allemandes. *14–18, aujourd'hui. Today. Heute.* no.2: 84–93.

Leese, Paul. 1999. *A social and cultural history of shellshock, with particular reference to the experience of British soldiers during and after the Great War*. Milton Keynes: Open University Press.

Ludlow Collective. 2001. Archaeology of the Colorado Coal Field War 1913–1914. In *Archaeologies of the contemporary past*, ed. Victor Buchli and Gavin Lucas, 94–107. London and New York: Routledge.

de Meyer, Mathieu and Pype, Pedro. 2004. *The A19 Project, archaeological research at cross roads*. Zarren: AWA. Publications.

Nora, Pierre. 1989. Between history and memory, les lieux de Memoire. *Representations* 26: 7–25.

Novick, Peter. 1999. *The holocaust in American life*. Boston and New York: Houghton Mifflin Company.

No Man's Land. 2006. "Looking for Wilfred".
http,//www.redtwo.plus.com/No Man's Land/p_serre.htm.

Piedalue, Giles. 2003. "Beaumont-Hamel, Le site mémorial Terre-Neuvian".
http://brea.culture.fr/sdx/bsr/voir.xsp?id=F1980199800007&q=q45&n=7.

Pollard, Tony and Banks, Ian. 2007. Not so quiet on the Western Front: Progress and prospect in the archaeology of the First world war. *Journal of Conflict Archaeology* 3(1): iii–xvi.

Porter, Peter. 1983. *Collected poems*. Oxford: Oxford University Press.

Price, Jon. 2004. The Ocean Villas Project: Archaeology in the service of European remembrance. In *Matters of conflict, material culture, Memory and the First World War*, ed. Nicholas Saunders, 179–191. London and New York: Routledge.

Samuel, Raphael. 1989. Introduction, the figures of national myth. In *Patriotism, the making and unmaking of British national identity, volume III national fictions*, ed. Raphael Samuel, xi–xxix. London and New York: Routledge.

Samuel, Raphael and Paul Thompson. 1990. Introduction. In *The myths we live by*, ed. Raphael Samuel and Paul Thompson, 1–21. London and New York: Routledge.

Saunders, Nicholas. 2001. Matter and memory in the landscapes of conflict, The Western Front 1914–1999. In *Contested landscapes, movement, exile and place*, ed. Barbara Bender and Margot Viner, 37–54. Oxford: Berg.

—. 2002. Excavating memories, archaeology and the Great War 1914–2001. *Antiquity* 76: 101–108.

Schudson, Michael. 1992. *Watergate in American memory, how we remember, forget and reconstruct the past*. New York: Basic Books.

Shackel, Paul. 2000. *Archaeology and created memory, public history in a national park*. New York: Kluwer Academic / Plenum Publishers.

Sheffield, Gary. 2002. *Forgotten victory, The First World War, myths and realities*. London: Review.

Smith, Laurajane. 2006. *Uses of heritage*. London and New York: Routledge.

Smith, Leonard, Stephane Audoin-Rouzeau and Annette Becker. 2003. *France and the Great War*. Cambridge: Cambridge University Press.

Stummer, Robert. 1998. The war we can't let go. *The Guardian*, November 7, *Weekend Magazine*.

Terraine, John. 1980. *The smoke and the fire, myths and anti-myths of war 1861–1945*. London: Sidgwick and Jackson.

Todman, Dan. 2005. *The great war, myth and memory*. London: Hambledon.

Wertsch, James. 2002. *Voices of collective remembering*. Cambridge: Cambridge University Press.

Wilson, Ross. 2007. Archaeology on the Western Front: The archaeology of popular myths. *Public Archaeology* 6(4): 227–241.

—. 2008. The trenches in British popular memory. *InterCulture* 5(2) http://interculture.fsu.edu/index.html.

Winter, Jay. 1995. *Sites of memory, sites of mourning*. Cambridge: Cambridge University Press.

CHAPTER SIX

ARCHAEOLOGY AND THE CULTURAL HERITAGE MANAGEMENT "TOOLKIT": THE EXAMPLE OF A COMMUNITY HERITAGE PROJECT AT CAWOOD, NORTH YORKSHIRE

KEITH EMERICK

Introduction

In this chapter, I intend to examine and discuss both the role of the archaeologist as expert and the use of archaeology as two of the key elements in the developing field of "community heritage" in Britain. I will consider whether archaeology has to be repositioned or relocated so that it is seen clearly as one of a number of *possible* approaches to be used in community heritage work or, more critically, whether it is the role of the archaeologist as community heritage expert that needs to be reconfigured. Reference will be made to an ongoing community heritage project in Cawood, North Yorkshire, to illustrate what can be achieved by reappraising the role of the heritage expert. This will also illustrate the complexity of the concept of "participation" and demonstrate the pitfalls of making assumptions about the ideas of "community" and "heritage".

To start, however, questions need to be asked as to whether the idea of community heritage or the archaeologist as "expert" is something that needs revision. The dominant idea of archaeology in the community is perhaps that of the archaeologist conducting excavations, undertaking field-walking, earthwork, geophysical or buildings surveys in a community context and doing so with the assistance of the community members. Once the work is concluded the archaeologist can then explain why the place is important and what the finds/results mean, all of which can then be added to the sum of human knowledge. Surely, this can only be a good thing?

Beneath the terminology of "archaeology", "expert", "community heritage" and "community", however, is a raft of developing government social policy that focuses upon the elimination of social exclusion and the encouragement of participatory initiatives at the local level (Department for Culture, Media and Sport (DCMS) 2001, 2002, 2004a,b, 2005, 2007; Department for Communities and Local Government (DCLG) 2008, 2009). These initiatives refer to inclusive actions taken by government departments, government agencies, local government, public institutions, and, indeed, any organization in receipt of public money. Those in receipt of such money (archaeologists in particular and the heritage profession in general are one such group) have to demonstrate that they are meeting government targets on inclusion and have responded to the government message. However, there are a number of issues to consider: is the government message clear; does the response to the message signify that there has been a comprehensive reappraisal of what heritage professionals "do" and how they relate to the community; and is the adoption and espousal of inclusive aims genuine or a marriage of convenience?

In addition to developing government policy, there is also an emerging discourse within the archaeological and heritage management disciplines on the subjects of "heritage" "expertise" and "participation" (Smith 2001, 2004, 2006; Marshall 2002a; Jones 2006). Although this debate will be discussed below, it can be summarized by reference to an analysis made by Kate Clark (2000, 37):

> A clear divide is beginning to emerge. On the one hand there is the traditional European model of heritage as a centralized, bureaucratic activity whose values pivot on the old, the monumental, the aesthetic, with an emphasis on attribution, connoisseurship, style, and national values. On the other hand, a newer model is emerging from the experience of the third world, Australia, Africa, and the USA that acknowledges that heritage is multi-vocal, contested, and difficult. The latter model incorporates cultural diversity, and works with communities, emphasizes places rather than monuments and has more in common with environmental conservation than the conservation of works of art.

There are a number of general points to make in relation to this analysis. First, the traditional model stresses that "fabric" (buildings, objects, artefacts) is of overwhelming significance and has "inherent" value and needs to be interpreted by "experts". Importance or significance in this sense is related to national importance. The "newer model" considers that fabric is important because of what it represents and means to people. In this latter sense, "cultural significance" is about the way in which meanings emerge, change, come into conflict and are used in the present, and therefore the task of the expert is to manage "conflict over the meanings given to heritage" (Smith et al. 2003, 67). Second, when heritage professionals undertake community heritage, or community archaeological projects, and claim to do so in line with government policy on exclusion and community, the aim should be to carry out that work according to the principles of the "newer model". In contrast, however, I suggest that community heritage work is currently undertaken according to the older model, whilst simultaneously purporting to be the "newer model". Why is this so? In some cases there is a lack of knowledge that there are alternatives. Similarly, there is a lack of training in new approaches. However, the greatest impediment to change is the power, solidity and resistance to change of traditional models, which Smith (2006) suggests are regulated by what she has termed the "authorized heritage discourse" (henceforth AHD). There are examples of the "newer model" in Britain, but they are far from common and it remains the case that the majority of the published case studies illustrating examples of a new approach to community archaeology/heritage are from Australian and New World contexts rather than British or European practice (Marshall 2002b). Therefore, case studies from Britain, and analysis of associated heritage management practices, are particularly valuable at the moment.

The aim of this paper, therefore, is to provide such an example, so as to explore the possibilities for engagement with community heritage groups (and in this paper community heritage groups is taken to mean local archaeological, historical, heritage clubs and societies, community groups as well as parish councils) and provide those tools which respond to community need, rather than sectoral desires, and allow any community to generate dynamic, sustainable and participatory cultural engagement in the areas of their choosing. In order to develop this argument, this paper will first examine the policy background and then consider the subject of community archaeology as it is and could be, by looking at issues such as capacity building and participation. This will be followed by an examination of the role and impact of "expertise", which will then lead into the case study of Cawood Castle, where a community heritage group has taken on the management of a nationally important monument. A final discussion will make connections between these sections of the paper. Before going further, it is important to identify how I am defining "heritage". My position is that "heritage" is concerned with identity, place, memory, history and story, but, following Harvey (2001), Clavir (2002), Jones (2006) and Smith (2006), it is also about "process" rather than "product"; "heritage" as "verb" rather than "noun". In this sense, cultural heritage and how we understand and engage with the past is all about "doing", rather than being about a fixed building, object or fabric, but importantly this process takes place in the present and is thus also about change and dynamism. Therefore, "heritage" is about how we use the past in the present and how—and why—we attach meaning and value to the past.

Social Inclusion and other Policy Issues

One of the mechanisms identified by government and its agencies as a means of generating "social inclusion" and the promotion of healthy communities is a greater appreciation and use of "heritage". However, when the word "heritage" is used in these various governmental position papers, they invariably refer to a type of "heritage" Smith (2006) associates with the AHD: established heritage places and sites, and the exploration of a shared, national history: in short, "the past". This has happened because heritage policy is created by ministers and civil servants advised by heritage professionals who continue to promote the AHD. And because archaeologists deal with the past, they therefore are thought to be best able, and have volunteered, to lead the community archaeology initiatives. The archaeologist in Britain has become, by default, an "expert" in community heritage issues. But does "community heritage" actually deliver its intended aims and are those aims "clear" in the first place?

Social inclusion and community initiatives became a major part of the current Labour government programme following the murder of the black teenager Stephen Lawrence and the subsequent publication of the Macpherson Report in 1999 (Macpherson 1999). Successive British governments have attempted to come to terms with multiculturalism, social exclusion, European integration, economic change (from heavy engineering to service economies), inner city decay, and agricultural and rural change, but it was both the murder and the content of the report, which talked of institutionalized racism and widespread social exclusion, that provoked the government into action. The report asked that government departments and agencies specifically consider implementing community and local initiatives aimed at promoting cultural diversity, combating social exclusion and addressing racism. For DCMS, the government department which leads on issues of culture and heritage and funds the heritage sector, combating social exclusion was about enlarging access to those traditionally left out of cultural activities—whether physically, intellectually, financially or in terms of race and gender. It was acknowledged that involvement and empowerment were essential to successful community and economic regeneration in the urban and rural spheres whilst the importance and recognition of, and respect for, cultural diversity was made clear (DCMS 2002).

Individual government ministers spoke on issues of heritage and identity, stressing the need for fresh thought. In November 1999, Chris Smith, then Secretary of State at DCMS, presented the opening address at a Museums Conference in Manchester entitled *Whose Heritage?* His speech was on the subject of the need for heritage professionals to address cultural diversity and the ways in which government initiatives were supporting that drive:

> We can make a difference through, for example, the funding agreements we are putting in place between DCMS and its sponsored bodies. We should be ensuring that those bodies have strategies in place to enable everyone to understand and appreciate their own culture and heritage, and to experience that of other people (DCMS, 2nd November, 1999. Extract from speech by the Rt. Hon. Chris Smith).

This meant that agencies would not receive any government funding if they failed to put the desired strategies in place. Other initiatives were reported by the Minister: the delegation of grant aid by the Arts Council of England to Regional Arts Boards; positive discrimination in favour of people from ethnic minorities putting their names forward as museum trustees; the Public and Commercial Services Union "black challenge" to promote the idea of a career in museums and galleries among black and ethnic minorities; regional devolution in Scotland and Wales, the new Regional Cultural Consortiums and local government cultural strategies. Because of this imperative, new definitions of community archaeology and "engagement" rapidly became discernible in the heritage sector, brought about by the very clear linking of financial grant to the delivery of explicit social and political aims, particularly that of combating social exclusion. In this context, "outreach" or "engagement" initiatives became essential parts of all archaeological projects.

Following on from the Macpherson Report, the government, in February 2000, announced its intention to undertake a review of current historic environment policy (English Heritage, *Conservation Bulletin*, 37, March, 2000). English Heritage, as the national lead body and advisor to government on heritage and conservation issues, was given the role of coordinating the consultation with the public, other funding bodies, local authorities and as full a range of interested groups as was possible. The process was managed by a Steering Group with five Working Groups covering different aspects of the historic environment.

The principal aims and objectives were the production of: a long term vision (at least 25 years); a shorter term agenda (with broad targets for the next 10 years); a broad, holistic and comprehensive definition of the historic environment (integrated with concerns such as biodiversity and countryside character); more efficient and effective instruments to protect and enhance the historic environment; ways to allow economic growth; a framework of new research; and further access. In addition, several themes were identified for consideration: a holistic definition of the environment; cultural diversity and inclusion; subsidiarity (from European to local levels); the balance between public and private involvement; the role of community and interest groups; closer integration of the historic and natural environment; improved databases; and improved working connections between organisations. As a starting point, the historic environment was presented in quite radical terms as: knowing no chronological limit; knowing no thematic limit; knowing no geographic limit; knowing no limit to scale (the locally-distinctive as worthy of consideration as the internationally significant); and knowing no limits of culture or ethnicity.

As a product of this review process, English Heritage published *Power of Place (PoP)* (English Heritage 2000). This was effectively the conclusions of the Steering and Working Groups and formed the core of the submission to the DCMS. *PoP* consists of three sections, with the bulk of the text contained in Part Two, *Needs and Priorities*. Part One (*The Power of Place*) contains fourteen extended bullet points covering "place"; the historic environment as a source of information; places needing to evolve and grow; the need to better understand places and the value and significance people ascribe to them; the need for knowledge about the condition of the historic environment; and the need for value-based decision-making to be consistent and transparent. Collectively, the presented text veers from fabric to value and back to fabric, and ultimately accepts that the historic environment is about "the past" and an inheritance to be handed on, as exemplified by the following extract: "It [the historic environment] is all about us. We are the trustees of that inheritance ... Most of our towns and cities, and all of our countryside, are made up of layer upon layer of human activity. Each generation has made its mark ..." (English Heritage 2000, 4). The terms "value" and "significance" are used as concepts to assist in the planning process, rather than as ideas that could be central to a new approach to cultural heritage management: "They [Character assessments] afford the information to make the whole spatial planning system a better and more creative process. The most significant elements of the historic environment will always need individual designation ..." (English Heritage 2000, 5). However, who is to determine which are the most "significant elements of the historic environment"?

Part Two extends the statements made in Part One and contains sections on conservation-led renewal, reinvestment, prevention and maintenance, widening values, managing change and enhancing character, the need for increased knowledge to inform conservation work, and the provision of leadership-specifically at the local level. Each section concludes with a short set of recommendations. The section that deals with value, people, broadening audiences, and inclusion, *People and Place: Reflecting Wider Values*, is sandwiched between sections on the economics of the historic environment and the management of change. The section begins with a series of positive statements:

> But many feel powerless and excluded. The historical contribution of their group in society is not celebrated. Their personal heritage does not appear to be taken into account by those who take decisions ... If the barriers to involvement can be overcome, the historic environment has the potential to strengthen the sense of community and provide a solid base for neighbourhood renewal (English Heritage 2000, 23).

The subsequent text and recommendations, however, return to a focus on the need to extend education, outreach, universal access and improve the "offer" and welcome at established heritage sites. Although these are desirable outcomes, by themselves they fail to signal a change in established heritage management practice and fail to address *how* the changes ("Find out what people value about their historic environment and why, and take this into account in assessing significance" (English Heritage 2000, 27)) can be made.

In December 2001, the DCMS set out the government's response to *PoP* and its vision for the historic environment. Entitled *The Historic Environment: A Force for our Future,* it accepted the conclusions of *PoP* and reiterated government commitment to social inclusion, participatory initiatives and the need to rethink the designation system and the way in which its content is constrained by professionals:

> ... the designation system does serve to reinforce the sense that the historic environment can be defined precisely, quantified even, in terms of formally listed buildings or scheduled monuments. These decisions are taken by central government on the advice of professionals within a framework of national criteria but do not always take account of other factors which might be important to the local community. Yet the value a community

places on a particular aspect of its immediate environment might be a
critical factor in getting that community to engage in local planning or
regeneration issues (DCMS 2001, 30).

Building on the need to stimulate social inclusion, the principal action
points from the document included and referred to: leadership; realizing
educational potential and access; increasing community participation;
instituting a review of the case for integrating the several heritage controls
into a single regime; and optimising economic potential. Critically, the
government also promised a second policy document: *People and Places:
A Draft Social Inclusion Policy for the Built and Historic Environment*
(DCMS 2002) and a major conference to allow "… everyone concerned to
agree how best to take forward this challenging agenda [social inclusion,
participation and responding to the public's widening perceptions of what
constitutes their heritage] and to set in hand the action required" (DCMS
2001, 25).

Although the two documents made it clear that heritage professionals
were no longer to act solely as "heritage police" and were to think of
themselves as "facilitators" and "enablers", they failed to explain how this
was going to happen and left it to the various heritage organisations to
solve, without the resources to "re-educate" heritage professionals and
their managers. If the existing system was constructed, maintained and
executed by professionals exercising their idea of value, what was the
likelihood that those same people and institutions would reinvent
themselves?

A number of policy documents have since been issued and the thrust of
those papers has remained focused on the historic environment as a
collection of buildings and sites and the need to support social inclusion
and participation to facilitate good and sustainable design, and
regeneration. In these documents, "place" and "place-making" have
become familiar terms. The 2002 *People and Places* document, for
example, stated that:

> The built and historic environment can also help connect people to their
> culture, both past and present. This document shows how people can be
> more effectively engaged with the contemporary and historic built
> environment as a cultural and educational experience (DCMS 2002, 4).

It also stated that "[i]n order to achieve these goals, a shift in practices,
aspirations and attitudes is required from many sectors" (DCMS 2002, 4).
However, the key policy objective of the document was, "to make social
inclusion a priority for all these organisations and agencies, and to achieve

the widest possible access to the contemporary and historic built environment as part of the cultural heritage" (DCMS 2002, 4). This explicit reference to the need for a change in practices and aspirations "from many sectors" is one of few, but in general the tone and content of the documents remain the same with an increasing stress on fabric, place and regeneration (DCMS 2004b; DCLG 2008), resulting in a message for change that is far from clear.

The AHD, Community Archaeology and Social Inclusion

In her 2006 book, *Uses of Heritage*, Laurajane Smith coined the term the "authorized heritage discourse", which she identifies as a dominant professional heritage discourse stressing the monumentality of heritage and privileging the role of archaeological expertise in the management of material culture. Within the AHD, national "heritage" is represented by a limited collection of heritage assets, all of which are used to deliver a comfortable and consensual national historical narrative. In this discourse, the often repeated "our" of "our heritage" and the "we" of "we British" are never questioned or unpacked, nor is the word "national". However, how embedded is the AHD, and if it is deeply embedded what is its impact on the professional and public status and behaviour of archaeology and archaeologists, and what does it suggest about the perspective that archaeologists "bring" to heritage issues? If we believe in the idea of "value" and the multiplicity of "values", and we accept that heritage professionals need to shift practices and aspirations in order to deliver social inclusion aims, we might expect that a heritage professional might ask whether "their" values (professional and personal, but chiefly those values which are about "evidence" and fabric) are more significant than other values.

One of the tools used most frequently in establishing the significance of places and initiating community engagement is the Conservation Plan (CP). CPs tend to be used in advance of, and to inform, conservation or development projects and their production is often linked to the receipt of grant aid, usually with the CP being the first stage of a project. Because they are linked to something that is "testable", such as the staged payments of grants, the drive for their production is towards the production of knowledge and evidence—which privileges archaeological expertise. CPs originated in Australia and are a product of the Burra Charter (Australia ICOMOS 1979, revised 1999). The Burra Charter presents a template for the management of "important places" using a simple process of: assessing the cultural significance of a place in terms of its history and fabric condition; understanding the different values attached to the place; developing conservation policy and strategy to enhance that cultural significance; carrying out the strategy (Australia ICOMOS 1979, 14). The Burra Charter introduced three key elements. The first was that the cultural significance of a place is defined as the sum of the values attached to it, and here the listed value groups were aesthetic, historic, scientific and social, although it was noted that other groups could be used (Australia ICOMOS 1979, 73). Second was the revised role of the professional (Australia ICOMOS 1979, 18), who has to ensure that different views are taken into account, and third was the role of the community (Australia ICOMOS 1979, 18), who were expected to participate in the process and express their views about the place. It was stressed that for a management document to be effective and useful, it has to be based on dialogue and participation. The CP approach builds on the Burra process but makes the steps more explicit: (1) understand the place; (2) state its cultural significance; (3) identify threats to the significance; (4) define policies to protect and enhance significance; and (5) action. Again, consultation and dialogue remain critical and the final text of a CP has to be agreed by all parties.

The CP process has been in use for many years in Britain and tends to be managed by archaeologists, architects or buildings historians. As the AHD is so ingrained, however, it becomes very difficult to use CPs as a tool that could satisfy inclusion and participatory needs. The Burra Charter, and by extension conservation planning, and its relationship to social inclusion has been critiqued (Waterton et al. 2006) on account of the language used in the Charter and the manner in which this language continues to sustain and reproduce the AHD. In Britain, it is clear to see that this failing also applies to the way in which CPs are used, as the following all too common example highlights, which is taken from the "Assessment of Significance" section of a draft CP for Ayton Castle, North Yorkshire:

> There are several elements of Ayton Castle that are nationally important and should make it valued by the owners, academic researchers, members of the local community and wider society … The criteria that will be taken into account when determining the significance of parts of the fabric and landscape are as follows: Age and rarity of the fabric: Generally, the older and/or rarer the fabric, the greater significance it will have …[1]

There are a number of assumptions embedded in the above, but most worrying is the assumed role of the heritage specialist. The entire section, from which this extract comes, is about heritage specialists telling communities what is of cultural significance, and why they should value it. The section begins with the concept of "national importance", which "*should* make it [the place] valued …" [my emphasis]. Therefore, the author is pointing the reader towards a particular definition of cultural heritage, without suggesting what the alternatives might be. The piece concludes with the assertion that the older and rarer something is "the greater significance it will have", but to whom? Again, we are being told that we *must* appreciate the old and rare, but by doing so the author devalues and de-legitimizes the values attached to the place by the existing community (particularly the children) who used the place in the recent past and the present for activities such as sledging and snowballing. The implication of this is that communities have to be dependent on experts to tell them what is culturally significant about their own backyards. It also ensures that the community will always consider that they must look to the expert to set "their" heritage agenda. The quotation above illustrates two issues: one is the prevalence of the AHD, its relationship to national importance and stress on evidential value; and the second is the weakness of the CP approach when used uncritically. The format of a CP indicates that examination of the history of the site should be chronological, commencing with the earliest period. Usually the medieval or early modern periods tend to be the longest and the modern period (today) is the shortest, but this privileges the AHD, the archaeologist as heritage manager and evidential value, because of the particular range of skills and knowledge required. CPs are usually written because there is an issue in the present, and therefore if the sequence was reversed, or the modern period came first and then reverted to a chronological approach, the writers would have to *begin* with the community and it might alter the perspective of the analysis. Similarly when the different types of value (historic, aesthetic, scientific and social) are being evaluated they are normally ranked in a descending scale beginning with international, national, regional, local and negative importance. Such a system immediately reinforces the AHD because it relies on the extent of academic knowledge. A different approach might be to think of ranking in terms of "critical to an appreciation of cultural significance", "important to an understanding of cultural significance", and so on, which could place something that was locally significant on an even playing field with something that was nationally important because appreciation of the local item might be "critical to" an understanding of the place. This technique has been used with some success by the heritage consultants Atkins, but there is room for further development. This approach will be referred to again in the Cawood case study.

What is important here is that heritage professionals assume that because they are *involved* in a participatory exercise about value, they are therefore *being* participatory and inclusive. What happens instead, however, is that they end up superimposing their own values onto a given situation, whilst failing to understand that this conflict is a direct result of how they use their expertise. The increasing use of CPs and the stress on outreach as a solution to social inclusion issues has also generated new interest in community archaeology and community heritage ventures, but the same lack of change in practice and aspirations persists. Extending outreach is seen as the solution, because people believe it *is* the solution or they feel that changing the fundamentals of what they do is not an option (or necessary), and inclusion can be met by outreach. Both outreach and community archaeology have now become essential elements of established heritage practice, but they could be the project itself instead of adjuncts to a principal project. There are, of course, good examples of community archaeology. The work of Kevin Cale in North Yorkshire and the Greater York project (see Kenny this volume) are particular examples, and it must be remembered that community archaeology has a long pedigree in Britain, although it was usually considered a poor relation to rescue and research archaeology (see Start 1999).

But what would define good community archaeology in the context of participation and social inclusion? Because of the lack of examples from Britain and Europe, we have to look further afield. The starting point, which also addresses the desire for change in practice and aspiration from the DCMS, is that archaeologists need to understand how their expertise is constructed, what it does and accept "the reflexive and socio-political nature of archaeological research" (Clarke 2002, 250). To do this would "make research practice more accountable, relevant and interesting for the communities in which it takes place" (Clarke 2002, 250) and, as Clarke notes, "archaeology is generally carried out in other people's social space" (Clarke 2002, 262). Community work should respond to community need and the community agenda. Greer et al. (2002, 268) make the important point that community-based work responds to questions of identity rather than knowledge, which runs counter to the privileged position of archaeological expertise and its stress on evidential value. Therefore, as suggested by Moser et al. (2002, 229, quoting Derry 1997, 24), the community has to define the questions to be asked, otherwise the answers are likely not to interest them. Thus, the relationship with a community has to go beyond consultation. The aim should be to empower a community to interrogate, define and manage its own (and an individual) cultural heritage and unlock the knowledge and skills that reside within that community. This takes time and commitment and moves the expert away from repeated summer excavation seasons towards capacity-building, which brings us back to the important issue of expertise.

Expertise

The Outreach Team at English Heritage undertake, encourage and produce brilliant work (see, for example, *Remembering Forgotten Heroes: Exploring the Indian Army Contribution to the First and Second World Wars, through the Personal Memories and Photographs of Ex-serviceman Living in Slough,* English Heritage April, 2005). However, the corporate commitment to "outreach" stops with the Outreach team when, in fact, every piece of casework and every project undertaken or initiated by English Heritage should be "outreach", and thus informed and driven by the same ideas and principles of inclusivity. Similarly, there is a problem with the different roles of the various heritage professionals. The Outreach specialist starts from the perspective of being a "facilitator" and "enabler" who recognises that many diverse aspects of cultural heritage are legitimate. The Inspector, officer or Local Authority Archaeologist, by contrast, starts from a position in which their particular discipline is pre-eminent, and therefore they are less likely to accept other perspectives as legitimate. Moreover, outreach projects tend to be concerned with identity, rather than the type of knowledge that clarifies national importance. English Heritage would argue that their casework remit is limited to those things which are nationally important and the vast majority of subjects tackled by outreach do not fall into that category. Similarly, they would argue that the pursuit of outreach elements in casework would be a distraction from the time specific nature of much of the work. However, the problem here is that no one is prepared to say what enabling, facilitation or inclusivity in cultural heritage might look like, when it is in fact the role of a national organisation like English Heritage to explore and define those words and the ideas behind them, and set a national standard. In such a situation, it would be invaluable to share the different types of expertise, but this has yet to happen. The reality is that it has been easier to take those elements of *Force for our Future* and *People and Places* that synchronize with the preferred remit of a national body and reinforce its expertise, rather than embark on a journey that would challenge both expertise and the primacy of national importance. This disjunction between the word, idea and its execution is commonplace in the new uses of "community" and "engagement"; many archaeologists consider that the only heritage reality is that which is on or could be added to the county

Historic Environment Record, whilst "engagement" is limited to explaining a project to a local history or archaeological society rather than trying to engage and empower a wider audience or provoke discussion on what constitutes heritage. Thus expertise, certainly in a British context, is linked to national importance, either in the role played by experts, or the level at which they become engaged: national importance is the "trigger point" and rationale. Anything below that level is difficult to fund or support and those things that are seen by heritage experts as both "heritage" or "culture" (historic buildings and sites) and contributory to the national picture form an extremely limited set.

One scheme that brought about considerable, but temporary change was the Local Heritage Initiative (LHI), although this scheme has now closed following the merger of the grant holding body with other agencies. This scheme was part of the Heritage Lottery Fund but administered by the Countryside Agency. It offered grants of £25,000 to community groups to explore those aspects of their place that were of particular importance to them (and it deliberately offered a wide definition of the word "heritage" to encompass the historic and natural environment) but below the national importance threshold (for archaeological and historical items). The grant was specifically for those projects that had been "unfundable". One of the unforeseen results of the scheme was that it turned archaeologists and heritage managers into "commodities" (Smith 2001), as community groups had the money, often for the first time, to employ an archaeologist to do exactly what it was *they* wanted, and it was specifically stated in the LHI documentation that professionals would be employed in order to *train* community groups, rather than have an archaeologist approach a community to undertake a project that the professionals wanted to do. The village of Cawood, North Yorkshire was one example of a LHI project that kept community interests as its focus (see Waterton 2008), but what can we learn about archaeology and heritage from their example?

Cawood, North Yorkshire

Cawood village (Figure 6.1) is located 10 km south of York and 4 km north, north-west of Selby, strategically sited on the south bank of the River Ouse 1 km from its confluence with the River Wharfe.

It has a population of about 1,500 and is slightly above the national average regarding social and economic categories and those relating to levels of qualification. There is some agricultural and other employment locally, but considerable numbers commute to, and work in, York, Selby,

Leeds and Hull. The village is also home to at least three professional archaeologists.

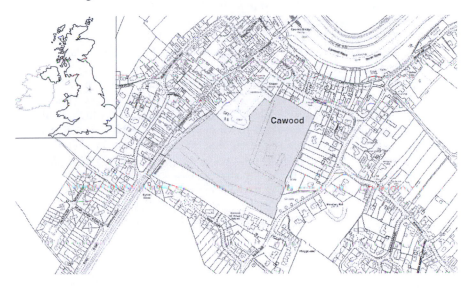

Figure 6.1 Location of Cawood village (source: English Heritage 1994)

A large portion of the village has been designated as a Conservation Area, whilst there are also two Scheduled Monuments in the centre of the village. The smaller of the two is that of Keynesbury, the site of a medieval moated manor house, and the larger, Cawood Castle Garth, represents the remains of a partially destroyed castle, archiepiscopal palace and its associated garden or "Garth". The standing fabric comprises the castle gatehouse and banqueting hall, both now owned by the Landmark Trust. The former is used as holiday accommodation. The site is chiefly renowned for the fact that it was the medieval residence of the Archbishops of York. The Garth is an open grassed area of relict orchards, earthworks and fishponds with remains of some more recent buildings such as concrete bases for Nissen huts. In the recent past, it was part of an agricultural holding and was used for pasture, but is now considered amenity space for the village.

The Garth is so valued by the village that they collectively agreed an increase in their rates to purchase the area for the village, for their communal use, but whenever the community (through the Parish Council) enquired about consent to undertake works associated with community events, they were infrequently told that such events and the related works were not permissible because the site was protected (Scheduled) as a Nationally Important ancient monument under the provisions of the 1979 *Ancient Monuments and Archaeological Areas Act*. In 2000, Neil Redfern and I (two English Heritage Inspectors involved with the site) received a series of applications for works on the Garth that we felt should be permitted, but which also seemed to indicate that people in the village had a vision for the site. As a consequence, we felt that it was important to meet with the village and ask them how they wanted to use the site. In response to our request to meet, the Parish Council created a representative sub-group called the Cawood Castle Garth Group (CCGG), which would be, and remains, the contact point for discussions about the Garth. At one of the early meetings it was suggested that that the community should try and produce a CP for the Garth that would clearly set out why the place was valued, by whom and would also include "actions" to help them develop their vision for the site. There were a number of reasons for this. First, we knew that if the CCGG wanted to apply for grant aid in the future, one of the conditions would be the production of a CP. Second, there was some surprise that English Heritage staff were interested in the multiplicity of values attached to the site, rather than the purely archaeological, and we felt that discussion about values through the CP process might be beneficial to all. Third, both Neil and I wanted to explore different ways of writing CPs, such as letting the community write it themselves, starting the analysis with the modern period, using different ways of ranking values (such as "critical to ...) and accepting that the CP might not be completed at the first attempt, but concentrating on the process and the discussions about meaning. This might seem like using the community for experimentation, but it was our feeling that the CP process was perhaps the best available for exploring ideas of value and meaning. Thus, we might learn something about their more effective use from the community, and of course this was discussed with the CCGG. The CCGG also temporarily included two of the villages' professional archaeologists, they were asked to write the text, and here we wondered whether the archaeologists, who were real members of the community, might write something that was not led by evidential value. In order to provide the group with some heritage management expertise, English Heritage suggested that they use the services of Emma Waterton, then a PhD student at the University of York, who would act as a facilitator for the project, collating ideas and arranging and advising on different heritage activities. The purpose of this from the English Heritage perspective was that it would be an attempt to understand what the terms "facilitator" and "enabler" might mean or involve, and also indicate the level of commitment that would be required from English Heritage for any future projects.

Taking several months in 2003, the CP gradually developed, and as the ideas of value, local pride and identity began to emerge, the CP became more about the village than the Garth itself. Consultation with the rest of the village took place through local meetings, community survey, the use of tools such as oral history (undertaken by the residents themselves) and the Common Ground "ABC of Local Distinctiveness", versions of which were produced by adults and children alike.

In order to better understand the archaeological deposits on the Garth, the CCGG applied for and received a grant from the LHI, which was used to employ geophysicists and archaeological surveyors to map the Garth, the results of which were then used to define areas where communal activities (such as fetes) and interventions (the construction of a bridge and insertion of footpaths to extend public access) could take place without impacting on the significant archaeological deposits, some of which the CCGG and others wanted to excavate in the future. The nature and location of the interventions were debated communally and recorded in a Management Plan, which also included a Research Strategy for the Garth covering prospective projects on excavation, oral history, building surveys, documentary research and natural heritage projects. However, not all of the communal activities were easily agreed upon. The Garth had been purchased by the community to protect it from development and some felt that a bridge and path were "creeping" development. The need for the path and bridge were the subject of a village questionnaire and the projects provoked some critical response. The issue from the perspective of the Parish Council and CCGG was that now the village "owned" the Garth there was a legal duty on the Council and CCGG to ensure that there was an appropriate level of access. The Garth is heavily used for dog-walking, casual amenity space and as a route from one side of the village to the other, principally as a route to and from the Primary School. Therefore, a path and a bridge over one of the deeper ditches were proposed to extend the access. An all-weather, low impact path was created, and now several elderly residents who have not had access to the Garth for more than ten years (on account of the difficult ground conditions) have been able to walk there, and have expressed their thanks that the Garth has been "returned" to them. Others were unhappy with the idea of excavating some of the Garth and wanted to focus on non-invasive archaeological techniques or the exploration of its natural heritage. It was only in 2008 that limited excavation using small one-meter square trial holes was agreed by the Group.

Several years after the completion of the CP it is clear that the document never became the cornerstone of management that specialists expect CPs to be, which in itself is quite revealing. It may be that the CP is not the most appropriate tool for such situations or it may be that the idea of placing value and meaning in the foreground, rather than archaeological and historical knowledge, was unfamiliar. This, combined with the novelty of actually allowing a community to manage its own heritage, was perhaps too daunting. But it might also have been thought of as irrelevant at that stage in the undertaking. However, over the years, CCGG members have amassed a huge amount of information and stories about the place, only a small portion of which can be placed on interpretation boards and there is now a desire to know where this information can go. Discussion has begun with the CCGG about a review of the CP and it may be the case that because there is in excess of five years management experience within the community and a familiarity with different types of meaning and value a more appropriate type of document might be produced which actually addresses their emerging needs.

However, the Conservation and Management Plan processes acted as a capacity building exercise that thereafter made additional participation and activities possible because the Plans began with fundamental questions about meaning and value, rather than throwing the residents in at the deep end of pottery types or flint flakes. The vast majority of community archaeological projects in Britain begin and end with archaeological value, and although people enjoy being involved in an archaeological project, at the conclusion there is nothing "beyond" that involvement. In Cawood, the various Plans also released a huge amount of creativity, skills and excitement: people with an interest in, or experience of, natural history came forward to help make the trails and do the surveys; people with video cameras filmed events which are then shown on Heritage Days; and farmers offered their fields for field-walking. The CCGG, with different parts of the village, undertook a natural history audit and trail, and has now added wildlife significances to the Garth; interpretation in the form of boards or hand-outs have been produced whilst interest in particular details—such as the fruit varieties in the relict orchards—has led to different specialists being brought to the village to share their knowledge (thereby extending the idea of "expert as commodity"). Neil and I both felt that our role as facilitators had to include listening to the community, and when they wanted to know something that was outside our area of expertise our job was to find those people who could best answer their needs. The example of fruit identification has been particularly creative, because numerous varieties of apple and pear first recorded in the mid-seventeenth century have been discovered, leading to the assumption that fruit growing in the village might have been on a commercial level in the post-medieval period. This knowledge, rather than being logged and stored away, has been acted upon and seized as an indicator of identity for the village. Numerous residents now want to have their own fruit tree stock identified, and has also led to an interest in planting more varieties which continues the historic and developing connection between Cawood and its orchards and may lead to the production of cider, jams, preserves and chutneys in the present

But what of the archaeology in Cawood? The interventions on the Garth (the creation of a footpath and bridge) both required watching briefs and it was agreed that the CCGG could undertake the watching brief for the creation of the path, supervised by one of the professional archaeologists from the village. The construction of the bridge required insertion of a footing into one of the in-filled ditches; this was watched by the same archaeologist who noted that water-logged deposits were likely to be evident at greater depth. This observation resulted in the employment of an environmental specialist by the CCGG to undertake an augur survey across various parts of the site (assisted by village residents) to address specific questions posed in their Research Strategy.

One of the most successful schemes was a molehill survey that involved children from the village school. Members of the English Heritage archaeological field survey team and Mick Atha from the University of York visited the site and explained the various field survey techniques to the children. A long tape was then set out across the Garth and children, working in pairs, carefully excavated each molehill and saved any archaeological contents of each. Using the long tape, the location of each molehill was plotted to scale on a site plan, using off-setting and triangulation. On completion of the project, it was possible to detect a clear clustering of locations where brick, roof and floor tile and mortar were particularly evident, which could then be set against the geophysics and earthwork surveys to locate possible structures or building platforms. The teaching staff was immensely happy with this project as a way of demonstrating the practical application of mathematics and the molehill survey is now a regular event on the Garth, with each phase of activity extending the original survey. In addition, the brief for each archaeological technique (such as geophysics) includes the conditions that the work can only be conducted during term time, must cover the school grounds and must include school children.

Local metal detectorists were invited to the village through the Portable Antiquities Scheme, where they presented and discussed their discoveries to the school children. Again, the invitation included the condition that the school grounds should be detected. The relationship between the Garth group and some of the detectorists has developed to the extent that the detectorists have provided a great deal of information concerning their finds from the fields around Cawood, which has added to the context for the Research Strategy.

However, the archaeological work detailed above is carried out either as an adjunct to the management proposals (that is, those management interventions that the village decide they want because they extend access and use of the Garth) or is geared towards the research objectives selected by the residents. As far as is possible the residents undertake the archaeological work, but they also agree *not* to undertake some projects. Along the bank of the River Ouse at Cawood there is an alignment of substantial vertical timber stakes that probably represent a wharf of some antiquity. Initially, the residents wanted to date the timbers but when they discovered how many would have to be extracted to establish a reliable date, they discussed it amongst themselves and then agreed that, as the stakes were a prominent and distinctive local feature, they would prefer to keep the stakes in place as a focus for imagination and discussion. Similarly, as the cultural heritage capacity building has developed within the village, so an increasing number of people have come forward with ideas of their own-surveys of vernacular buildings, fruit tree surveys, examination of the written resources, a history of the several crashed Second World War bombers from around the village, extending the oral history work and liaison with other community heritage groups to discover common areas of interest—there is a particularly strong bond developing between Cawood and Bishop Wilton, East Yorkshire, which has a similar Garth site. The developing relationship with other community heritage groups has been particularly important as it has led to the sharing of tools and techniques, ideas for study, and is a general self-help and capacity building network which expands and sustains itself. An increasing number of people in the village have begun to discuss, present, construct and contest those ideas about the past and the present that until now were the province of the heritage expert. When a proposal was brought forward from one member of the community to build a car park on part of the Garth, this was rapidly opposed from a variety of quarters. From their initial and scatter-gun requests for consent, the residents of Cawood have built their own cultural heritage project which, although it initially focused on the Garth, has developed into an assessment of what the Garth means in the present and how the Garth can be used; but it has now spread to driving engagement in other stories and opportunities across and around the village.

Conclusion

So, did the Cawood example take "archaeology" out of "heritage"? Not really, but the work at Cawood made it clear that archaeology was one of several tools that could be used by a community to explore ideas of heritage and place. Importantly, the use of archaeology was *negotiated* by the village. They agreed *not* to excavate objects and only agreed limited excavation on the Garth after much discussion. The different survey approaches were more readily embraced because they were non-intrusive, and in that sense they lacked the finality or the sense of "no going back" implied by excavation, but the surveys also provoked story-telling about the Garth or individual buildings, which gave a greater sense of participation. However, there were some issues to address. One of the geophysical teams comprised postgraduate (MA) and undergraduate archaeology students. They argued that they would not discuss their findings first with the CCGG, preferring instead to present the results to the village. The problem here is that the team were actually arguing for retention of their expertise and control of the data: the engagement was to be on *their* terms. When the CCGG failed to make the contractors understand the nature of the community initiative at Cawood they had to appeal directly to the University, after which the situation was resolved. Although this was a limited incident, it was an effective illustration of the way in which expertise is exercised, and the distance still to be travelled in terms of meaningful participation. There were also some interesting assumptions to counter. When Neil and I first approached the Parish Council and the CCGG there was an assumption that, because we were archaeologists, we would immediately organize a series of excavations. Some were resistant to the assumption, others wanted to know how they could be involved, but this was then overshadowed by some suspicion when we began by asking people what it was they most valued about Cawood and the Garth, which seemed a long way from archaeology. We explained that the long-term projects of most interest to them needed a focus on more than archaeological value and were in fact to do with management—which they could undertake. The second assumption concerned "community". The various government papers and policy documents referred to above lead on community, community engagement, community participation and so forth, but the underlying assumption is that a community is a fixed, stable and homogenous body. The Cawood example, and the case-studies documented by Marshall (2002a), illustrate that communities are complex, far from homogenous and do not respond well to one-response-fits-all approaches, which takes us back to the earlier discussion of social inclusion policy and the role of expertise.

In considering whether professional aspirations have changed and social inclusion and its related desirables (regeneration, participation and sustainability) have become embedded in the heritage sector it is necessary to remind ourselves of the government aim taken from *People and Places* (DCMS 2002):

> ... to make social inclusion a priority for all these organisations and agencies, and to achieve the widest possible access to the contemporary and historic built environment as part of the cultural heritage (DCMS 2002, 4).

A problem here has been that the heritage sector has readily seen that the historic environment is both "built" and "historic", but has avoided the idea that it is only "part of the cultural heritage". The outcome of this is that the plethora of things, places, events, activities, memories and stories that make up "heritage" are dispatched to the margins of professional activity to be mopped up by outreach. In this sense, "access" to cultural heritage is about offering access to existing and formal heritage sites and places, where the engagement is always determined by the professional. It could be argued that the message from government needs to be clearer, but that message relies on professional advice. The AHD ensures that either only those elements of the message that reinforce AHD expertise are acted upon, or that the message acknowledges that there are other parts to the cultural heritage but does not suggest what they are, how they might become mainstream or how expertise needs to transform itself.

At present, archaeology and "heritage" are seen and portrayed as synonymous, while archaeology is used as the primary mechanism for addressing "heritage" issues. The social inclusion agenda has been picked up by archaeologists who are keen to see and portray themselves as "community archaeologists" doing "community archaeology", but there is no awareness that there needs to be a professional transformation— whether this is in terms of understanding what expertise does, or in terms of questioning existing assumptions about terms such as "community" and "participation". Participation, sustainability and conservation are meaningless without capacity building—not only *giving* people the tools so that they can explore their own identity, but also *releasing* the tools and skills that people already possess. So, although central government, local government and the various representatives of the heritage sector appear to have signed-up to a new definition of heritage that emphasises the local, the all-embracing extent of the cultural environment and the need for community, there has yet to be an explanation of *how* this revision is to take place. An intellectual and methodological argument is beginning to be put in place as archaeological theory is converted into theoretical approaches to cultural heritage management (Smith 1994), but there is as yet no comparable work on how to turn theory into practice, nor any suggested training programme for heritage specialists introducing them to these new theoretical approaches.

Archaeology's stress on the past and recreating the past works against the creation of meaning in the present—a fundamental part of cultural heritage—because archaeology consigns "heritage" to the past. Community archaeology needs to be carefully considered to ensure that it builds capacity, responds to community need and, ultimately, is a vehicle that allows a community to manage and explore its own cultural heritage. So why take the approach that we took at Cawood? The Cawood example showed that capacity building is not easy and, certainly for archaeologists or building historians, requires negotiation and people skills that are not taught at degree level. In addition, it illustrated how the institutions that might be involved need to think in a different way. Capacity building takes time and it needs regular involvement because the trajectory can undulate, moving from excitement to frustration and back again as understanding and confidence peak and trough. Communities deserve more than to be picked up and dropped as projects come and go. The aim is that as capacity for participation (and confidence) grows, so the volume of meetings should decrease. In this picture, engaging with communities is about "facilitation"; empowering people and providing the circumstances in which existing skills and knowledge can be released; only in this way can sustainability and inclusion become embedded. The most important change is to stand back and think critically about the values and ideas that shape your own discipline and its rationale for engagement.

Notes

[1] This quote was taken from a draft text of the conservation plan. The revised text does not include this quote.

Works Cited

Clark, Kate. 2000. Hard times. *Conservation Bulletin* 37: 37–8.

Clarke, Anne. 2002. The ideal and the real: Cultural and personal transformations of archaeological research on Groote Eylandt, northern Australia. *World Archaeology* 34(2): 249–64.

Clavir, Miriam. 2002. *Preserving what is valued: Museums, conservation and First Nations.* Vancouver: UBC Press.

DCLG. 2008. *Communities in control: Real people, real power.* London: HMSO.

—. 2009. *Guidance on building a sense of belonging.* London: HMSO.

DCMS. 2001. *The historic environment: A force for our future.* London: HMSO.

—. 2002. *People and places: Social inclusion policy for the built and historic environment.* London: HMSO.

—. 2004a. *Government and the value of culture.* London: HMSO.

—. 2004b. *Culture at the heart of regeneration.* London: HMSO.

—. 2005. *Better places to live: Government, identity and the value of the historic built environment.* London: HMSO.

—. 2007. *Culture on demand: Ways to engage a broader audience.* London: HMSO.

Derry, Linda. 1997. Pre-emancipation archaeology: Does it play a role in Selma, Alabama. *Historical Archaeology* 31 (3): 18–26.

English Heritage. 1994. *Schedule entry copy—Cawood Castle and Castle Garth: Residence of the medieval Archbishops of York and associated enclosure containing gardens, five fishponds and a quarry pit (National Monument Number 20539).* London: English Heritage.

—. 2000. *Power of place: The future of the historic environment.* London: English Heritage.

—. 2005. *Remembering forgotten heroes: Exploring the Indian Army contribution to the First and Second World Wars, through the personal memories and photographs of ex-serviceman living in Slough.* London: English Heritage.

Fredericksen, Clayton. 2002. Caring for history: Tiwi and archaeological narratives of Fort Dundas/Punata, Melville Island, Australia. *World Archaeology* 34(2): 288-302.

Greer, Shelley, Rodney Harrison and Susan McIntyre-Tamwoy. 2002. Community-based archaeology in Australia. *World Archaeology* 34(2): 265–87.

Harvey, David. C. 2001. Heritage pasts and heritage presents: Temporality, meaning and the scope of heritage studies. *International Journal of Heritage Studies* 7(4): 319–38.

Jones, Siân. 2006. "They made it a living thing didn't they ...": The growth of things and the fossilisation of heritage. In *A Future for Archaeology*, ed. Robert Layton, Stephen Shennan and Peter Stone, 107–26. London: UCL Press.

Macpherson of Cluny, Sir William. 1999. *The Stephen Lawrence inquiry: Report of an inquiry by Sir William Macpherson of Cluny.* London: HMSO.

Marshall, Yvonne. (ed) 2002a. Community archaeology, *World Archaeology* (Special Volume) 34(2).

Marshall, Yvonne. 2002b. What is community archaeology? *World Archaeology* 34(2): 211–19.

Moser, Stephanie, Darren Glazier, James E. Philips, Lamya Nassr el Nemr, Mohammed Saleh Mousa, Rascha Nasr Aiesh, Susan Richardson, Andrew Conner and Michael Seymour. 2002. Transforming archaeology through practice: strategies for collaborative practice in the Community Archaeology Project at Quseir, Egypt. *World Archaeology* 34 (2): 220–248.

Porter, Libby. 2004. Unlearning one's privilege: Reflections on cross-cultural research with Indigenous peoples in South-East Australia, *Planning Theory and Practice* (5)1: 104–8.

Smith, Laurajane. 1994. Heritage management as postprocessual archaeology? *Antiquity* 68 (259): 300–10.

—. 2001. The archaeologist as a commodity: Re-appraising the role of archaeologists and their knowledge in CHM. Paper presented at the Fourth Cambridge Heritage Seminar, March 2001, in Cambridge, United Kingdom.

—. 2004. *Archaeological theory and the politics of cultural heritage.* London: Routledge.

—. 2006. *Uses of heritage.* London: Routledge.

Smith, Laurajane, Anna Morgan and Anita van der Meer. 2003. Community-driven research in cultural heritage management: The Waanyi Women's History Project. *International Journal of Heritage Studies* 9(1): 65-80.

Start, David. 1999. Community archaeology: Bringing it back to local communities. In *Managing historic sites and buildings*, ed. Gill Chitty and David Baker, 49–59. London: Routledge & English Heritage.

Waterton, Emma. 2008. Invisible identities: Destroying the heritage of Cawood Castle. In *An archaeology of destruction,* ed. Lila Rakoczy, 107–127. Newcastle-upon-Tyne: Cambridge Scholars Press.

Waterton, Emma, Laurajane Smith and Gary Campbell. 2006. The utility of discourse analysis to heritage studies: The Burra Charter and social inclusion. *International Journal of Heritage Studies* 12(4): 339–55.

CHAPTER SEVEN

WHAT ON EARTH IS ARCHAEOLOGY?

DON HENSON

Introduction

Archaeology seems to be a well defined body of theory and practice, and a profession with well structured organizations of representation and authority that lend coherence to its identity. It is often taken for granted that *we* know what an archaeologist is, and that *we* stand within a mutually recognized community of scholars or practitioners. This chapter seeks to explore whether these positions hold any validity, and does so in the belief that archaeology as practised is inherently elitist. Moreover, it argues that archaeology can only find a more democratic base, and a greater place in society, by better understanding that it is part of the wider field of heritage studies and practice. To do so, we first need to understand what archaeology is, and what it is not. Various definitions of archaeology will thus be explored in order to see if there is any agreed description of our disciplinary boundaries. Exploring these boundaries through the self-definitions of archaeology allows us to see how archaeologists envisage their relationship to heritage. If it is less easy to establish what archaeology is than it should be, then our relationship to heritage becomes rather more nuanced and less oppositional than we might suppose.

Archaeology, it will be argued, is a set of practices carried out in various contexts that provide us with positions in a hierarchy of power and influence, and that there are deep divisions within archaeology. In so doing, this chapter seeks to make clear that archaeology is somewhat porous. It has boundaries, although these differ according to context (for example, are museums part of archaeology or not?), and shade into other areas of study related to the past or to people's relationships with each other and the environment. It is a study of the past, but other disciplines also deal with the past, such as history. It is a study of people, but other disciplines also deal with people, such as sociology or anthropology. It is a study of past environments, but the environment is also the object of other disciplines, such as geography. The key aspect that makes archaeology unique is that it deals with the physical remains of past human life. But how does it deal with these remains?

Archaeology grew out of antiquarianism through the application of modernist methodologies. Carman (2002, 192–3) has applied Foucault's delineation of modernist sciences as a conceptual space bounded by biological, philological and economic approaches as a way of categorizing archaeological practices. The biological approach focuses on taxonomy and function (the basic activities of field archaeology), while philology deals with symbols and meaning (the interpretive role of archaeology), and economics covers control and rules of access (the domain of archaeological heritage management). Archaeology is thus a process that transforms the remains of the past from something that is a record of the past, to a resource needing preservation for future study, to a heritage conserved for all to enjoy (Carman 2002, 17–8). Archaeology and heritage, as Carman suggests, are therefore intimately connected. Yet, we shall see that archaeology is often separated from heritage, usually within academic contexts (privileging the philological approach, "those who think", over the biological and economic, "those who do").

Definitions of Archaeology

The archaeological discipline developed as part of the Western and European engagement with tangible cultural heritage since the Renaissance (Schnapp 1996), but clearly heritage is something much wider than simply tangible culture. The UNESCO World Heritage Convention (UNESCO 1972) treats *heritage* as a term that covers both natural and cultural objects and places. In the same convention, tangible cultural heritage consists of monuments, groups of buildings or sites. Archaeology is mentioned specifically under sites rather than the other categories. The Council of Europe also treats archaeology as a distinct form of cultural heritage, for example, through separate conventions on archaeology (Council of Europe 1992) and architecture (Council of Europe 1985). The Council creates a specific subset of heritage, the archaeological heritage, which includes structures, constructions, groups of buildings, developed sites, moveable objects, monuments and their contexts. It is clear that archaeology is not coterminous with heritage, but is a specific part of a wider notion. Heritage is something that comes to us from the past. It is handed down from one generation to another. It is the continuity of human experience and expression that binds people together in the great chain of being human. Archaeology clearly deals with aspects of heritage, and yet heritage is something wider than archaeology. Heritage is fundamentally about human relationships and what it is to be human. If archaeology is really devoted to exploring our engagement as people today with the remains left behind by people in the past, then archaeology must be part of heritage, and therefore be a humanistic discipline. Of course, archaeologists would have to develop an active relationship with the historic environment, and not see it as a set of physical attributes to be conserved. The relationship that people have with the past is complex (see Lowenthal 1985 for a comprehensive exploration of this). Yet, archaeologists are only dimly aware of the past as a relationship. Much more common is to see the past as a resource. The emphasis in archaeology on exclusive rights to validate, conserve and study the archaeological resource has led archaeology to be elitist and exclusive. If archaeology can reconnect with a wider heritage perspective, and reorient its relationship to the past, then we may begin to break down the barriers and make archaeology a more open and diverse discipline.

But what is archaeology? This is not a frivolous question. As archaeologists, we work in the public domain, we receive public funds, and what we do matters to a wider audience. But then, so do many others; others who also claim to work in areas we often regard as our own, or which could be seen by an outside observer as allied to us, such as art historians, building conservators, historical geographers or anthropologists. We also seek to influence public policy in various areas relating to our discipline, in which others also have a legitimate interest. It behoves us to think therefore exactly what *is* our area of interest, how does it relate to those of others, and are there limits to what we can claim?

Archaeology can be defined very simply as a study of the human past through examining physical evidence of that past. There is a general understanding that this evidence can consist of a variety of different things, both above and below ground. Can we refine this definition? What do we find when we look at self-definitions of the discipline by archaeologists themselves? There is no single such definition of archaeology, but there are various attempts at definition that reveal an awareness of boundaries between archaeology and other areas of study or practice. Curiously, some of these seem to limit archaeology only to part of the physical evidence for the human past. The Association of Local Government Archaeological Officers, for example, "embraces all aspects of the historic environment including archaeology, built environment and historic landscapes" (ALGAO n.d.). If archaeology is different to the built environment and historic landscapes, then this suggests that archaeology is discrete buried sites. The ALGAO statement also suggests that the object of study of archaeologists can be characterized by the term *historic environment* and that this is wider than *archaeology*. The objects of study within this term, *historic environment*, beg the question as to what is the specific archaeologists' concern with the built environment that is not that of architectural historians, or of the historic landscape that is not covered by historical geographers. English Heritage also recognizes a distinction between archaeology and other areas of study. Its website has a section headed "Archaeology and Buildings", which distinguishes between archaeology and architectural history:

> Archaeology is the study of past societies and individuals through the physical remains they have left us. Architectural history is about understanding buildings and their surroundings in their wider cultural, historical and social context.[1]

It is hard to see from this definition how architectural history is really any different from archaeology.

A different kind of distinction is provided by the Archaeology Forum. This is a group of organizations in the United Kingdom that are active in archaeology as national bodies. The Forum defines itself as "a grouping of independent bodies concerned with the archaeological investigation, management and interpretation of the historic environment—both buried remains and standing structures" (The Archaeology Forum 2005, 4). Here, archaeology refers to the processes of investigation, management and interpretation, while the object of these processes, the physical remains of the past, is referred to as the historic environment. This is similar to the stance of ALGAO, wherein archaeology is what archaeologists do and the object of their study is the historic environment. Archaeology as practice deals with a body of evidence, the physical remains of the past. These are encompassed by the term *historic environment*, yet this seems inadequate in that it generally refers to buildings, structures and remains in the landscape while excluding, for example, human remains and artefacts. The whole archaeological resource, then, is wider than, but includes, the historic environment. It is important to note that as far as the Forum is concerned, archaeology is more than simply the study of the past. It is also concerned with managing and interpreting that historic environment.

The most comprehensive statement of what is archaeology is perhaps that of the benchmark statement for archaeology issued by the Quality Assurance Agency (QAA) for teaching undergraduate honours degrees in British universities. This was written by the archaeological higher education community, and defines archaeology as:

> ... the study of the human past through material remains (the latter is an extremely broad concept and includes: evidence in the current landscape, from buildings and monuments to ephemeral traces of activity; buried material, such as artefacts, biological remains, and structures; and written sources).[2]

This brings archaeology back to being the study of physical remains of the past, not their management and interpretation. The objects of study also include written sources, which historians would surely see as being in their domain rather than part of archaeology. This academic restriction of archaeology to the process of only investigating the past accords well with the separation of archaeology in higher education from other subject domains. However, if we restate the historic environment as the object of study of archaeology, as the physical traces of human activity handed down from past generations to the present, we can see that what archaeologists study is only a special example of tangible cultural heritage. We might then logically seek academic research and teaching in the management and interpretation of the historic environment within the separate field of heritage studies. Indeed, only a few departments of archaeology successfully cover the wider definitions of archaeology provided by ALGAO and the Archaeology Forum.

Where is archaeology placed within the spectrum of academic disciplines? Which other disciplines are its natural bedfellows? Is heritage studies the natural partner for archaeology? These are not easy questions to answer, yet asking them should lead us to consider whether archaeology has a role to play in relation to heritage. Archaeology is not the only discipline that deals with the past, nor indeed is it the only discipline that deals with the historic environment. It may be that a wider notion of heritage studies that could include, and yet be wider than, archaeology may serve it better than a concern with disciplinary demarcation as *archaeology*. The academic subject domain is divided up and classified in different ways for different purposes. The Research Assessment Exercise (RAE) of the Higher Education funding councils in 2008 placed archaeology as a sub-panel in its own right alongside architecture, town planning and geography. For the QAA Subject Review, archaeology is a separate subject. Yet within the Higher Education Academy, it is placed in a single subject centre with history and classics, albeit with its own subject director and advisory panel. Archaeology is seen, therefore, as having a disciplinary coherence, yet allied to other subjects (albeit with no agreement as to which subjects it is allied with). Neither the RAE nor the subject review included heritage studies within or alongside archaeology, and this agrees with the limited definition provided by the QAA benchmark for the subject.

The location of archaeology as an academic discipline is equally confused in the Joint Academic Coding System used by the Higher Education Statistics Agency and the Universities and Colleges Admissions Service, which places archaeology within historical and philosophical studies, but recognizes that archaeological science needs to be placed elsewhere; with forensic sciences. The Qualifications and Curriculum Authority (QCA) place both archaeology and archaeological sciences within history, philosophy and theology as part of their Sector Subject Area Classification System for the education of 14 to 18 year-olds. In none of these, is a link between archaeology and heritage studies recognized.

The most comprehensive mapping of subjects is probably that of the government's Learn Direct Classification System (LDCS) of academic and vocational subjects (for the purposes of the education of 14–18 year-olds). Archaeology is included in the subject area of history, archaeology, religious studies and philosophy, but also includes archaeological heritage management under the heading of archaeological conservation (QCA n.d.). However, museum studies are under a separate subject area of museum, gallery, conservation skills and studies, while heritage is also covered by the separate subject area of arts, culture and heritage administration. The LDCS thus includes heritage, and introduces us to the idea that there is an *archaeological heritage*. Presumably, this is meant to denote the historic environment and at least restores to archaeology the practices involved in managing and interpreting that environment that were included by ALGAO but excluded by the QAA. On the other hand, aspects of what may be considered the heritage industries are separated from archaeology. As we shall see, this has echoes in the relationship between different areas of archaeological practice.

We can see from the above that there is no single, agreed definition of archaeology. Instead, we have a confusing plethora of definitions and exclusions. This is hardly helpful and reveals a latent contradiction in our attitudes towards the study of the remains of the past, and the treatment of those remains in the present.

Domains of Archaeological Practice

If definitions of archaeology are unsatisfactory in helping us to establish the boundaries of the discipline, can we turn to look at what archaeologists actually do? The practice of archaeology helps to define what archaeology is and establishes a conceptual space related to that practice (Carman 2002, 192–3). One problem we run into is that there is no one profession or job of archaeologist. The term is used to describe various positions in widely differing kinds of organization, pursuing radically different aims and objectives. Research by the IfA (Institute for Archaeologists) estimated that 57% of archaeologists work in field investigation and research, 26% in historic environment advice and information, 12% in academia or education, and 5% in museums and visitor services (Aitchison and Edwards 2008, 66–8). This research also indicated that there were 428 different job titles, which could be grouped into 38 post profiles employed in an estimate of nearly 900 organizations (72% of which employed less than 10 people). Nevertheless, there are some clearly identified sectors within which archaeologists work. The various employment sectors in archaeology have their own power and funding structures, as well as discourses. They define for themselves their portion of the archaeological landscape. Although they may accept that they share this landscape with others (for example, through shared membership of the IfA or other umbrella organizations), they inevitably create specific archaeological discourses that fracture the overall discipline. Archaeology is not one profession but several, and it is in the nature of professions that they seek to define themselves and create boundaries through standards and working practices (Carman 2002, 79, 191). These professions include the contracting sector of field archaeology units, the curatorial sector of local authority planning services, museums and academic institutions. Archaeology is of course more than a profession. It is also a discipline practised widely by the voluntary sector and these must be included in any understanding of how archaeology is defined. Indeed, it is in the voluntary sector where the boundaries of archaeology may be the most porous. We can say then that there are many types of archaeological discourse: including the curatorial, field, academic, museum and volunteers. They differ in their forums of engagement, their languages, their practices and their theoretical bases.

Field archaeology, for example, is the province of a wide range of commercial and charitable organizations. The workforce is largely based on short-term contracts, fluctuating in response to the demands of developer funding and the strictures of the archaeological curators based in planning authorities. Older professionals in supervisory and managerial positions have been lucky to get permanent contracts, and many in senior positions have been with the same unit for most, or all, of their working lives. The lot of these senior archaeologists is project and organizational management rather than archaeology. It is their workforce that engages in archaeological process in order to provide a report to the developer, which allows the developer to carry on with their more profitable development scheme. The world of field units, the contractors of archaeological fieldwork, is defined by the working practices they adopt and the standards they follow (including for many the guidelines laid down by the IfA). They find common cause through membership of the Federation of Archaeological Managers and Employers, and some professional acceptance through being registered archaeological organizations of the IfA. Field archaeology is defined by a concern for archaeological process, management and commercial development. Field units benefit from the principle that developers now pay for archaeology, and the number of jobs in archaeology continues to grow. This yields its own tensions, however: whom does the archaeologist serve, the developer, the rest of the discipline or the public? There is a delicate balance between commercial confidentiality and the diffusion of knowledge. With notable exceptions, allowing public access is difficult, and dissemination of results to the public is patchy.

The curatorial sector is based largely in local authority planning departments. It engages in regulation, control and public service mediated through council bureaucracy and political management. The archaeological process itself is less important than the planning process. Curators are explicitly there to manage the conservation of the historic environment. Active investigation of the past is less of a concern than conservation of the historic environment. They could be said to be conservation professionals rather than archaeological professionals, if we accept the academic position that archaeology is the *study* of the physical remains of the past. Yet, many curatorial archaeologists are also members of the IfA, and share in its framework of standards and delineation of archaeology as a profession. A sense of common identity for the curatorial sector is given by membership of the Association of Local Government Archaeological Officers. The curators quite rightly focus on conserving a scarce archaeological resource for the future: however, not for the public but for the benefit of future archaeologists with better techniques of investigation. Chapter 13 of Planning Policy Guidance 16 (Department of the Environment 1990) is explicit in stating that archaeological excavation is to be seen as a second best option to preservation in situ, and that the reason for this is to allow future and better archaeological techniques to have access to the archaeological resource. This could be seen as contradicting the public service setting of most curatorial archaeologists, based as they are within local authorities or government funded organizations. The world of the curator is the world of planning control rather than public accountability. Of course, some do try to look outward to the public. For example, Historic Environment Records (HERs) are being made increasingly available online. Such remote access can serve in place of potentially damaging physical access to the historic environment, yet this falls a long way short of a meaningful engagement and dialogue with the public.

Alongside conservation, a natural bedfellow for this sector would seem to be presentation and interpretation. The activities of organizations like the National Trust, English Heritage, Historic Scotland, and so forth, reveal the link between the two in that they are charged as public bodies with the conservation and care of historic sites for the public benefit. Interpreting and presenting these sites to the public is part of that benefit. Yet, as far as local authorities are concerned, the link between conservation and presentation is largely the domain of museums rather than the local authority archaeology service. Of course, not all local authorities have museum services, and many have made these services independent trusts rather than support them with limited local government funding. The museum profession includes archaeologists, and there is a Society of Museum Archaeologists. But archaeology is only one aspect of what museums cover. What many archaeologists outside museums would regard as the proper domain of archaeology, the post-medieval and modern worlds, is firmly regarded by museum professionals as part of social history, with archaeology restricted to earlier periods of time. The borders of archaeology have therefore been narrowed to a more restricted field than most outside the museum walls would accept. This would remove archaeology from any connection with the remains of the most recent past; a past still accessible through living memory and family experience.

The professional world of museums is a separate world from archaeology (Carman 2002, 87), with its own career structures, recruitment and training. It is, moreover, separated by the context of professional practice, whereby archaeological remains are treated within a non-archaeological (for example, museum) context where they are decontextualised from their original relationships to each other (Carman 2002, 87–8). They become publicly visible collections and manipulated material culture (objects for manipulation as part of display with purposes and messages often far removed form their original meanings). The museum world has been dominated by the care and display of collections. The educational and outreach functions of museums have improved greatly since the 1960s, led by the work of the Group for Education in Museums (GEM). However, as late as 1999, less than 400 out of 1,700 museums had any education staff, and most put collection management and display as their main priorities (Anderson 1999). There has been no similar survey since 1999, but education has been given greater priority through the Renaissance in the Regions programme (Resource 2001, 36–42), funded by government since 2003. Only a very small proportion of collections are ever put on display and for most people the museum experience is one of passive visitation, invited to gaze upon the wonders of the past. We must wonder, are the artefacts we dig up destined to be no more than curiosities for the display cabinet or museum storage box? Museum displays themselves are increasingly more adventurous, but still cannot quite escape the distancing effect of boundaries, and separation between the display and the observer. The public are welcome, but only as passive observers and units for the cash till.

The final part of the profession of archaeology is the academic sector. Induction into the discipline begins for most archaeologists with their entry to university. Teaching and research within higher education are a major part of archaeology. At one time, it would have been easy to find archaeologists in universities by seeking out separate departments of archaeology. The move towards larger, thematic schools and divisions within universities has led to the merger of some separate archaeology departments into wider units, where they share resources and space with allied disciplines. While the higher education RAE, and earlier subject review for teaching quality, classified only 26 departments as covering archaeology (with disagreement over exactly which departments were included in the 26), there are 59 wider departments, schools or faculties in UK universities that offer single or combined degrees in archaeology at undergraduate and/or postgraduate level. Only 23 of these departments have archaeology in their title. The allied disciplines that archaeology is teamed with in wider departments include history, classics, art studies, geography, conservation studies, European culture and languages, materials and medical sciences, life sciences, environmental management, and critical and contextual studies. Although neither management of the historic environment nor heritage studies are covered by the QAA benchmark for archaeology, a few archaeology departments do cover these in their teaching. There are a few departments that have archaeology in their title offering courses in conservation (of objects or of the historic environment), heritage management, museum studies or just generally archaeology and heritage. Academic archaeology is clearly beginning to engage with both archaeological practice and with wider relations of archaeology with heritage (in research as well as teaching). However, the degree of overlap between archaeology and heritage studies is still small (just four departments of archaeology). There are many more heritage degrees offered by a range of other departments, covering heritage conservation, heritage management, heritage tourism, museums and galleries, for example departments of architecture, planning, built environment, history, environmental studies, arts/media and culture, business and tourism.

In spite of a restricted definition of archaeology in the QAA benchmark statement for archaeology, heritage is recognized as a potential career area for graduates. Yet, the statement itself focuses entirely on archaeology, so that heritage management, conservation etc. are not listed among the body of knowledge or skills required of an archaeology degree. Archaeology is thus taken as a process of investigation, and priority and prestige within academia lies firmly with research. Links with the world of employment outside the academic walls are somehow resisted as part of an imagined opposition between academic and vocational education. Whether such a stance is rational is open to question, and is certainly not shared by all academics. Nevertheless, there is a strong tendency in academia towards protection of its status and identity. The often voiced opinion that to be an archaeologist necessitates having a university degree is a reflection of this. Archaeology in the university sector is popular, growing from 19 universities in 1961 teaching undergraduate archaeology to 43 universities in 2008. The government wants our universities to be world class research institutions, and it is research that has the highest prestige and priority. Publications and conferences serve the needs of the scholarly discipline itself and peer review of publications serves to keep the discipline tightly knit and highly selective.

We can see, then, that the processes involved in doing archaeology have created a particular pattern of sub-professions and fragmented perspectives within archaeology, each with its own careers, language, practices and theoretical underpinnings. Each also tends towards exclusivity and exclusion of the non-inducted. There is also, however, a vernacular discourse outside the sector boundaries outlined above, and largely outside the radar of the academy. Perhaps the greatest gulf in archaeology lies not between the different professional sectors but between the professional sectors and the voluntary sector. This can be characterized as a disjunction between academic and vernacular discourses. The use of the term discourse implies communication as a key aspect of identity. The problems inherent in archaeological discourses have long been noticed. As far back as 1968, Jacquetta Hawkes observed that archaeological discussions were:

> ... so esoteric, so overburdened with unhelpful jargon, so grossly inflated in relation to the significance of the matters involved, that they might

emanate from a secret society, an introverted group of specialists enjoying
their often squalid intellectual spells and rituals at the expense of an
outside world to which they will contribute nothing that is enjoyable,
generally interesting or of historical importance (Hawkes 1968, 255).

Hawkes effectively highlighted the tendency of archaeology to become a
self-selecting clique, defined by references to itself and reinforced through
adopting particular methods of communication and practice. If we are
seeking a broad, encompassing understanding of archaeology, then we
must include the vernacular discourse (or, more properly, multiple
vernacular discourses). These vernacular discourses are visible in the large
voluntary sector engaged in archaeology. If we widen our perspective to
include this sector, then we begin to break down the boundaries that are all
too easy to establish around professions and academic disciplines.

The voluntary sector includes old established county societies, such as
the Sussex Archaeological Society founded in 1846, and more recent and
more local societies like the Bath and Camerton Archaeological Society
established in 1946 or the Uttoxeter Archaeological Society founded in
2002. It thus seems fairly easy to define where volunteer-led archaeology
takes place. On the other hand, some local societies cover more than just
archaeology, for example the Isle of Wight Natural History and
Archaeological Society, or the Leighton Buzzard and District Archaeological
and Historical Society. Furthermore, although many of these societies have
a long established reputation and good relationships with professional
archaeology, there are some groups whose relationship to archaeology has
been more problematical. Since the 1960s, there has been a steady growth
in groups using metal detectors to explore the landscape for artefacts. The
growth of metal detecting led to an angry response among many
professional archaeologists (Gregory 1983, 1986; Dobinson and Denison
1995). The STOP (Stop Taking Our Past) campaign of 1980 sought to
restrict the use of metal detectors on archaeological sites in highly emotive
terms. The use of the word "our" is highly interesting; whose past is under
discussion here, the archaeologists' or the public's? The very use of the
word seems calculated to be ambiguous. The campaign stimulated a strong
adverse reaction among detectorists and many years of poor relations
between the two sides. More recently, the impossibility of stopping
detecting as a hobby has led to greater acceptance and cooperation, with
the Portable Antiquities Scheme being set up with government funding to
provide a network of finds liaison officers to work with detectorists and
others to record the artefacts being found, which has wide support, and a
Code of Practice agreed by both sides. Nevertheless, Gregory's
characterization (1986, 26) of professional archaeology as a middle class,

university educated pursuit rejecting populist engagement with the working class is still uncomfortably close to the mark for some, as it is a profession whose members are almost without exception possessed of at least one and sometimes two university degrees, and still tend to be drawn from the white middle-classes.

What all these voluntary groups have in common is a concern with recovering archaeological material and information, through survey, excavation, fieldwalking and collection. They are concerned with archaeology as a process, less so with managing, conserving or presenting the historic environment. Concern with management of the historic environment tends to fall within the activity of other kinds of voluntary sector groups, such as the Civic Trust (with c.900 local civic societies), the Society for the Protection of Ancient Buildings, the Garden History Society and the National Trust. Of course, it is not just buildings that galvanize volunteer efforts. There are also historic railways run by volunteers, groups looking after maritime heritage, clubs and volunteer museums concerned with historic vehicles etc. Conserving the past through ownership and management is an increasingly important task of the voluntary sector. Some, but only a very few, archaeology groups have also been active in this kind of work, for example, the Sussex Archaeological Society with its properties like Michelham Priory. All of these groups operate in the sphere of the historic environment and are engaged in a relationship with tangible cultural heritage. There are, of course, many more people engaged with local history, genealogy, family history and other intangible forms of cultural heritage. When the government placed the 1901 UK census online in 2002, the webserver was so overloaded by people logging on that it had to be shut down after just four hours (The Register 2002).

Voluntary sector efforts are less prone to respect the boundaries between disciplines than the professional sectors. There has been a growth recently of newer, more intensely localized heritage groups, stimulated by funding from the Heritage Lottery Fund since 1994, and by Local Heritage Initiative funding from 2000 to 2006. Archaeology is often only one component in the activities of such groups. One example of these newer heritage groups is the Badsey Society[3], a joint winner of the 2008 Marsh Community Archaeology Award. The society covers local history, archaeology, folklore, flora, fauna and geology. Their enclosure map project, for which they won the Award, integrated archaeology with local history through a study of the nineteenth century enclosure maps.

The popularity of the past among the voluntary sector, and the inclusion of archaeology within wider heritage activity, ought to be

welcomed by professional practitioners as providing a broader base of
support for the profession. It should also be welcome in helping to build
bridges with other disciplines such as local history, historical geography
and for helping us question our relationship to heritage as a set of
relationships between past and present. Yet, there is no doubt that
professional attitudes towards voluntary engagement are mixed. In part,
this is the natural reaction of self-selected and defined power groups
(Clarke 1993, 193). Allowing access to archaeological knowledge and
skills beyond the boundaries of the profession threatens to dilute the
exclusivity and control of the profession over the archaeological resource.
It threatens professional identity.

Hierarchy, Heritage and Humanism

A further reason for the exclusion of the vernacular discourses from
what might be considered the core of archaeology is the processual
underpinning of archaeology as an objective, rigorous discipline. The New
Archaeology of the 1960s and 70s did much to revitalize archaeology, yet
it too easily leads to the view that only the qualified can do it; those who
have the necessary training and skills (those with a degree). It tends to
exclude the amateur, and narrows the object of study to what is validated
within academic research. It is therefore natural for the academy to
exclude heritage management, even though this forms an important
context for professional practice (Smith 2004, 42). The vast majority of
professional archaeologists are university educated and much of field
archaeological practice and curatorial historic environment practice is
underpinned by the processual model of archaeological theory, whereby
archaeologists objectively seek to recover information about a past that
once existed and privilege the historic environment as an archaeological
resource for them to validate and own (Smith 2004, 107–8). The
archaeologist becomes the expert guardian of proper archaeology, and
archaeology retreats into being an exercise in data recovery and university-
based analysis, divorced from the uses of the past in the world outside the
academy.

Challenges to the scientific paradigm of New Archaeology have come
in the form of so-called post-processual theorizing, which focuses on
interpretation and construction of narratives about the about past within
the present. This has much in common with constructivist models of
learning and interpretation and is much more evident in the world of
museums and heritage sites (Copeland 2004), as well as within academia.
It might be thought that post-processual archaeology, with its call for a

more open and contested form of interpretation, would help to widen archaeology's perspectives and be more inclusive and welcoming to heritage. This, however, has not been the case (Carman 2002, 7). Post-processual theorizing has been an academic exercise, pursued using strategies of academic positioning and clique creation that exclude as much as they include (Smith 2004, 50–1). Indeed, Smith (2004, 34) has noted how both sets of archaeological theory are highly self-referential and inward looking; having little to say about the practice and use of archaeology outside the academy, even though practice is itself a reflection of attitudes derived from academic theory.

The one area of practice that has embraced a more open position is the world of museums, where displays have begun to explore multiple and contested meanings. A recent example of this is the exhibition based around the Lindow Man bog body at the Manchester Museum in 2008. This has made explicit its desire to take into account a post-processual position:

> Since those earlier exhibitions the Manchester Museum has introduced new ways of working in the development of its temporary and permanent displays, which place more emphasis on inclusiveness, on consultation and on making publicly visible the processes by which we create exhibitions. The museum accepts that it does not hold a monopoly on the interpretation of the objects it puts on display and that there is no one single authoritative voice which speaks through the displays. This reflects changes in the theory of knowledge or epistemology and in approaches to exhibition both within the museums profession as a whole and within the Manchester Museum.[4]

Such an approach has also led to some museums seeking to widen the notion of what is worth curating and displaying, and, therefore, what is the object of study. Croydon Museum, for instance, found that public consultation on what it should contain showed an overwhelming desire only for the recent, and therefore most personally relevant pasts, rather than an archaeologically recovered past (Merriman 2004a, 7). It is noteworthy, of course, that the extent to which museums are part of the archaeological domain remains uncertain (Carman 2002). A post-processual positioning within museums has to look outwards through the medium of the museum display. Similar post-processual positioning in academia has no such medium of public engagement and looks inward rather than reaching out. It remains true that archaeological theory still limits the possibilities for what archaeology is, and where its boundaries lie, since it is the different sectors of archaeological practice that allow the articulation of boundaries and determine how theory is related to practice.

Archaeology is not simply the technical study of tangible cultural heritage, of material things, it is the study of people and the places occupied and affected by people over time. This is the conceptual space of our study. There is also a domain of archaeological practice: the study of the past by people in various places across time. This time aspect of what we do is to bring the past into the present through our interpretations, and ensure that the past has a future as a conserved historic environment or archaeological archive. The places in which we work determine the kind of work we do. Our dispersal through various employment contexts, and between professional and voluntary sectors, ensures we have a fragmented discipline with multiple perspectives and contrasting discourses. When we think about the people who practice archaeology, we encounter a majority of people who are white, middle class and male. Research by the IfA has shown than 99% of professional archaeologists are white, 59% are male and only 1.6% of them have a disability (Aitchison and Edwards 2008, 47–52). On the other hand museum archaeology has a majority of women, 63% (Aitchison and Edwards 2008, 48), while people from more excluded socioeconomic backgrounds are to be found within parts of the voluntary sector such as metal detecting. Research by the Portable Antiquities Scheme, which has a majority of users from the metal detecting community (Portable Antiquities Scheme 2006, 120–1), has shown that 47% of people reporting finds are from socioeconomic categories C2, D and E, which cover people who in another age would have been described as the skilled and unskilled working class (Portable Antiquities Scheme 2006, 3).

We also encounter a hierarchy. This is seldom explicit but often implicit in many people's minds, and might run from lower to higher along a scheme such as metal detectorists—local amateur archaeologists—museum archaeologists—field archaeologists—local authority curators—academics. The more male, middle class and educated the archaeologist, the higher they tend to be in the hierarchy. Such a hierarchy is, of course, unjustified, but reflects the privileging of academic over vocational status in education, the supposed superiority of the paid professional over the unpaid amateur, and the inevitable class consciousness that elevates more highly educated and highly paid social groups over others. Importantly, hierarchy involves power—the power to define the object of study and what is or is not archaeology. The archaeological hierarchy is also based on the treatment of archaeological heritage as an objectified past, which fossilizes attitudes and power relations that exclude socioeconomic, ethnic or gender groups that lie outside the dominant discourse of the profession; what Stuart Hall characterizes as colonising the past (Hall 2008, 221). The lack of ethnic minority archaeologists is a recognized problem in the profession, as is the imperfect reflection of gender within the various sectors of archaeology (Aitchison and Edwards 2008, 51–2). Issues of exclusion from, and by, archaeological practice are often starker elsewhere in the world and perhaps less theorized in relation to British archaeology, but are nonetheless real and urgent in the United Kingdom (see Merriman 2004b and Smith 2004 for excellent explorations of this).

Archaeology is in reality defined by its domains of practice, and the enervating effects of fragmentation and hierarchy will not be overcome until we accept that archaeology is both a domain of heritage studies as well as set of professional historic environment practices. While many archaeologists accept that theory and practice are intertwined, this seldom reveals itself in practice. The key property of archaeology is that of time: invisible yet all pervading. It is the physical remains of the *past* that we investigate from within our *present*. Time is the tie that links people then with people now. It was Sir Mortimer Wheeler who insisted "that the archaeologist is digging up, not *things*, but *people*" and that archaeology "must be seasoned with humanity" (Wheeler 1954, 13). If we agree with Wheeler, we have to accept that an archaeology embedded within heritage will be a strengthened archaeology. The notion of heritage comes to the aid of archaeology by highlighting the relationship between past and present, rather than treating the past simply as an object of study. It can help us to better articulate what we do, and why we do it. We can restate our purpose to use the objects of the past to investigate and understand human behaviour and expression, now and in the past. We can use the notion of heritage to articulate why we do it, as a way to connect ourselves with previous generations and to express the humanity we are part of. It can also help us to realize that we share a conceptual and practical space with other disciplines that also share the heritage space with us. In sharing space with other disciplines, we can draw strength from the differing perspectives and challenges they offer without feeling threatened. We have been told this before, albeit in the language of another era:

> I envy the new generation its great opportunity, as never before, to dig up people rather than mere things, and to enable us, in the fullness of time, to view the past and the present as a single, continuous and not always unsuccessful battle between Man [sic] and his Environment and, above all, between Man and himself [sic](Wheeler 1954, 246).

Notes

[1] http://www.english-heritage.org.uk/server/show/nav.1134
[2] http://www.qaa.ac.uk/academicinfrastructure/benchmark/statements/drafts/arc
haeologydraft06.asp
[3] The Badsey Society homepage: http://www.badsey.org.uk/Society/
[4] http://www.museum.manchester.ac.uk/aboutus/ourpractice/lindowman/

Works Cited

Aitchison, Kenneth, and Rachel Edwards. 2008. *Discovering the archaeologists of Europe: United Kingdom. Archaeology labour market intelligence: Profiling the profession 2007/08.* Reading: Institute of Field Archaeologists.

ALGAO. n.d. "Association of Local Government Archaeological Officers UK: Homepage". http://www.algao.org.uk/.

Anderson, David. 1999. *A common wealth: Museums and learning in the United Kingdom.* London: DCMS.

Carman, John. 2002. *Archaeology and heritage: An introduction.* London: Continuum.

Clarke, Annie. 1993. Cultural resource management (CRM) as archaeological housework: Confining women to the ghetto of management. In *Women in archaeology: A feminist critique*, ed. Hilary du Cros and Laurajane Smith, 191–4. Canberra: Australian National University.

Copeland, Tim. 2004. Presenting archaeology to the public: Constructing insights on-site. In *Public archaeology*, ed. Nick Merriman, 132–44. London, Routledge.

Council of Europe. 1985. *Convention for the protection of the architectural heritage.*

Council of Europe. 1992. *The European convention on the protection of the archaeological heritage (revised).*

Department of the Environment. 1990. *Planning policy guidance 16: Archaeology and planning.* London: Department of Environment.

Dobinson, Colin, and Simon Denison. 1995. *Metal detecting and archaeology in England.* London and York: English Heritage and the Council for British Archaeology.

Gregory, Tony. 1983. The impact of metal detecting on archaeology and the public. *Archaeological Review Cambridge* 2 (1): 5–8.

—. 1986. Whose fault is treasure-hunting? In *Archaeology, politics and the public*, ed. Colin Dobinson and Roberta Gilchrist, 25–27. York: York University Archaeological Publication 5.

Hall, Stuart. 2008. Whose heritage?: Un-settling "the heritage", re-imagining the post-nation. In *The heritage reader*, ed. Graham Fairclough, Rodney Harrison, John H. Jameson Jr and John Schofield, 219–28. London: Routledge.

Hawkes, Jacquetta. 1968. The proper study of mankind. *Antiquity* 42: 255–62.

Lowenthal, David. 1985. *The past is a foreign country*. Cambridge: University Press.

Merriman, Nick. 2004a. Involving the public in museum archaeology. In *Public archaeology*, ed. Nick Merriman, 85–108. London: Routledge.

—. ed. 2004b. *Public archaeology*. London: Routledge.

Portable Antiquities Scheme. 2006. *Annual report 2005/6*. London: Portable Antiquities Scheme.

Resource. 2001. *Renaissance in the regions: A new vision for England's museums*. London: Resource.

QCA. n.d. "Qualifications and curriculum authority: Homepage". http://www.qca.org.uk/qca_8488.aspx.

Schnapp, Alain. 1996. *The discovery of the past: The origins of archaeology*, trans. Ian Kinnes and Gillian Varndell. London: British Museum Press.

Smith, Laurajane, ed. 2004. *Archaeological theory and the politics of cultural heritage*. London: Routledge.

The Archaeology Forum. 2005. *Archaeology enriches us all*. http://www.britarch.ac.uk/archforum/enriches.pdf

The Register. 2002. *1901 census site closed for urgent repairs*. http://www.theregister.co.uk/2002/01/03/1901_census_site_closed.

UNESCO. 1972. *Convention concerning the protection of the world cultural and natural heritage*.

Wheeler, Sir R.E Mortimer. 1954. *Archaeology from the earth*. Harmondsworth: Penguin Books.

CHAPTER EIGHT

THE DILEMMA OF PARTICIPATING

MARJOLIJN KOK

Introduction

This chapter explores the dilemma of participating in heritage projects explicitly connected to wider politics of identity and heritage management. Since Michael Shanks and Chris Tilley (1987) authored *Re-Constructing Archaeology* some twenty years ago, most archaeologists have realized that what they publish has consequences outside the archaeological discipline. How we should deal with this awareness is, however, less clear. In the (western) Netherlands, there is little public awareness of the archaeological heritage present, especially when dealing with the prehistoric period. This is partly due to the fact that nearly all archaeological remains are invisible as they are beneath the surface (Figure 8.1). Another reason for the lack of general knowledge about archaeological heritage is the limited amount of public outreach that has taken place. In recent times, however, several national policies have given heritage a central position in environmental planning; based partly on the development of the *European Convention on the Protection of the Archaeological Heritage* (Valetta) in 1992, and partly on the idea that knowledge of local heritage enhances the quality of living (Feddes 1999). Dutch archaeology has become a booming business at such a fast pace that we have not been able to rethink our position. Archaeologists were just glad to have a job, as we were told during our education that only ten percent would be so lucky. As large amounts of public money are put into archaeology, it is reasonable that the public should get something in return. In itself this is not an unusual demand, but what we should "give" is less clearly defined.

This chapter focuses on the development by the province Noord-Holland of a book—*The Land of Hilde*—(Dekkers et al. 2006) that accompanied a local exhibition—*Treasures Beneath Your feet*—about the "unknown" archaeological history of the Oer-IJ area (Figure 8.2) and the involvement of the academic researchers of the Oer-IJ project. First, a theoretical background and an overview of the Dutch situation and the Oer-IJ project in relation to provincial politics and the public is given, followed by a discussion of the dilemma that arose when the book and exhibition came into being. The different participants and their agendas are discussed in order to try and answer the question: do I, as an archaeologist, want to participate in this kind of project?

Figure 8.1: A typical (nearly) invisible archaeological monument in the Oer-IJ area, the Netherlands

Theoretical Background

Archaeologists construct narratives about the past based on archaeological data, which is not the same thing as archaeological "facts". Archaeological knowledge is a specific type of knowledge that is constructed within a specific practice. There is always an element of interpretation that starts when we collect data. We judge the validity of an archaeological narrative not on the truth of its content, but on how it deals with the known archaeological data. This leaves room for multiple interpretations, and narratives have to be valued in relation to what Shanks and Tilley (1992, 104) call a "network of resistance" of archaeological data. The position of the interpreter will also be of significance when a narrative is being valued. Archaeologists, when they doubt the validity of a narrative, will look at the data before making any judgement. Nonexperts, such as public audiences, usually have no access to the data and make judgements on different grounds. These judgements can be based on how the narrative relates to their own experiences, or on the view that the expert will have made the right choice based on a professional standard. Our position as so-called "experts of the past" gives us a certain authority within the public domain of heritage management. Even though this authority may be contested, we should not downplay our responsibility for what we narrate when we are in a position of authority (Bender 1998, 9; Skeates 2000, 89; Joyce 2002, 14; Smith 2004, 198). The choice for a specific narrative and narrating style should therefore be examined critically as it has an effect in the public domain.

Furthermore, over the last decade many archaeologists have felt that communities should be able to participate within heritage projects (Bender 1998; McDavid 2000; Skeates 2000; Carman 2005; Smith 2006). Our archaeological interest in the past should not overrule the desire of others to participate in their heritage. The type of discourse used by archaeologists can be excluding or including for other participants. How we use language and discourse has therefore become an important part of studies that want to involve more people with heritage (Bender 1998; Joyce 2002; Smith 2006). More inclusive discourses embrace multivocality and multiple narratives, as this will give different groups a voice, including differing archaeologists (Bender 1998, 158; McDavid 2000, 223; Joyce 2002, 128). If we combine the multi-interpretable aspects of archaeological data with the desire to include more people in heritage practices than multiples narratives are possible and desirable. So, if I am aware of the political dimension of all archaeological narratives, and think that multiple narratives are not only possible, but even desirable, how, then, did the dilemma of participating occur?

Background to the Dutch Situation

With the implementation of the *Belvedere* policy in 1999 and the *Fifth Policy Document on Town and Country Planning* in 2001, both concerned with the embedding of cultural heritage into the planning process, archaeologists and other academics within the field of cultural studies have been asked for their input in the development of (local) planning and heritage policies (Groenewoudt and Bloemers 1997) and large environmental development projects (Elerie and Foorthuis 2003; Plasschaert 2005; Stam 2008). In Dutch archaeology, this was a new demand for academics. At first, it mainly involved archaeological resource management, which concentrated on the preservation or, if necessary, excavation of physical remains. This form of archaeological resource management was mainly based on the Convention of Valetta. Generally, the aim was to make archaeology known to a wider audience in order to safeguard archaeological remains in everybody's interest. More specifically, however, this mainly covered the interests of academic archaeologists and safeguarded their data for themselves or future archaeologists. This view of the management of archaeological resources was so self evident that there needed to be little debate about it. Thus, for a long time academia mostly withdrew from the debates about archaeological resource management. This was facilitated by the fact that by law only a few institutions could perform excavations, namely the universities, the State Service and the municipal archaeological services. The position of these institutes was so strong that no serious rethinking of their positions was undertaken even in the face of increasing commercial archaeology in the 1990s. Even when the processes of archaeological resource management was renamed (archaeological) heritage management at the turn of the century, little debate or reflection occurred on what this name change implied. For example, Willem Willems, the then director of the State Service, wrote in 1997 that "a truly commercial archaeology will probably not be allowed to develop in the Netherlands ..." (1997, 12). Private companies were regarded with suspicion; implicitly it was suggested that commercial interests and competition would lead to bad archaeology. This could be overcome with a single private initiative closely aligned with the State Service that could deal with most of the excavations and tasks that would be necessary under the Convention of Valetta. The State Service would focus on archaeological resource and knowledge management and the universities and museums would generate knowledge they believed to be of importance.

Within the last few years, the field of archaeology has, however, developed enormously. The biggest change to the system is that, since 2001, commercial companies can get a permit to excavate, and the majority of excavations are now performed by these companies instead of the old institutions. These companies employ the majority of archaeologists. Professional archaeologists are, however, all academically trained. The University of Amsterdam was the first to start education concerned with archaeological resource management and, in 2002, Tom Bloemers became the first professor in archaeological resource management, landscape and heritage. Currently, most universities with an archaeology department have taken up archaeological resource/heritage management in their educational programme.

National policies concerned with the quality of the environment in which we live (Feddes 1999), spatial planning (VROM 2001), the *European*

Landscape Convention (Florence Convention) and the Convention of Faro
have led to the development of a "Heritage sector" in the Netherlands from
the more general "Cultural sector". Archaeological resource management
is gradually becoming heritage management in the sense that we can no
longer focus purely on the management and preservation of archaeological
sites, but are also increasingly involved with what these sites mean as
heritage in present day society. This trend has taken place in other Western
countries as well (see for instance Smith 2004; Carman 2005, 45–61;
Fairclough et al. 2008).The change to heritage management is, however,
not a uniform phenomenon. When van den Dries and Willems write on the
subject of quality management, the participants involved with archaeological
management are developers, authorities and archaeological contractors
(2007, 52). The public is notably absent in their scheme as they focus on
legislation and contracts. The last issue of the main publication series of
the State Service (BROB 2006), before it merged into the "State Service
for Archaeology, Cultural Landscapes and Monuments" (RACM), shows a
similar focus on best practice within the archaeological field. The public is
not seen as people who actually interact with heritage, but as an abstract
concept perpetuated by the idea of "public interest". This means that the
management of archaeological resources is viewed as evidently beneficial
for all in society (Groenewoudt and Bloemers 1997, 121), and what that
benefit may be is hardly ever problematised or considered. Only two
articles in this issue (van Beek and Keunen 2006; Spek et al. 2006)
considered the public as active participants in the heritage process. It is
only when archaeological heritage management is closely associated with
spatial planning that the public takes a more prominent role as active
participants (van der Valk and Bloemers 2006; Elerie and Foorthuis 2003).
Here, opportunities for cooperation and development are emphasized
instead of a focus on protection and preservation of archaeological remains.

The heritage sector functions differently than the archaeological
resource management sector in the sense that interdisciplinary becomes
necessary. Policymakers and planners do not want to deal with heritage as
divided into separate disciplines. The disciplinary divisions between
archaeologists   (buried   monuments),   historian-geographers   (visible
landscape), architectural historians (historic buildings), and landscape
ecologists (natural and cultural heritage), clear to the academic, are often
less clear to other people. When dealing with heritage in environmental
development projects, policymakers and planners want centralized
experts/interest groups with whom they can easily deal, instead of
different experts/interest groups that have to be consulted separately (Tress
et al. 2005; van der Valk and Bloemers, 2006). Nor do the users of a

specific landscape ascribe meaning to a place along disciplinary boundaries. Furthermore, within academia the idea of landscape is often seen as interdisciplinary (Tress et al. 2005; van der Valk and Bloemers 2006). The need for interdisciplinarity in the heritage sector becomes important now that different institutions from the cultural sector are merging into single heritage institutions, such as the RACM in 2006. Although most academics/archaeologists see the advantage of interdisciplinary projects, the merging of the institutions was organized from the top down. In 2007, the organizations NCM (National Contact Monuments), SNA (archaeology), DIVA (Record and Information Management and Archives) and Erfgoed Actueel (Heritage Education) merged into Erfgoed Nederland. In 2008, the Dutch museum organization (NVM) joined Erfgoed Nederland. Erfgoed Nederland is an organization funded by the state. Another change has taken place in the sense that the individual organizations main interests were to lobby for the interest of experts and professionals and this interest has now shifted towards a public outreach function.

Policy associated with heritage, such as "Belvedere" (Feddes 1999), also influences the academic practice as the Dutch Science Foundation initiated the research programme "Protecting and developing the Dutch archaeological-historical landscape" specifically dealing with the embedding of heritage into spatial planning (Bloemers and Wijnen 2001). The case study below is part of this programme. The additional formation of three "Belvedere" chairs in different disciplines at different universities which are directly associated with this specific policy, deepens the relation between science and policy (Stam 2008). Whether this direct link is good for academic practice is not questioned widely. Even though Eickhoff (2003, 11) has warned about the tendency for the uncritical combination of policy, science and politics that encourage debate, little discussion is actually undertaken. No reflection on the desirability of the far-going mixing of policy and academia has taken place. The issue is simply not discussed. The influence of the Dutch government in the shaping of how and what elements of our history should be taught is increasing with the development of heritage policies, heritage institutions, a historic canon and a new national museum of history. For example, the prime minister has repeatedly said that what we need nowadays is a "VOC-mentality". These merchants, through bold entrepreneurial spirit, brought wealth to the Dutch in the seventeenth century. That they gathered this wealth through the slave trade, plundering and colonialism, a historically reality which could be painful for many Dutch citizens, is overlooked by the prime minister. Although, within the Netherlands, the cultural and historic disciplines participate in the public debates about the problematic nature of the political influences (Grever et al. 2006; de Bruin 2008; Palm 2008, 27), archaeologists are conspicuously absent from this debate.

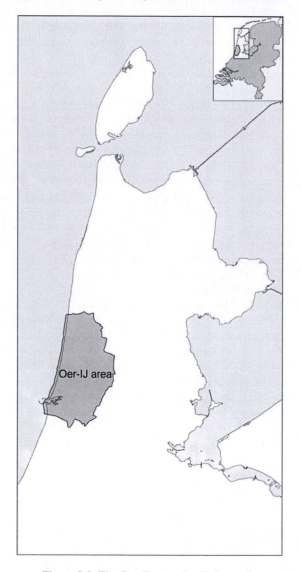

Figure 8.2: The Oer-IJ area, the Netherlands

Debates about the relationships between heritage, identity and public participation seem to take place mainly outside the archaeological field, and there is little discussion about the ethical and social implication surrounding the formation of identities through the use of heritage. In the Netherlands, archaeological work increasingly takes place within the field of spatial planning and heritage policies. Discussions centre around how to deal with the archaeological record in a way that archaeologists find important (Groenewoudt and Bloemers 1997) or how the integration of archaeological narratives in the planning process lead to a better quality of the living environment (van Loon et al. 2006, 236; Bloemers and Wijnen 2001). Public outreach activities mostly have an educational character in which the story of the past is told in an understandable way (van Ginkel and Cruyshaar 2003). How the public actively deals with this information in relation to the shaping of their identity or view on present-day affairs is left out. In general, there is no archaeological debate about the use of the past in the present within the Netherlands.

Project Framework: "Oer-IJ" and "Land of Hilde"

The Dutch Science Foundation's research programme "Protecting and developing the Dutch archaeological-historical landscape" (BBO) comprises four large regional projects and several small general research projects. All projects are concerned with the issue of how to embed academic knowledge into the planning process and related policies (Bloemers and Wijnen 2001). The Oer-IJ project—fully named: "From Oer-IJ estuary to metropolitan coastal landscape: assessing and preserving archaeological-historical resources from 4000 years living between land and water"—is one of the regional projects. From the start of the Oer-IJ project in 2001, there was a strong connection with the government at the provincial level. Both the University of Amsterdam and the Province had defined the Oer-IJ area (Figure 8.2) as a place of interest (Bloemers 2001, 3; Therkorn 2005, 90). At the time, the provincial government played a pivotal role in the execution of the national Belvedere policy for sustainable development of the archaeological-historical values in the research area (Bloemers 2001, 3). Another partner was the regional directorate of the Ministry of Agriculture, Nature and Fisheries, which had also committed itself to the Belvedere policy and was managing a large area in the Oer-IJ region as part of the ecological main structure (a structure that physically connects different nature reserves throughout the Netherlands so animals can move freely). The common ground for cooperation between the research program and governmental bodies was care for the archaeo-historical landscape (Bloemers 2001, 3).

It was recognized from the start that all participants had different time-schemes and policies. This was seen by the participants as inherent to any project where policies and research programmes were combined and the challenge would be to overcome these difficulties. The project leader Tom Bloemers proposed that adequate and regular communication about aims, methodology, planning, and results would lead to good results (Bloemers 2001, 3). The programme instigators saw the concept of the cultural biography of the landscape as central to cooperation. The cultural biography of the landscape was seen as a "fuzzy" or "bridging" concept. By not defining what the concept exactly meant, or leaving multiple definitions possible, all different participants would be able to talk to each other without immediate conflicts arising or endless discussions over definitions. In its most general form, the cultural biography of the landscape was seen as a way to tell an appealing story of a landscape and its transformations through time (Hidding et al. 2001). The province announced that it would participate as long as it fitted into their planning. They did not explicate what this meant exactly, but it was clear that they had a limited commitment. The researchers did not show any such reservations. This lack of reservation showed a certain naivety about the way in which non-academic projects are carried out.

The Oer-IJ project consisted of three different types of research with specific purposes. Conceptual research should lead to archaeological knowledge, strategic research should integrate archaeological knowledge into the policymaking process and study the process at the same time, while applied research should investigate technical questions concerning archaeological heritage management. The intention of the research programme was that, with these different approaches, all aspects of archaeological heritage management could be covered. Within the Oer-IJ project the conceptual research consisted of two PhD researchers who would write an archaeological thesis on the Oer-IJ, with one concentrating on the pre- and protohistory (Kok 2008), and the other on the medieval to the present period (Alders forthcoming). The two theses would provide building blocks for the strategic research in which a cultural biography of the region would be constructed. This cultural biography could be used as a bridging tool between academic knowledge and policymaking (van Londen 2006). The applied research analysed the physical preservation of the archaeological monuments, so that when decisions were made about what archaeological monuments to preserve adequate measures could be taken (van Heeringen et al. 2003).

The first few years of the project concentrated on the physical remains of archaeology, their management and incorporation into new developments and planning policies. Discussion arose especially around the usefulness of the concept of "cultural biography" in archaeological heritage management (van Londen 2006). Debates concerned such issues as: what archaeological elements were included in the narrative, and what would be the effect of the inclusion, or, for that matter, exclusion, of specific elements? Would the decision to research, preserve or destroy archaeology be dependent on a single narrative? Even if the narrative encompassed all archaeological periods, choices still had to be made as to what to enter and what to leave out, and who would make those choices?

In 2004, the province published a report on the preservation and management of archaeological sites in the Oer-IJ area (van Eerden 2004) that assessed known archaeological sites on the archaeological monument map and made proposals for their management. In this publication, it was stated that the policy for the preservation of archaeological sites could only count on public support when the public was made aware—through specific and active information and its dissemination—of the heritage present in the soil and that its loss would be regrettable (van Eerden 2004, 31). Furthermore, suggestion should be made on how this archaeological heritage could be an inspiration for the future (van Eerden 2004, 15). At the same time, the Province commissioned the University of Amsterdam to make an archaeological knowledge inventory (AKI) (Lange et al. 2004). Participants of the Oer-IJ project took part in this assignment. This inventory described known archaeological sites in their local context (ensembles), and the knowledge that existed in prior publications. One chapter described the archaeological developments through time, and the interpretative models that were used. Plus/minus charts were made that indicated if there had been sufficient excavations in a specific area and if the data gathered had been published. In this way, it became clear in which parts of the Oer-IJ area more excavation data and/or other knowledge through syntheses was needed to create a coherent picture of the development of the region through time. During this time the researchers of the University of Amsterdam felt they were thinking along similar lines about archaeological heritage management as the Province's policymakers. Policymakers were a bit disappointed about the chapter that described the archaeological development, due to its lack of catchy elements, but this was not seen as major setback as it was, at the same time, seen as very useful in the decision making process.

As the cultural biography of landscape was seen as a central concept in the BBO programme, the researchers were still discussing whether this concept was the best instrument for integrating archaeology, spatial planning and policy. The main point of discussion was whether the methods and definitions should be made more explicit within the biographical approach (Kolen and Witte 2006; van Londen 2006). On the one hand, it was felt that rigid definitions and methodology would hamper the development of relevant concepts (Kolen and Witte 2006, 133). On the other hand, it was thought that lack of definition and methodology would make it unclear what elements were taken up or left out in the biography of specific landscapes (van Londen 2006, 178). Heleen van Londen was part of the Oer-IJ project, and within this project her line of reasoning about the cultural biography was followed. The cultural biography could be used in shaping new developments and communication about archaeology when the reasons for choosing a particular story are explicated. However, the AKI, or similar documents, were better suited for the purpose of decision making concerning the preservation and/or development of archaeological heritage. Although the AKI may not read as easily as a biography, it would make the decision making process less dependent on the elements that fitted a chosen biography. If selection of archaeological sites for preservation or development were only chosen on the basis that they fitted within a specific biography, it would become quite difficult to choose a different narrative in the future. Furthermore, Van Londen warned against the dangers of the uncritical use of the cultural biography in the creation of identities. Politicians can seek to get academic legitimation for their creation of specific identities. When this identity is also expressed solely in ethnic terms a situation is created that takes us back to the controversial subjects of the use of archaeology by politicians in the 1930s (van Londen 2006, 175).

Figure 8.3: The reconstruction of Hilde that plays a central role in the exhibition
and the book of the Oer-IJ area

The Dilemma

As stated in their report of 2004, the province wanted to "reach" the
public and in order to do so a book and an exhibition on the archaeology
of the Oer-IJ area was produced. Both the exhibition and the book
revolved around a woman whose remains had been found in the area, and
of whom a life-size reconstruction was made (Figure 8.3). The woman was
named "Hilde" (Dekkers et al. 2006, 9). The book was written by
writer/journalists—including a representative of the province who was
also involved with the care of archaeological monuments—who were used
to writing for a general public audience. Different archaeologists (including

members of the Oer-IJ project) and geologists were asked to participate by giving information on their specialist subjects.

The first choice the province made was limiting the area and period the book would cover. The focus would be on the rural parts of the area, as these were least developed and the preservation of archaeological monuments was still possible. Large amounts of public money were about to be spent on the preservation of provincial monuments that were threatened by agricultural use instead of building projects. The prevention of the destruction of invisible archaeological monuments by normal agricultural activity is a new approach that has to be explained to the public (van Eerden 2005, 19).The rural area coincides with the remnants of the streambed of the Oer-IJ and its side branches. These are the lower parts of the landscape that were still heavily under the influence of the sea in the Iron Age. This automatically meant that the period in the narrative would also be narrowed down. The logical start was thus the Late Iron Age. The start of Christianization and the introduction of written sources from inhabitants/visitors in the area in the early medieval period around 750 A.D. was chosen as the end date. The lack of written sources means that all information about the area would be largely based on geology and archaeology. The aim was to characterize the area and period in both the exhibition and the book.

The dilemma arose when the archaeologists of the University of Amsterdam told a different story about the characterization of the area than what the policymaker had hoped. Within the Oer-IJ project, we had mainly focussed on how our narrative of the cultural biography could be used in spatial planning. The area is a former delta, and the present-day landscape is shaped by the former Oer-IJ. Most people will look at the area as flat meadow landscape with ditches, although it may not be clearly visible to the untrained eye, there are perceptible differences in height in this landscape. The old riverbed can be seen as a large depression that weaves its way between the different villages that are all situated on former coastal barriers and old dunes, many of the curving waterways are the remnants of old creeks or the Oer-IJ. Water not only has shaped the landscape, it is still a major part of the landscape as there are several lakes, and water is the main division between different pieces of land, such as meadows and fields. When discussing the theme for the cultural biography of the landscape water seemed an obvious choice. This choice of theme appealed to spatial planners and artists who were dealing with the shaping of the present-day landscape on the instigation of the Province. Spatial planning and archaeological, historical and cultural values would be incorporated as a pilot project (Plasschaert 2005, 8). Therefore, the researchers thought that landscape would be central to the narrative, as it was within the cultural planning project that the remains of the old landscape would be made visible (Plasschaert 2005, 34–41).

Furthermore, the researchers felt that a focus on the landscape was desirable in the context of constructing an identity for the area, as this would be less excluding to newcomers. The archaeologists told a story of multiple landscapes on top of each other. This was based on the specific geology of the region; the archaeological diversity within the area between the different locales; the time-depth of the history of the area in which the dry and wet parts both played a role; and the exceptional preservation of organic remains, which made the area rich in archaeology of a specific nature. These excellent archaeological conditions allow us to reconstruct the active engagement of people in the past with their landscape. The layout of settlements and fields, and ritual activities ranging from offerings in the wet-low-lying parts of the Oer-IJ, the construction of earthworks, to pits with depositions that formed star-patterns, make clear that the landscape was constantly reworked. Tradition and transformation were at the same time at play as the landscape changed through time due to natural and cultural factors. The policymaker/writers' interest in our story was minimal. It soon became clear that what was wanted was scientific approval or validation of a Frisian identity for the region. The Frisian identity wanted by the policymaker is, however, not so straightforward.

According to Tacitus, the Frisians lived on the west coast of the ocean, north of the Rhine (Mattingly 1948, 128). He divides them in to minor and major Frisians of which the minor Frisians could have lived in the Oer-IJ area. The Oer-IJ is often seen as the most northerly branch of the Rhine river system (Bazelmans et al. 2002, 23). This would mean that in Tacitus description the Oer-IJ area was a borderland between Frisians and Cananefaten. Whether the people in the Oer-IJ area perceived themselves as minor Frisians is a different matter. On archaeological grounds, the cultural traditions show both a link with the people to the south (Cananefaten) and to the north (Frisians), but in how far this shaped their identity is unknown. Besides the Oer-IJ area has its own distinct features that are unique for the Netherlands such as wall-ditch houses (Kok 2008, 115).

There is no textual evidence related to the Frisians between 300 and 600 A.D. From the seventh century onward, the Oer-IJ area becomes part of the flourishing Frisian Kingdom that lasted for five centuries. An enduring link between this Medieval Frisian Kingdom and the Frisians mentioned by Tacitus is untenable, as both a political and ethnic continuity seems unlikely (Bazelmans et al. 2002, 30–1). The emphasis on tribal affiliation for the pre- and protohistoric period is therefore of limited value from an academic viewpoint. Besides the Frisian identity is not just any historic identity, as a northern province of the Netherlands is called Friesland. This province has its own language—Frisian—and is officially bilingual. This means that all legal documents should be available in Frisian, and Frisian is taught in the regular school curriculum within the province. The Frisians are known for many traditions that non-Frisians admire or find interesting, such as "skûtje silen", a specific type of boat and associated races, and the "Elfstedentocht", a skating contest over 200 km long that passes through all the historically important cities of Friesland. In short, we were told by the policymaker that our academic story, in which the word Frisian was not used, would be retold as a story of the Frisians and how they lived within the Oer-IJ area. When asked about this choice for a Frisian story—as the link between the medieval Frisians and the people in the period under discussion was untenable—it was explained that it was felt that the public needed to identify with the people of the past. Romans, Vikings, and the like, were seen as strong identities (van Eerden, 2005). As the main part of the book and exhibition were dealing with the Roman period—and it had to be clear that the local people were not Romans—the use of the Frisian identity was seen as the best way to deal with this.

When we suggested that the creation of identities might exclude people or lead to unsavoury and exclusionary tendencies within current social debates, this was set aside. We were seen as overanxious, as there would be some explanation of the term Frisian in the first part of the book. It would be made clear that the use of the term Frisian had only limited use. Furthermore, other archaeologists used the term Frisian explicitly, so why were we against the use of this term? Our response that the archaeologists who used the term Frisian were usually speaking about a different period or used it as shorthand for a very broad group was not taken up. As we would not see the final text of the book, the people participating in the Oer-IJ-project decided that they would discontinue their support of the book and the exhibition. The information we had already given could be used freely, but we would not like to be mentioned in any part of the book that accompanied the exhibition. This was done in order to avoid the idea that we gave academic legitimization to the content. As it turned out, we were glad we discontinued support, as the word Frisian appeared continuously, and in the most unlikely places, with an average of 2.6 mentions per page, even when the book has many large illustrations.

The sad conclusion, however, was that we could not avert the excessive use of the word "Frisian" and the attempt to establish a Frisian identity, especially as the book is distributed freely to all schools in the area, and used as educational material. We could not convince the policymaker that the use and creation of ethnic identities can be dangerous, especially as the "integration debate" in the Netherlands is not what you can call friendly or sophisticated. Until the late nineties, debates about multiculturalism emphasized the existence of multiple Dutch identities and that both immigrants and Dutch inhabitants were responsible for the solution of social problems. However, since the turn of the century, the debate has focused on integration, and all responsibility for the solution of social problems has been put in the hands of immigrants (and their descendants) (Schinkel 2008). Schinkel (2008) has argued that this change to the term "integration" has in effect put immigrants outside Dutch society, instead of recognizing that Dutch society has changed into a multicultural society. Tillie (2008) describes Dutch society as self-referential. The strange belief seems to be that when all non-Dutch elements are taken away, societal problems will be solved. The construction of a Dutch identity has become a major political issue. This became clear when princess Maxima, at a public lecture in 2007, said that there is no such thing as *a* Dutch identity, just as there is not *an* Argentinean identity (her homeland). Her statement, which seems so valid in a multicultural context, was even discussed in parliament. If we view the construction of identities against this political debate, it becomes clear that the construction of identities is far from a neutral practice.

Some Points of Discussion

All participants involved with the creation of the book and exhibition made their own choices based on their own background, information and motivations. Here, I want to analyse some of the issues that have come to the fore and how we could deal with these issues in the future. It should also be clear that although we stopped participating with the book and exhibition, we did not end our discussions with the province of Noord-Holland. The first point of discussion is the emphasis on a Frisian identity. It became most obvious that both parties never assumed that the other party might have had different views on how to approach the subject of the characterization of the area, until it was too late. Identity was seen as important from the start. In previous cooperative discussions, identity referred to the recognizable characterization of the environment in which local people live. When the request from the province came for participating in a book and exhibition for the public, the researchers assumed it was from a similar perspective. The researchers sense of a desired construction of identity that would be inclusive of all inhabitants of the area never allowed for the possibility that other groups would see the landscape differently, or privilege different aspects over others. As neither party was aware of a possible conflict, each continued on their own path, although both had the aim of making the archaeology of the area known to the wider public. Van Eerden in his contact with the public when they visited the provincial depot was always asked about the Romans, Vikings or Middle Ages. Showing the artefacts (mainly pottery vessels) from large scale excavations from the pre- and protohistoric period often led to a feeling of disappointment by the visitors. The local inhabitants were viewed as poor pitiful farmers living in the "prut" (wet dirt). Visitors had difficulty with identifying with these farmers without a clear name. According to van Eerden, the naming of the past inhabitants as Frisians could fill the need for a recognizable people (2005, 17), which would be further aided by the reconstruction of a "real" person that would be named Hilde (Figure 8.3). Nowadays, nearly none of the inhabitants of the Oer-IJ area view the Frisians as part of their heritage, a public friendly book, it was felt, could change this (van Eerden 2005, 17). Besides, the term Frisian is used in academic studies such as Heidinga's *Frisia in the first Millenium* (1997) or Kramer and Taayke's *Friesen, Sachsen & Dänen* (1996), so why did we, as researchers, oppose the use of a Frisian identity in the book and exhibition? Our response that these books deal with a different period and that direct ethnic links are untenable were seen as of little relevance.

We cannot criticize the authors of the book *Het land van Hilde* for basing their narrative on academic and/or public friendly sources that were not of our choosing. Was it not what we tried to achieve, a co-operation between academics and policymakers? Here, a point of self-reflection is important as within academic debate in the Netherlands the use of ethnic names is hardly discussed. On the one hand, it is just seen as tool or shorthand for a specific type of material culture (van den Broeke et al. 2005, 20–1). In this use, it is understood by academics that there is no direct link between ethnic identity and material culture, but it makes the narratives easier to read. On the other hand, Dutch archaeologists usually assume that ethnic names are not something that is of any interest for present-day society. It is not felt that our academic narratives influence public opinion in an essential way, or help shape people's personal identities. The influence of archaeology on the present is seen in an abstract way as an improvement on general living conditions. Duineveld (2006) argues that Dutch archaeology could be viewed as a closed system in which the main reason to communicate with the public seems to be to make people aware of archaeology so they may be more inclined to think that the protection of the archaeological resource is important. In other words, Dutch archaeologists do want people to know about archaeology in the sense that they would be able to appreciate and enjoy their surroundings more. It is, however seldom stated that we think our narratives might change their general ideas about culture, history and identity. The absence of archaeologists from the public debate concerning identity and the national historical canon is telling in this respect. Our lack of critical engagement with present-day public debates makes archaeology a conservative discipline. Although we may see ourselves as "experts" of the past, we may loose our ability to speak within the present.

Extensive discussions in the Oer-IJ project made us conscious of how easily identities are used within Dutch archaeology and the Netherlands in general. Uncritical use of identities can lead to exclusion of minority groups within society. Van Londen (2006) had warned against the uncritical use of ethnic identity in archaeological narratives. This probably led to our strong reaction against the book and the exhibition, as here a strong Frisian identity was posed. That the authors of the book were surprised by our reaction and our eventual withdrawal should not have surprised us. The authors were unaware of the discussions that had taken place. When we tried to convince them of the dangers of the explicit use and propagation of the Frisian identity they were taken aback. First and foremost the authors did not have the intention of excluding anyone and were convinced that their story points to inclusion of everyone, as immigration is seen as integral to the Frisian identity. For example, van Eerden (2005, 19) explicitly takes a stand against the idea of "Blut and Boden" which was used by the Nazis to exclude and eventually destroy groups of people based on ethnic background in combination with a specific territory. The intention of the authors of the book was not to exclude people; however, we could not give, in all consciousness, academic legitimacy to the way concepts of Frisian identity were used. For even if we saw ourselves not as authorities the inclusions of our and the universities names was intended as academic approval of the narrative.

Another point of contention was the language use in the texts we read before publishing. The language had colonial, deterministic and repressive overtones, and although this may not have been the intention of the authors, the wording was often naive about the power of language and this is a problem with many popular texts on archaeology (Shanks and Tilley 1992, 259–65; Bender 1998, 117; Joyce 2002; Smith 2004, 27). Archaeologists are also hardly innocent of naive use of such language, as various authors have pointed out (Wailes and Zoll 1995, 24; Smith 2004,

27). The deterministic language used was partly caused by the defensive overtone within the book. As while an ethnic identity was created, there was a simultaneous attempt to show that no one needed to feel excluded by the books content. Besides, it had to be made clear that the local inhabitants were not only worthy to be called Frisians, but that this identity was important for understanding present-day society. The text, therefore, is sometimes contradictory. For example, within one page the authors do not want to exclude anyone, but promote the Frisian identity at the same time. They go on to state that the direct descendants of the Frisians can be easily found in the villages, whereas the people in the cities have few Frisian descendants (Dekkers et al. 2006, 112). The Dutch word used here for descendant is "afstammeling", which translated means coming from the same tribe. They could also have opted for more neutral words like "nazaat" or "nakomeling", which mean offspring. At the end of this paragraph, all characteristics associated with a Frisian identity, namely trade, water control, and immigration are, however, not part of the genetic makeup of the people but are anchored in the landscape. The change to landscape is maybe less excluding, but the landscape remains deterministic. Furthermore, although it may not have been the intention of the authors, the message given is that the people living in the villages belong more to the Oer-IJ area than the people in the cities. This genetic overtone was also present in the exhibition as one of the signs read:

> The Frisians lived in rough circumstances and spoke a different language than we do. But we also look like them. You can see that by looking at Hilde. *Her skeleton is of a real Frisian*. She is reconstructed in a special way and plays a leading role in the exhibition "treasures beneath your feet" (My translation and emphasis, see also Figure 8.3).

In a recent discussion with Van Eerden (policymaker and co-author of the book), it became clear that he was totally unaware of the overtones in the language used. On a positive note, he recognized the need for further discussions so as to avoid unwanted associations in the future.

Conclusion

Although it was a period of conflict, for me personally, the experience has been an enormous learning curve. Choices have to be made about whether we participate within a specific project or not. Withdrawal from participating in the heritage process all together is an option that I do not wish to advocate. Avoiding conflict may be a comfortable option, but, as

Butler writes, "Contestation must be in play for politics to become democratic" (2004, 39). Just as much as I am an archaeologist, I am a citizen who must engage with society. However, the goal of projects should not be stated in general terms, such as the care for archaeological heritage of a region. Before the start of a project, the motives for participating should be analysed or brought to the fore. This could be done by explicating expectations and the delineation of boundaries of the different participants. This should not mean that as soon as something is not exactly as you want it to be that you stop participating, but points of discussion are to be made clear and a baseline should be established. A similar goal like the preservation of archaeological sites should never mean that all actions are justified.

When new events take place within a project, their goal and the ways of meeting that goal should be discussed. Otherwise, different participants may think they are on the same track and notice too late that others have chosen a new direction. Furthermore, we should be more aware of the possibility that scientific work could be used to legitimize a policy or text that we may not support. I do not believe that scientists are objective in the sense that our work is free of any political or personal value. The choice of the type of things we investigate is never neutral. Questions we should ask are: do we want to align ourselves with the political parties in charge and their programs? Do we want to evaluate critically the stories they tell from an external position? Do we want to continue in a dialogue where we can have conflicting ideas and learn from each other?

Finally, due to the commercialization of archaeology, the money for syntheses are thinly spread. The number of students at universities has increased, as the number of teaching and research jobs have decreased, leaving little room for writing and research (KNAW 2007, xvi). However, if we want to be heard, we need to produce the stories we want to tell. Archaeologists should engage with public debates on identity and heritage from a critical position, and we should engage publicly. We should show the way in which we construct narratives and that multiple narratives are possible and desirable.

Acknowledgements

I would like to thank Elles Besselsen, Silke Lange and Heleen van Londen from the "Heritage and Landscape" research group for their close reading of and comments on the first drafts. I would also like to thank Rob van Eerden of the Province of Noord-Holland for our (still ongoing) discussion of the book and exhibition. All errors are mine alone.

Works Cited

Alders, Gerard. forthcoming. *Landschap en bewoning in het Oer-IJ-estuarium in de Middeleeuwen en Nieuwe Tijd*. PhD diss., University of Amsterdam.

Bazelmans, Jos, Menno Dijkstra and Jan de Koning. 2002. Voorspel. Holland in het eerste millenium. In *Geschiedenis van Holland tot 1572*, ed. Thimo de Nijs and Eelco Beukers, 21–68. Hilversum: Verloren.

Bender, Barbara. 1998. *Stonehenge: Making space*. Oxford: Berg Publishers.

Bloemers, Tom 2001. *Subsidie aanvrage strategisch onderzoek: Stimuleringsprogramma Bodemarchief in Behoud en Ontwikkeling*. (unpublished NWO-project proposal).

Bloemers, Tom and Mies Wijnen ed. 2001. *Bodemarchief in Behoud en Ontwikkeling: de conceptuele grondslagen*. Den Haag: NWO.

de Bruin, Ellen. 2008. Geen Turk, geen Duitser. *NRC Handelsblad*, August 23, 4–5.

Butler, Judith. 2004. *Undoing gender*. New York: Routledge.

Carman, John. 2005. *Against cultural property: Archaeology, heritage and ownership*. London: Duckworth.

Dekkers, Claudia, Gaston Dorren and Rob van Eerden. 2006. *Het land van Hilde: Archeologie in het Noord-Hollandse kustgebied*. Haarlem: Provincie Noord-Holland and Stichting Matrijs.

Duineveld, Martijn. 2006. *Van oude dingen, de mensen, die voorbij gaan: Over de voorwaarden meer recht te kunnen doen aan de door burgers gewaardeerde cultuurhistories*. Delft: Eburon.

Eerden, Rob van 2005. De Noord-Hollandse Friezen mogen er wezen. *Archeobrief* 9(1): 14–20.

Eickhoff, Martijn. 2003. *De oorsprong van het "eigene" Nederlands vroegste verleden, archeologie en nationaal-socalisme*. Amsterdam: Boom.

Elerie, Hans and Willem Foorthuis ed. 2003. *Dorp2000anno: De Hunze maakt geschiedenis*. Bedum: De Ploeg.

Fairclough, Graham, Rodney Harrison, John H. Jameson Jr. and John Schofield. eds. 2008. *The heritage reader*. London: Routledge.

Feddes, Fred. 1999. *The Belvedere Memorandum: A policy document examining the relationship between cultural history and spatial planning*. Nieuwegijn: Ministerie van VROM.

Grever, Maria, Ed Jonker, Kees Ribbens and Siep Stuurman. ed. 2006. *Controverses rond de canon*. Assen: van Gorcum.

Groenewoudt, Bert and Tom Bloemers. 1997. Dealing with significance: Concepts, strategies, and priorities for archaeological heritage management in the Netherlands. In *Archaeological heritage management in the Netherlands: Fifty years state service for archaeological investigations*, ed. Willem Willems, Henk Kars and Daan Hallewas, 119–72. Amersfoort: ROB.

Hidding, Marjan, Jan Kolen and Theo Spek. 2001. De biografie van het landschap: Ontwerp voor een inter- en multidisciplinaire benadering van de landschapsgeschiedenis en het cultuurhistorisch erfgoed. in *Bodemarchief in Behoud en Ontwikkeling: de conceptuele grondslagen*. ed. Bloemers, J.H.F. and M.-H. Wijnen ed., 7–111. Den Haag: NWO.

Joyce, Rosemary. 2002. *The languages of archaeology: Dialogue, narrative, and writing*. Oxford: Blackwell Publishing.

Kok, Marjolijn S.M. 2008. *The homecoming of religious practice: An analysis of offering sites in the wet low-lying parts of the landscape in the Oer-IJ area (2500 B.C. – A.D. 450)*. Rotterdam: uitgeverij lima.

Kolen, Jan and Mathijs Witte. 2006. A Biographical approach to regions, and its value for spatial planning. In *Multiple landscapes: Merging past and present*. ed. Wim van der Knaap and Arnold van der Valk, 125–45. Wageningen.

KNAW(Koninklijke Nederlandse Akedemie van Wetenschappen). 2007. *De toren van Pisa rechtgezet. Over de toekomst van de Nederlandse archaeologie*. Amsterdam.

Lange, Silke, Ellse Besselsen and Heleen van Londen. 2004. *Het Oer-IJ estuarium: Archeologische KennisInventarisatie (AKI)*. Amsterdam: University of Amsterdam-AAC/projectenbureau.

Mattingly, Harold trans. 1948. *Tacitus on Britain and Germany*. West Drayton: Penguin Books.

McDavid, Carol. 2000. Archaeology as cultural critique. Pragmatism and the archaeology of a southern United States plantation. In *Philosophy and archaeological practice: Perspectives for the 21st century*. ed. Cornelius Holtorf and Håkan Karlsson, 221–32. Göteborg: Bricoleur Press.

Palm, Jos. 2008. Het vadeland heeft weer grootheid nodig: het arcadië van het eigen verleden. *De Groene Amsterdammer* 41: 22–7.

Plasschaert, Anne-Marie. ed. 2005. *Beleving en verbeelding door culturele planologie: Twee jaar integratie van kunst en ruimtelijke inrichting in de provincie Noord-Holland*. Haarlem: Provincie Noord-Holland.

Schinkel, Willem. 2008. *De gedroomde samenleving*. Kampen: Klement.

Shanks, Michael and Christopher Tilley. 1992 [1987]. *Re-constructing archaeology: Theory and practice*. London: Routledge.

Skeates, Robin. 2000. *Debating the archaeological heritage*. London: Duckworth Publishers.

Smith, Laurajane. 2004. *Archaeological theory and the politics of cultural heritage*. London: Routledge.

—. 2006. *Uses of heritage*. London: Routledge.

Spek, Theo, Otto Brinkkemper and Barbara Speleers. 2006. Archaeological heritage management and nature conservation. Recent developments and future prospects, illustrated by three Dutch case studies. *Berichten van de Rijksdienst voor het Oudheidkundig Bodemonderzoek* 46: 331–53.

Stam, Marjo ed. 2008. *Op historische gronden: Erfgoed in een context van ruimtelijk ontwerp, planning en democratie*. Utrecht: Onderwijsnetwerk Belvedere.

Therkorn, Linda. 2005. From the Assendelver Polder to Oer-IJ Estuary Project. In *Innovatie in de Nederlandse archeologie: Liber amicorum voor Roel W. Brandt*. ed. Monique van den Dries and Willem Willems, 85–99. Gouda: SIKB.

Tress, Bärbel, Gunther Tress, Gary Fry and Paul Obdam. eds. 2005. *From landscape research to landscape planning: Aspects of integration, education and application*. Dordrecht: Springer.

van Beek, Roy and Luuk J. Keunen. 2006. A cultural biography of the Coversand Landscapes in the Salland and Achterhoek Regions. The aims and methods of the Eastern Netherlands Project. *Berichten van de Rijksdienst voor het Oudheidkundig Bodemonderzoek* 46: 355–375.

van den Broeke, Peter, Harry Fokkens and Annelou van Gijn. 2005. Een prehistorie van deze tijd. In *Nederland in de prehistorie*, ed. Leendert Louwe Kooijmans, Peter van den Broeke, Harry Fokkens and Annelou van Gijn, 17–31. Amsterdam: Uitgeverij Bert Bakker.

van den Dries, Monique and Willem Willems. 2007. Quality assurance in archaeology, the Dutch perspective. In *Quality management in archaeology*, ed. Willem Willems and Monique van den Dries, 50–65. Oxford: Oxbow Books.

van Eerden, Rob. ed. 2004. *Behoud en beheer van archeologische vindplaatsen in het Oer-IJ-gebied*. Haarlem: Provincie Noord-Holland.

van Ginkel, Evert and Anton Cruyshaar. 2003. *Archeologie presenteren: Ervaringen voorbeelden adviezen kosten*. Den Haag: College voor de Archeologische Kwaliteit.

van Heeringen, Robert, Sander Smit and Liesbeth Theunissen. 2003. *Archeologie in de toekomst: Nulmeting van de fysieke kwaliteit van het archeologisch monument in de Broekpolder, gemeenten Heemskerk en Beverwijk.* Rapportage Archeologische Monumentenzorg 107, Amersfoort: RACM.

van Loon, Marjo, Ceciel Nyst and Anneke van Mispelaar. 2006. The role of the cultural heritage in urban development projects. *Berichten van de Rijksdienst voor het Oudheidkundig Bodemonderzoek* 46: 225–42.

van Londen, Heleen. 2006. Cultural Biography and the Power of Image. In *Multiple landscapes: Merging past and present*, ed. Wim van der Knaap and Arnold van der Valk, 171–81. Wageningen: NWO/WUR-Land Use Planning Group/ISOMUL.

van der Valk, Arnold and Tom Bloemers. 2006. Merging past and present in landscape planning: Introduction. In *Multiple landscape: Merging past and present* ed. Wim van der Knaap and Arnold van der Valk, 21–33. Wageningen: NWO/WUR-Land Use Planning Group/ISOMUL.

VROM. 2001. *Ruimte maken, riumte delen. Vijfde Nota over de Ruimtelijke Ordening 2000/2020.* Den Haag: VROM.

Wailes, Bernard and Amy L. Zoll 1995 Civilization, barbarism, and nationalism in European archaeology. In *Nationalism, Politics, and the Practice of Archaeology.* ed. Philip Kohl and Clare Fawcett, 21–38 Cambridge: Cambridge University Press.

Willems, Willem. 1997. Archaeological heritage management in the Netherlands: Past, present and future. In *Archaeological heritage management in the Netherlands: Fifty years state service for archaeological investigations.* ed. Willem Willems, Henk Kars and Daan Hallewas, 3–34. Amersfoort: ROB.

AN INTERVIEW WITH MARGARET BREARLEY AND CAROLE BIRTWHISTLE (SECRETARY AND CHAIR, CAWOOD CASTLE GARTH GROUP)[*]

Could give us some examples of working with archaeologists that have been both unsuccessful and successful?

CB: We've worked with our Local Heritage Initiative Funding and we've got a variety of experts in to help us with the different bits of the projects. We've had students from the University of York. We've had issues trying to get specialists, so for example, Hull University—we were trying to get core sampling and we found it really difficult to make contact with them. Or rather we made contact with them but they wouldn't return our calls. But that has been the exception, really. Most of it has all worked well.

MB: Yes, we've particularly been successful with the York Archaeological Trust. The community archaeologist [archaeologist A] has supported us a lot, with helping us to do field-walking, coming along to our history day and identifying finds. He's been good and we've worked quite a lot with him now. In the early days, our relationships with some archaeology students didn't go quite so well. I'm not really sure what happened, whether they took advantage of us or not, but they tried to charge for their expertize, but actually when they were here they stood and watched while we did all the work. I had to call the university in the end to try to get that sorted out and it was a shame really. That put us off a little bit [...] so next time we thought we would pay for a professional team to come in—West Yorkshire Archaeological Services—but it didn't prove to be that successful, did it?

CB: No, we were able to narrow down the areas that we wanted to look at, rather than do the entire site. But they did take the original geophysics data and incorporate it in the final report, but at the end of it, we didn't get

---

[*] Interviewers: Laurajane Smith and Emma Waterton

much out of that and we paid quite a lot of money for their services.

MB: Well, let's put it this way, the students wouldn't take a risk in saying what they found in the surveys, so that wasn't really helpful to us. I mean, we were absolute beginners, so had no experience of what to look for, and I understand why they wouldn't take the risk, but we thought that by paying a professional organization that they might take more of a risk and say what the features were. But they didn't.

MB: The other practical experiences we've had has been core sampling with [archaeologist B], which was very successful and it was an introduction for us to see some real, practical archaeology. The archaeologist was very enthusiastic. EH came along as well to supervise. I suppose there have been quite a few people who have been really helpful.

MB: One of our main aims was to involve the whole community and that included children too. I was really impressed with our meeting with the archaeologist from the Portable Antiquities Scheme, and [archaeologists C and D] – they were really good with the children when we did molehill surveys/sifting. I'll never forget, I think it was [archaeologist D] standing there, when he asked the children what they thought our site was? He was trying to get them to say it was a rich man's garden, and I'd never thought of it like that and I don't think the children had and he really inspired them to look at the Garth and appreciate the site more. This is an important aspect of what we try to achieve isn't it?

CB: Yes.

MB: We want the children to grow up enjoying and appreciating the Garth because they've got to be the one's to look after it in the future. Importantly it is a community site. The village saved it and paid for it. We all paid extra on our rates so it belongs to everybody. [Archaeologist D] has continued to support us, but funnily enough the last couple of weeks I've been doing some research into the Bishopdyke canal and the historic transporting of stone through Cawood to build York Minster. I found in the York Minster Fabric Rolls a reference to an unloading place, a wharf "at some distance from the river", and I know for sure there is one, and I think I've found where it is—I think it's in the castle garden. There are the remains of staithes in the pond but I'm arguing with [archaeologist D] about it. There is a little bit of "he knows better than me"—, he said he would need to see the Latin. So I shall get him the Latin, but I'm not going to give up, because he's not necessarily right. I've read the translation of this particular example.

Is he willing to debate with you?

MB: Yes, he is. And he wants me to prove it to him. I'd love to prove it. The other interesting thing that's happened recently is we did three test pits last July and found many pieces of brick and pottery. In December, I went to the Yorkshire Museum on a course on identifying Bricks and Tiles and the tutor identified one of our finds as a Roman roof tile. Now, we believe that the finds in this particular pit are the cleaning out of our large moat, called the New Cut. What if that is Roman? This could potentially be very exciting but no one will commit to saying it could date the moat from a much earlier period than we had originally thought.

How important has archaeology (or archaeologists) been to realizing the aims of your community project?

MB: Well, we couldn't do it without archaeologists. We need to access those with more expertise and training than we have in this field as we are just learning about archaeology. The archaeology of the site is very important to our aims. It is the main reason we formed the group. The Garth is full of earthworks, moats and other features, which the community would like to find out about. We have not been allowed to investigate the site before due to it being a Schedule Ancient Monument, but we all want to explore its history and find out what happened in the past.

CB: What is holding us back is the interpretation boards. We are unwilling to commit things to paper because there is still more things that we want to investigate, so there is a sense of frustration that if we do go to press with what we've got now and then we get more stuff from our finds day in July and the last three of the test pits then we'll have missed the opportunity to say what we've found in the last bit of the project.

MB: I think the other thing is getting people to commit to dates of objects. In one of our test pits we found Roman pottery. The archaeologist said not to tell me because I'll get too excited and it was too small to say for certain, but *Time Team* can fill a whole program on one tiny bit of pottery and say, "This site is Roman". The archaeology is there and the village doesn't know about it yet. We don't know anything about it, really, as there has been very little done. There has been no actual practical digging on the Garth except for the moles. One of our group actually found a George III silver shilling in one of the molehills last year. Getting the finds properly identified is a problem, even with [Archaeologist A]. He's taken it all to his office and I think it's just there in the corner of his office still. It is very slow to get any data about the site.

How did you find communicating with archaeologists?

MB: I thought it had gone quite well at first. We met with some archaeology students and discussed ground rules from both sides—what they would do and what we expected—and I seem to remember making it really clear that we had no money. We hadn't actually got our grant at that point, but what we could do for the students was provide them with food and drink, a proper lunch everyday, and we took that in turns and we were happy to do that. And then it turned sour. They started asking for travelling expenses, yet I was sure I'd made it clear there was no finance at this time available. We fulfilled our part, but it felt like they took advantage of us. I thought we'd communicated clearly. On reflection, I think we should have put it on paper. We should have set out both sides and our expectations, and I think that was our big mistake. We got friendly and people take advantage of that. They showed us what to do, and it was a good experience, but...

You've talked about communicating with archaeologists on technical issues, what about in terms of communicating with them about the actual archaeology, the knowledge and the things that interest you about the Garth and so on?

CB: We did a lot of that in the beginning, when we were putting the grant together. It was difficult to know what we could do on the Garth at first. We had to ask for permission from English Heritage to do anything on the site. Not being archaeologists ourselves we did not know which methods of investigation we should use to determine the use of the features on the site or to find what was hidden below the grass. Eventually we worked out the right questions to ask and then we were guided to the right method of investigation.

MB: Now if we invite [Archaeologist E] to one of our meetings, we'll ask what we should do next and he'll always turn it around and want the community to come up with the questions. Now, I think I understand why that is, but I think initially we didn't understand what he was doing. And we really wanted to be lead a bit by the hand.

CB: I think [archaeologist E] has always directed us to do our own thing.

MB: He has always got us to think for ourselves even if we didn't want to!

CB: Yes, he's always advised us to put things in writing and get it agreed by the group: the conservation statement and the management plan, for example.

MB: They were actually really hard to do, very difficult for us at first. Because we had no idea what we were doing. Even to the point that if we ask [archaeologist A] "where shall we put the next pit", he'll say, "Well, I think [archaeologist E] will want you to come up with that answer". But we don't know! We did come up with something in the end. We had to submit questions for Scheduled Monument Consent. Archaeologist E doesn't want to dictate to us and tell us to do this, this and this. I think he wants us to say "We want to do this, this and this", but even if we say that, we don't always know how to achieve it and we don't know where to go to achieve it. I do understand what he is trying to do—he wants us it to be a community led group.

CB: I can think of one example, where [archaeologist D] raised the issue of the staithes in the river and said that we should get them dated. As a group we got quotes for doing that, but then we found out that the testing involved would decimate the staithes. At least one fifth of the archaeology would disappear, and as a group we decided we didn't want to be responsible for the destruction of that. And actually, I think if we did go ahead and do that, and a man came in with a chainsaw, I don't think the village would like it. They would want to know the date of it, but not like that. That is one of the things we have found, that archaeology destroys by doing it. So that was a step too far for us. We've learnt that. Test pits don't cause the same amount of concern.

MB: I don't know that we will find what we want from test pits. We would like more definite answers. We would like the rest of the country to appreciate the site—we are told it is of national importance and it is one of perhaps only four remaining medieval gardens in the country. We haven't really investigated this part of the site yet. I would like to raise the profile of the site but by doing that you end up destroying some of the archaeology.

How would you define heritage?

CB: I think it is natural and people-made heritage, but we've also been looking at the more verbal heritage, like oral histories. There are different bits of heritage.

MB: I think it is about where you've come from, where we are today, defined by where we've been before. It's also what's physically left; I think, as in earthworks, castles, interesting buildings, parklands, archives and important events from the past perhaps too?

CB: It is people's stories.

MB: Heritage is very hard to define really.

How would you define the heritage of Cawood?

MB: Very long and very interesting. Some amazing things have happened here: there have been battles, Kings and Queens visiting, Vikings and Archbishops lived here. Let's take the Vikings for instance. My house is right next to the river and when the Vikings came they moored their boats out there. I rather like that. There were so many Viking long ships in 1066 that they occupied 3 miles of the river. I'm not saying my house was here then, but something might have been, and I like that; It is the heritage of my house. There is no reference to Cawood in the Doomsday book and I have a theory—it was written just after the Vikings came and I reckon if 300 Viking ships came into your village one day, you wouldn't hang around! You'd be off! Hence no one here to put in the Domesday Book! It's just a silly theory, but that is something that I would consider heritage, even though it is all hearsay—there is nothing on the ground to see though.

CB: The Cawood sword.

MB: The Cawood Sword is heritage too, but it is heritage we didn't know about. When it was rediscovered recently the Yorkshire Museum asked us

166

if we would like to see it. I don't think I've ever known a museum ring someone up and ask if you want to come and look at an artefact. Not only that, but they invited our group to a private visit. We get to go and get involved in that, which is really nice. And then, later we had the history day coming up and I asked [museum curator] about bringing the sword to that. He was so enthusiastic and so helpful and obliging, and I think we picked up his enthusiasm, because he wanted the village to experience this wonderful artefact. And I notice that they are now using it in their advertising material that hangs outside the museum. It was a really wonderful experience for us all. The written history of Cawood goes back to at least 963. So many things have happened here that we are proud of and we like that fact that they happened here and it makes us different from the other villages which makes it feel a special place.

Are archaeology and heritage the same?

MB: I think it is part of it, but not the total whole.

CB: I think the people's side of heritage brings things more alive. Certainly seeing people touching the sword was important.

MB: It was amazing, wasn't it?

CB: People were genuinely connecting with an inanimate object.

MB: They were queuing out the door, weren't they?

CB: Yes.

MB: I've never seen so many people at a History day before. It was just incredible. I think people are also part of heritage as well, and if you were to think of your own heritage through your family line, you may be only agricultural labourers, but every body wants to have somebody famous, and I guess they are heritage, aren't they, the people who have lived before. I do a lot of family history and I go to places not so far from here, we drive through them, and I always think about my great grand parents and they have no idea who I am, but I know that they were farming this land and they were living in this part. I went in to the public house were my great grandmother was born and it was a very strange feeling to sit in the building where she was born. So I guess that is your heritage as well. It connects you in some way, but for Cawood it is something we should shout from the rooftops about, I think. We have so much, and it is not just the archaeology in the ground. It is the documents, the lives, the stories of the people who were here before.

CB: And there is a lot of interest here, we did a survey to find out who was interested and we found that there were about 20 people within the village who were looking at different aspects of heritage. As we have collected more and more stuff, in terms of putting it out to the community, we're probably going to try and put on exhibitions. We haven't done that outside of the village yet. There is a move to have a new community centre and maybe we can try to put a permanent display or at least have some storage space there.

Who do you think is important to manage heritage? Who should be looking after this?

MB: I think some of it should be the community. But you've got to be realistic. There is no way that we could keep the Cawood Sword because it is too valuable. But, from that point of view there is no way that we could have that, but I did read your bit about Castleford (Smith and Waterton 2009: 95–101, 110–112) not having their heritage and I do think that there are some things that should stay local. Generally, everyday though, it needs to be somewhere, doesn't it? I use the information we have collected and give it freely, but actual photographs, finds, most of it is in my greenhouse, but what do you do with it? The Yorkshire Museum wouldn't want them, anyway, but then we would lose access to them. Yes, I think ideally it would be best to keep it in the community, but that is an expensive thing to do. We have this wonderful Banqueting Hall in the village that would make a fantastic museum, but would the Landmark Trust let us have it? No they won't.

Can you summarize what you think the importance of community projects like this one is?

CB: For me it is giving people a sense of place, of their place in history and what's happened.

MB: It is a very hard question to answer. We initially started just to get some funding to investigate the Garth, and I don't think we knew in the early days what we were taking on and how difficult it would be to do these things. I guess the other side of it is that we have grown as people through the skills that we have learnt. The interest and enthusiasm that we have shown, is slowly getting the village more and more involved and I hadn't expected that when we first started. It takes a very long time to do anything! It is so time consuming to get things right! The project has been important to the community because it has involved so many different people from the village in the various activities that we have held. We have investigated and recorded the wildlife on the Garth, molehill sifting for finds, done oral history recording, practical archaeology in the test pits, developed a wild flower area, built a bridge and footpath to help the disabled and many more activities for everyone to take part in. Hopefully, the project has brought people together, involved them in community life and given them a more of a sense of place as well as having a good time!

Further Reading

Smith, Laurajane and Waterton, Emma. 2009. *Heritage, communities and archaeology*. London: Gerald Duckworth.

Waterton, Emma. 2007. An institutionalized construction of the past in the UK' in *Which past, whose future? Treatments of the past at the start of the 21st century*, ed. Sven Grabow, Daniel Hull and Emma Waterton, 31–40. Oxford: Archaeopress.

—. 2008. Invisible identities: Destroying the heritage of Cawood Castle' in *An archaeology of destruction*, ed. Lila Rakoczy, 107–127. Newcastle-upon-Tyne: Cambridge Scholars Press.

PART III:

ARCHAEOLOGY AS HERITAGE?

Chapter Nine

Devil's Advocate or Alternate Reality: Keeping Archaeology in Heritage

Martin Newman

Introduction

> Cnut [Canute] put to sea with his fleet, and the unhappy people were thus left in the lurch by him: he sailed southward until he came to Sandwich, and there put ashore the hostages which had been given to his father, and cut off their hands and their noses.... In this year, on St. Michael's eve [28 September], the swolen incomming timde swept far and wide through many places in this land; and it ran further inland than it had ever done before, submerged many homesteads and drowned a countless number of human beings (*Anglo-Saxon Chronicle*, 1014 A.D., Garmonsway 1972, 145).

Why take archaeology out of heritage? What is heritage without archaeology, or the historic environment without archaeological knowledge? Does archaeology really dominate in the way that Smith and Waterton (this volume) suggest, and, equally, are archaeologists as proprietorial as is implied? True, archaeologists have their "databases", but those who curate them see themselves in a very different light to that suggested by Waterton and Smith; working to share information, encourage access, to be inclusive and engage with a range of publics. Is this another example of the great theoretical and practical divide? Is archaeology really institutionalized by its associations with government authority? Perhaps some definitions of heritage management, focused on the mitigation of conflict between preservation and development, are too limited. Curatorial archaeologists are often wide-ranging heritage managers dealing with differing expectations of the past from differing groups in an environment of post-modernist, cultural relativism. Could removing archaeology from this wider view of heritage create a vacuum, and be to the detriment of the discipline? This chapter aims to address some of these issues from the point of view of a heritage practitioner involved in data curation, so as to show curators in a more reflexive and public-focused light than their development control remit suggests. It is illustrated with examples drawn from the English National Monuments Record (henceforth NMR), and local Historic Environment Records (henceforth HERs). The NMR is the public archive of English Heritage which, as well as curating physical archive items such as photographs, is responsible for maintaining the national inventory of the historic environment previously maintained by the former Royal Commission on the Historical Monuments of England (RCHME). Local HERs, maintained by local authorities, were originally set up as a planning tool. However, they now fulfil a far wider remit. From this perspective, taking archaeology out of heritage is viewed very differently as it is the curatorial side of the discipline that has worked so hard to get it included. Take archaeology out of heritage, why would we want to?

Telling someone you were an archaeologist used to be the norm. Now, however, it is commonplace for someone who would have described themselves as such to say they are a "Heritage Manager" or an "Historic Environment Professional". It is interesting to note that in *Profiling the Profession* (Aitchison and Edwards 2003, 105), a range of job titles appeared using terms such as "Heritage Management" and "Historic Environment" that had not appeared in the same survey four years earlier (Aitchison 1999, 108). Additionally, the four grouping terms in the later report ("field investigation and research services", "historic environment advice and information services", "museum and visitor/user services" and "educational and academic research services") do not specifically mention archaeology. The most recent report on archaeological employment shows a continuation of this trend with an even wider range of job titles using the terms "Heritage" and "Historic Environment" rather than "Archaeologist" (Aitchison and Edwards 2008, 212–3). Is this just semantics and management speak, or does it represent something more fundamental about the changing nature of the profession? Could it be that the roles and titles have changed to reflect the position of archaeology within something wider called "heritage"? The topic for this volume, *Taking Archaeology out of Heritage*, and the job titles mentioned above, would suggest that this is a position taken up, to some degree at least, within the heritage sector. Matthews (2004, 5) comments that "the identity of being an archaeologist has changed from an isolated researcher to a more engaged citizen of what may be termed the research polity". However, this itself may be too limited an interpretation considering the work archaeologists currently undertake and the scope of archaeology as a whole.

This chapter does not set out to answer the question posed in its title "Devil's Advocate or Alternate Reality?". That is left for the reader to consider. What it does aim to do, however, is set out the case for keeping archaeology in heritage by suggesting that this is of mutual benefit to archaeology, and the wider heritage sector. It will also raise a few points to consider concerning the implications and ramifications for archaeology of taking it out of heritage, considering the potential impact on the perception and funding of archaeology as well how this would relate to the growing momentum of integration across the historic environment sector.

When the original *Taking Archaeology Out of Heritage* session at the Theoretical Archaeology Group (TAG) conference (held at the University of York, 2007) was proposed, it proved quite provocative to those engaged in the curatorial side of the discipline and was the subject of informal discussions at meetings involving members of the Association of Local Government Archaeological Officers (ALGAO). In true post-modern tradition, there is more than one viewpoint from which to look at the arguments. It would seem unlikely that many of those working in the curatorial archaeological sector would see themselves as operating in the propriatorial way implied, both in the original TAG session abstract and the introduction to this volume, given the efforts currently being carried out by this sector in outreach. Many curators are using their unique position to reach out and engage with a diverse range of publics, tackle issues concerned with social inclusion and utilize the new methods of dissemination made available by developments in information technology. Equally, it can be argued that curators are not as far removed from archaeological theory as might be imagined and are contributing to an holistic, democratized and inclusive vision of archaeology, heritage and the historic environment.

Does archaeology risk losing its nose like the hostages of 1014 only by its own hand to spite its face, or equally would taking archaeology out of heritage be like the Canute of legend, standing in the way of an unstoppable tide? Only in this case, a tide of integration across the sector rather than the literal waves of fable.

Definitions and Perceptions

To argue the benefits of the archaeological sector's conflation with heritage it is necessary to first consider the nature of both heritage and archaeology, and consider that heritage itself could be a meaningless concept without archaeology and that archaeology itself needs the heritage label. It is also important to put things into the wider political context and consider the changing environment in which the archaeological discipline finds itself operating.

If taking archaeology out of heritage is to be considered, then as a prerequisite to making an objective decision it is important to start by defining what is meant by these terms, and not just what professionals and academics mean by them, but what those outside the discipline understand them to mean. Only then will it be possible to decide whether this is desirable or even achievable. The Oxford English Dictionary defines heritage as "that which has been or may be inherited" or "that which comes form the circumstances of birth" (Simpson and Weiner 1991, 760). This is potentially very wide ranging. More useful here, perhaps, is the definition of cultural heritage contained in Article 1 of UNESCO's World Heritage Convention. The list this provides consists entirely of components that would be classed as part of the Historic Environment (UNESCO 1972). Though this does not quite sum up its totality, the former Vice President of ICOMOS has suggested that:

> ... the definition of built heritage may have to be expanded to include mountains, caverns and other repositories of these [rock art] galleries of art which are expressions of multiple viewpoints. Indeed these sites are more than geomorphological expressions but are the domicile of the living, the dead and the supernatural (Munjeri 2003).

Although discussing intangible heritage in Africa, these suggestions have wider application for the interpretation of landscapes by archaeologists, something that this chapter will return to later.

Moving on from defining heritage to archaeology, the Collins Dictionary of Archaeology defines archaeology as "the study of the past through the systematic recording and analysis of material culture" (Bahn 1992). However, what constitutes material culture is itself open to interpretation (as will be demonstrated later in this chapter through the example of landscape characterization and archaeology) and it should be remembered that the intangible elements of cultural heritage are reflected in its material culture and the surrounding landscape that a culture interacts with. Consequently, if delegates to a conference such as TAG were to be asked what was meant by "archaeology" there could be a wide range of answers encompassing many areas, simply reading the programme and abstracts demonstrates this. With sessions covering areas ranging from "Animal Bones" to "Landscape and Memory", TAG demonstrates what a "broad church" the archaeological sector is. However, if someone on the proverbial "Clapham Omnibus" was to be asked the same question, what would the answer then be?

Work by Cornelius Holtorf (2007, 52–4) has shown that television is the main way people get their information about archaeology. If you are lucky, you will get an answer relating to the activities of *Time Team*. If you are not, you might get something closer to Indiana Jones or Lara Croft, or the latest fictionalized portrayal of archaeology, *Bonekickers*. This latest dramatization features a team from a university in the south west of England who are involved in a series of increasingly improbable investigations, starting with the finding of a piece of "the true cross". This raises concerns for the image of the discipline, and was the subject of discussion before it was aired (Bailey 2008, 38–9) as well as much criticism afterwards, summarized in *British Archaeology* (Council for British Archaeology 2008, 27). Such fictional depictions could further distort public perceptions of archaeology (and archaeologists), although the archaeological advisor to *Bonekickers* believes it had the opportunity to "excite viewers about history and archaeology" (Horton 2008, 7). Neither can the documentary genre on television be guaranteed to provide a balanced view of archaeology, from the views of pseudo-archaeologists to serious documentaries that target the more sensational aspects of the past. Although, as has been observed, this can work well with the "conversion of the sensational into the banal" (Taylor 2007, 187–200), this is still selective of the portion of the past to be publicized.

Four separate surveys have shown that people mainly associate archaeology with digging and excavation (Holtorf 2007, 56). Whatever the range of answers received from the general public about the nature of archaeology, they would certainly be nothing like the areas covered in the archaeological literature and actual research. Indeed, much of what archaeologists actually do and engage with would be unfamiliar to the lay person and not recognized as being relevant to popular definitions of archaeology. Supposing, instead, you were to pose a different question and ask: "What does heritage mean?". You may well get a very different, and far wider ranging, set of responses than the narrow responses associated with archaeology. Answers covering areas as diverse as buildings, local history, music, family history, folklore, the recent past, and so forth, could all be expected. If you look at the answers to questions "When you think of 'heritage' and the 'historic environment' what sort of things do you think they refer to?" in the *Attitudes to the Heritage* survey conducted by Mori (2000, 13), that range comes over very strongly. Overall, this survey indicated that 98 per cent of those who participated thought that "heritage is important to teach us about our past" (Mori 2000, 4). The Mori survey also asked what the public associate with "heritage" and the "historic environment", and, unprompted, archaeology was mentioned in a mere eight per cent and 11 per cent of the responses respectively. In Smith's Country House Visitors Survey, when asked about the meaning of heritage, archaeology did not feature at all (2006, 132). So, the notion of heritage is unique to every individual and comes "from the bottom up" as well as "the top down".

Archaeology is not universally regarded as part of heritage by the general public because it is associated with digging things up, which is only part of the discipline. However, it could be argued that all the areas that the public considers as coming under the heading of heritage are all subjects that could be seen as being within the remit of archaeologists working in the discipline. Buildings archaeology, for example, is a growth area within archaeology, yet standing buildings are not recognized by the general public as being within the remit of archaeologists. Research suggests that it is the archaeological staff in local authorities who are giving most of the advice in the planning process rather than conservation officers, especially with regard to non-listed industrial structures (Gould 2004, 25 and 2005, 12). Another example of the expanding remit of archaeology is Schofield's research on popular music (2000, 131–55). Similarly, at the NMR a recent desk-based recording project was undertaken on 1960s music venues (Page 2007, 36–7). A further example was the excavation of a Ford Transit van, which included as one of the deliverables a film, hardly what is usually thought of as archaeological publication (Newland et al. 2007, 16–21). These examples beg the question when does archaeology start anyway?

The NMR, along with three quarters of the local HERs, do not have a cut off date for the antiquity of the monuments they record (Newman 2002, 10–11): taking a "history starts yesterday" approach where even the most recent physical remains of our past can be regarded as worthy of recording and as of historic value. In fact, it can be argued that as the built environment continues to develop and new items of material culture are created, so the past becomes a renewable rather than a finite resource (Schofield 2006, 11). Similarly, if you consider the range of what the NMR and the HERs regard as within their remit and, therefore, what they actually record, it can be seen that, as with cut off dates, the type of monument recorded goes far beyond what has traditionally been considered archaeology. For example, over 90 per cent of HERs include built heritage as within their remit, and half include sites implied by place name evidence. The change in figures from 2002–2004 (Figure 9.1) shows how this wider remit is spreading amongst the records maintained by local authorities (Newman 2002, 10). This can be seen as part of a longer trend when compared to Baker's earlier assessment of the content local Sites and Monuments Records (SMRs, the previous name for HERs) (1999, 20). This, together with case studies such as those given at an Institute for Archaeologists (IfA) conference session on HERs in 2005 (Newman 2005, 15) and included in the HER guidelines (Gilman and Newman 2007), demonstrates why the change in name from SMR to HER is more than just semantics, as opposed to the suggestion that they are still mainly archaeological (Whitehouse 2008, 39–41). This demonstrates how the remit of archaeology has changed and is continuing to expand and is at odds with more widely held perceptions of what archaeology is and archaeological records are.

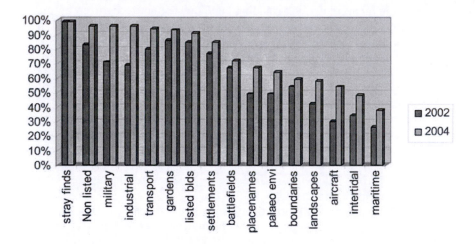

Figure 9.1: Areas that HERs regard as being within their remit in 2002 and 2004. This is based on the 2002 Content and Computing Survey and data collected by the author during the HER Trends Survey 2004 as part of research for *Heritage Counts*

Neither is this wider remit of archaeology just a very recent phenomenon. For instance, Colin Renfrew includes linguistics (not something traditionally associated with archaeology) in his research on the archaeology of language (Renfrew 1987). The same will be true for every new technique or area of study within archaeology, as each will have pushed the boundary of what archaeology was considered to be about. Industrial archaeology, for example, shows how the discipline has evolved. One of the latest developments to challenge our perceptions of ways of looking at archaeological sites and to impact on HERs is the development of historic landscape recording and characterization projects. Historic Landscape Characterization is an English Heritage research and recording programme carried out by HERs, they follow a "GIS-based archaeological method for defining the historic and archaeological dimensions of the present day landscape" (Fairclough et al. 2002, 69). These are changing the nature of HERs by treating the landscape as an historical artefact in its own right, effectively an item of material culture shaped by human activity. This breaks away from the traditional concept of monuments seen in isolation from each other as unconnected points. This poses challenges for the creation of an integrated and interoperable geographical data set placing monuments within wider temporal landscapes. This change in approach is (alongside the broadening remit mentioned earlier) fundamental to the SMR to HER transition (Dyson-Bruce 2004, 3–7). The inclusion of multimedia recording elements, which lends itself to internet dissemination and engagement with lay audiences, further changes the nature of these records of the historic environment. The SeaScapes projects which are characterizing the marine historic environment are a good example of this (Tapper 2008). Additionally, there is the potential for the use of virtual reality, particularly in relation to the interpretation and dissemination of information (Haig 2003, 5–6).

This all underlines the argument that virtually whatever you think of as heritage can be interpreted through archaeology, and therefore falls within the scope of archaeologists. The first conclusion reached in this chapter, therefore, is that the remit of archaeology is very broad but its public perception is poor when compared to that of heritage.

Relationships

There are two ways of representing the archaeology to heritage relationship. Both can be modelled using an application of set theory as weighted Venn diagrams where the sets are symbolic representations of the concepts being considered. As Clarke observed when considering the relationship of set theory to archaeology "we are consciously or unconsciously working within the field of Set and Group theory" (1968, 55). It would therefore seem appropriate to use it to provide schematic representations of the interpretations to be discussed here as a visual aid to their comparison. First, it is necessary to use the arguments already put forward about the scope of the archaeological remit to justify the statement "archaeology encompasses the study of the totality of the historic environment" rather than just thinking of material culture as objects. To enable this the historic environment should be seen to encompass all that remains of any period of the past from the earliest hominids to the most recent, including the landscape they help to shape. Archaeology can then be viewed as the method by which these remains of the past are studied. Once accepted, then the relationship to heritage can be considered. If the definition of a set as applied by Orton (citing Stoll 1961, 2) so that it constitutes "any collection of definite, distinguishable objects of our intuition or of our intellect to be conceived as a whole" and "what defines a set is its members" (Orton 1980, 221) is accepted, then this can be used to represent the relationship between archaeology/the historic environment and heritage.

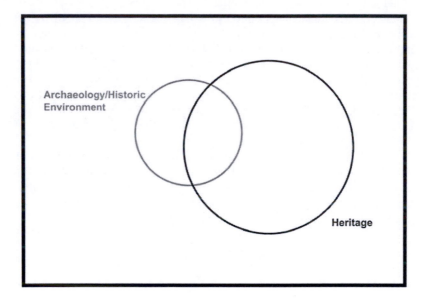

Figure 9.2: Venn diagram model representing archaeology and the historic environment as a minor component of heritage

The first model (Figure 9.2) represents an impression of the archaeology/historic environment relationship implied by Waterton and Smith (this volume). In this model, the union between archaeology/historic environment and heritage is relatively small, enabling archaeology to be removed intact from heritage, leaving the heritage sector largely unaltered.

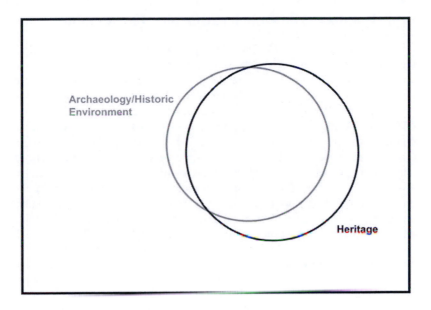

Figure 9.3: Venn diagram model representing archaeology and the historic environment as a major component of heritage

The second interpretation (Figure 9.3) represents the relationship envisaged here. In this interpretation the archaeology/historic environment set is larger than in the first interpretation. Consequently, the union where heritage could also be regarded as historic environment and studied through archaeology, is larger to the point where the area of the heritage set that does not form a union with archaeology and the historic environment is very small. Similarly, there is little which archaeology does that does not comprise part of the heritage set. It could even be argued that this, itself, is too limited an interpretation and archaeology/ the historic environment is itself a sub-set of heritage. This application of Occam's Razor will be perfectly logical to some, where as others may regard this as an example of hyperbolism. The nature of the overlap is open to debate, but it is the principle that archaeology and the historic environment largely cover the same areas as heritage that is important. This leads to the second conclusion that you can not take archaeology out of heritage simply because they are largely one and the same. Archaeology is the study of the historic environment, and the concept of heritage is an empty one without the components of the historic environment and the contribution made to it by archaeology.

Databases, Post-modernism and Dissemination

As the *Attitudes to the Heritage Survey* (Mori 2000, 4) has demonstrated, the general public value heritage. However, archaeology comes way down the list compared with other areas of heritage that archaeologists would see as being within the remit of their discipline, but these areas are not recognized as archaeology by the general public. Taking archaeology outside of heritage would be cutting the discipline off from the wider public who ultimately finance archaeology, whether directly through taxation as in the case of local authorities, university study and the work of national bodies such as English Heritage, or indirectly through passed on cost incurred as a result of developer funding. Therefore, this approach can be applied to the curatorial situation. If the statement that "archaeologists have been very successful in protecting what they perceive to be their database" and the question "is archaeological data actually heritage?" (volume introduction, p. 1) are taken, they then need to be assessed as to how curators might view them. Firstly, curators would not see themselves in such a proprietorial light. If a literal view is taken of what is meant by an archaeological database rather than a discussion of the totality of the archaeological resource available, then this can be assed in terms of the work undertaken by the HERs and the NMR in England. Those who curate these resources are very keen to engage with the public, make their data fully available, including both online and offline interactions through outreach projects that address cultural, socioeconomic and intellectual barriers to access and understanding. There are now some excellent case studies published demonstrating what can be achieved such as *Unlocking Somerset's Past* project (Bagwell 2007, F.24–F.31), which as well as online dissemination included promotional material, a roadshow, lectures, events and work with local schools.

What is particularly impressive is the way HERs, in particular, are utilizing the opportunities presented by electronic dissemination to break down intellectual barriers to accessing archaeological data (Newman 2007, 67–74). The way hyperlinks have been utilized to link records, glossaries and essays facilitates non-linear reading and engages with the way people now surf for their information. This has potential implications for understanding, including the potential breaking of the hermeneutic circle, where understanding of a text as a whole can only be achieved through its constituent parts and understanding of the individual parts is by reference to the whole. However, these are wider issues rather than just for archaeology. Some record curators are starting to embrace Web 2.0 concepts, giving users the opportunity to comment, record their reminiscences and personal stories of the monuments recorded, thus increasing engagement and ownership and enabling multivocality. Further, the combination of structured indexing to facilitate retrieval and free text linked to sources enables these records to combine objective and subjective elements, presenting differing interpretations that allow users to weigh up suggestions and evidence rather than presenting authoritative fact. This potentially makes these a truly post-modern record, which, together with the outreach and feedback mentioned earlier, challenges the concept of the Authorized Heritage Discourse (AHD) as set out by Smith (2006, 29–34), where professionals hand down to the public their interpretation of the past as solid facts promulgating the official storyline.

Taking an approach that stems from concepts of post-modernity and looking at the user bases of these records suggests a wide range of publics with differing interests in and interpretations of the past, all of whom need to be served by the same curators with the same information. Data from the English NMR's National Inventory is available via the PastScape[1] website managed by English Heritage. Similarly, the Royal Commission on the Ancient and Historical Monuments of Scotland (RCAHMS) and the Royal Commission on the Ancient and Historical Monuments Wales (RCAHMW) have also made their records available online via *Canmore*, *PASTMAP*[2] and *Coflein*[3]. Many such outreach projects, for example Durham and Northumberland *Keys to the Past*[4], have been supported by the Heritage Lottery Fund, which required market research to show local demand for the information and elements of the project designed to tackle social inclusion (Heritage Lottery Fund 1999; English Heritage and ALGAO 2005). The *Unlocking Somerset's Past*[5] and *Keys to the Past*[6] projects are good examples of this.

This data from HERs is now being drawn together for the first time with that of the NMR via the *Heritage Gateway*[7] website, which is a collaboration between, English Heritage, ALGAO: England and the Institute of Historic Building Conservation (IHBC). This promotes interoperability between national and local records, including cross searching and disseminating information to a range of audiences (Cload and Clubb 2008, 23–4 and Cload 2008, 42–43). These (especially the Web 2.0 initiatives) are hardly the activities of archaeologists who are protective of their databases. In fact, quite the opposite, it is the democratization of heritage. This represents a major development from when Smith (1994, 301) observed that "little progress has been made towards entering into a so called "politically democratized discourse with non-archaeological interests". Things have changed so much that they have led the Director of the *Institute of Ideas* to note that "people who know about heritage are so defensive about their role that they give over decision-making about what matters to those who don't" (Fox 2004, 9). This is being defensive over concerns that heritage professional might be seen to be handing down a list of what constitutes heritage to the public. The elements of the historic environment profession leading these innovations in the democratization of the past are those with an archaeological background, members of ALGAO and those working on a national level in government agencies including the three NMRs.

Curators find themselves in an interesting and possibly unique position in heritage where they form a bridge to fulfil both the "legislator" and "interpreter" roles as discussed by Smith (1993, 62–3). But do they really have authority, as some suggest, through their association with the state? Most would wish they had. Could this partly be an issue of perception amongst elements of the publics with which they deal? In reality, curators also explain and interpret the historic environment and its importance to those in the decision making positions, as authority does not deal well with uncertainty, ambiguity and differing hypotheses. However, they do not make the eventual decision despite how their role in the decision making process might be perceived. This issue of perception is something that the outreach and engagement sides of the curator's role is helping to address.

Models that show heritage as a feature of authority or government control through the handing down of approved authoritative interpretations of the past to the public may apply well to some situations. The notion of the AHD may have particular relevance in post-colonial areas where those working in heritage are primarily from the ethnic group of the former colonial power. There are well documented accounts of conflicts that have arisen from differing views of the past (see Smith 2004). Such models, however, do not fit so well into twenty-first century Britain, where those individuals that such interpretations would suggest are in authority in reality have little power and are engaging with the public.

Further, as has been argued elsewhere (Newman forthcoming), the workings of HERs can be described in a reflexive way critically analyzing biases in data, recording priorities and choices. Hodder's recursive model for excavation and on site recording where each area dug improves the planning of the investigation of the next area (1998, 98–102) can be adapted to explain the way HERs operate (Figure 9.4). So using this approach to explain information flows for recording within HERs, data from fieldwork enhances the HER and allows better judgments to be made when new planning applications arrive, leading to further fieldwork enhancing the HER. There are other loops which can be applied to this model, one of which is the dissemination loop where feedback from users enhances the HER. Further the cyclical process of HER Audits (Newman 2001) could themselves be seen as another reflexive loop.

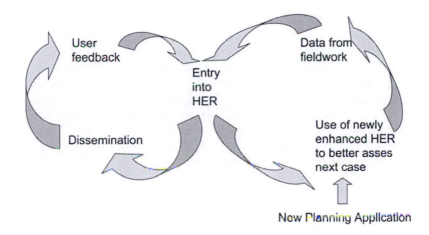

User feedback

Data from fieldwork

Entry into HER

Dissemination

Use of newly enhanced HER to better asses next case

New Planning Application

Figure 9.4: Recursive information flows within HERs demonstrating a reflexive model (Source: Hodder 1998, 102)

So, in fact it is curators who are pushing forward the theorizing of data through developments such as the CIDOC Conceptual Reference Model, which provide a formal structure for describing concepts and relationships in cultural heritage documentation as part of an extensible semantic framework (International Council of Museums (ICOM) 2008 and Crofts et al. 2005). If curators are moving forward in this way, democratizing archaeology, developing a holistic past with the potential to develop theoretical understanding, where is this more negative view of heritage, the historic environment and curatorial practice coming from? Perhaps this is an issue of the traditional divide between academia and practice? It might also be that the kind of data classification through indexing inherent in HER management and subsequent interrogation conjures up images of the more processualist approach of the *New Archaeology*. Certainly the structured organization of information, the inclusion of scientific data (de Moulins 2004, 8–11) and the analytical use archaeological data facilitated by storage in information retrieval systems does inevitably lead to databases such as HERs appearing to lean more to the science side of the discipline rather than the arts, which is more associated with theory, and cultural and political debate. In

general, theory has traditionally been less involved with subjects such as
archaeological science and curatorial practice than other areas, although
some examinations of these in theoretical terms have appeared, for
instance in the work of Jones (2002) and Smith (1993, 2004). Jones
demonstrates how the scientific study of material culture enables wider
interpretation of the thought process that creates the biography of an
artefact and how the archaeological process itself can be analysed. This
has the opportunity to benefit both the theoretical and practical sides of
the discipline. As Smith observes, "if we accept that practice and theory
inform each other then the practices of CRM [Cultural Resource
Management] cannot be dismissed as insignificant" (2004, 2). A modern
heritage database has much to offer a post-procesualist reflexive and
recursive approach. By engaging the general public, offering differing
hypotheses and providing data to enable individuals to draw their own
conclusions, curators in England are proving they have nothing to hide
and are democratizing the past, rather than handing down an approved
official version as Smith's (2006) proposition of the existence of the
AHD would suggest. Further, the explanation of curator's roles as part of
this outreach makes it less likely that they will be seen as an instrument
of state authority. This leads to the third conclusion, which is current
curatorial practice in Britain does not conform to the model of
archaeology's relationship with the state set out by the AHD, and has the
ability to contribute to theoretical debate, the development of the
discipline and its relations with the general public in a way that is not
constrained by the AHD.

Wider Implication and Politics

The wider ramifications of suggesting we take "archaeology out of
heritage" in the current environment in which archaeology operates should
also be considered. Might attempting to take archaeology out of heritage
be pointlessly swimming against a fast incoming tide of integration?
SMRs are changing to become the more holistic HERs, and are proposed
to become a statutory responsibility of local authorities in the Draft
Heritage Protection Bill (DCMS 2008). The Bill also proposes sweeping
reforms of heritage protection, replacing Scheduling, Listing, landscape
registration and Protected Wrecks with a single integrated list of Heritage
Assets. The *Management of Archaeological Projects* (known as MAP2,
Andrews 1991) has been replaced by the *Management of Research
Projects in the Historic Environment* (MoRPHE) (Lee 2006). At English
Heritage, Archaeology Commissions is now the Historic Environment

Enabling Programme (HEEP) underpinned by an integrated research strategy (English Heritage 2005a and 2005b). In 2008, instead of launching its annual Buildings at Risk gazetteer, English Heritage launched its first integrated *Heritage at Risk* report combining all historic assets with plans to expand the scope in future years (English Heritage 2008). The IfA hosted a seminar on "Convergence in the Historic Environment Sector" (Hinton and Dawson 2008a, 10–1, 2008b, 53–4), and has clarified the eligibility for membership to emphasize that it includes the totality of the historic environment profession. There has also been debate within the Institute about the name and whether it truly still represents the membership and whether changing the "F" from standing for "Field" to "for" should just be an interim step. Thus the fourth conclusion to be drawn is that the integration of the historic environment (including archaeology) is taking place across the sector and it is interwoven with heritage; this cannot be halted by attempting to take archaeology out of heritage.

Conclusion

Archaeology as a profession currently lacks critical mass, and if it wants to maintain and increase influence within government and other decision makers that is an issue that needs to be addressed. "Taking archaeology out of heritage" in this environment would lose influence. Heritage, on the other hand, has the opportunity to influence decision makers through its perceived relevance to the lives of the general public. Archaeology alone does not. Heritage has a voice. Without the heritage label, archaeology runs the risk of being marginalized and viewed as a minority discipline that gets in the way of development, and thus relegated to a meaningless academic discipline. What knock on effects might that have on the ability of the discipline to reach a variety of audiences and, crucially, funding? Does archaeology really want to cut itself off in this way?

This chapter has four main conclusions that can be summarized as follows. Firstly, it must be emphasized that the remit of archaeology is very broad, but its public perception is poor when compared to that of heritage. On the other hand, archaeology is the study of the historic environment and the concept of heritage is an empty one without the components of historic environment, and this means you cannot take archaeology out of heritage because they are largely one and the same. Further, current archaeological curatorial practice in Britain does not conform nor adhere to a single authorized heritage discourse, as Smith

(2006, 29–34) defines it, and has the ability to contribute to theoretical debate and development. This becomes particularly important given that an unstoppable tide of integration is taking place across the historic environment sector that will ultimately be of benefit to archaeology as a whole.

Many in the profession have worked hard to have archaeology recognized as a crucial component of heritage in order to deliver benefits to archaeology. If archaeology is to be taken out of heritage then the wider implications for the future of the discipline need to be considered. This is not pragmatism, nor an example of "real politik", but an argument that fundamentally has its roots in the theoretical side of the discipline. It can be argued that there is no such thing as heritage because what you are actually talking about is the historic environment and its study through archaeology. The convergence of the historic environment sector including archaeology under the heritage label with the engagement of the general public is the current zeitgeist. Archaeology will be marginalized if it is not included as a vital component of heritage. Take archaeology out of heritage? Why would archaeology want to leave?

Acknowledgements

I would like to thank Dr Laurajane Smith and Dr Emma Waterton for giving me the opportunity to speak at the original *Taking Archaeology out of Heritage* session at TAG in York, as well as inviting me to contribute to this volume. I would also like to thank the colleagues at the NMR with whom I discussed my thoughts for the original TAG paper and this chapter, in particular Dr Gillian Grayson, Nicholas Hanks, Edmund Lee and Robin Page.

Notes

[1] English Heritage, "Pastscape" [Online] Available at:
http://www.english-heritage.org.uk/pastscape
[2] RCAHMS, "Canmore" [Online] Available at:
http://www.rcahms.gov.uk/search.html; RCAHMS, "PASTMAP", [Online] Available at: http://www.rcahms.gov.uk/pastmap.html
[3] RCAHMW, "Coflein", [Online] Available at: http://www.coflein.gov.uk
[4] Durham and Northumberland County Councils [Online] Available at:
http://www.keystothepast.info/k2p/usp.nsf/pws/keys+to+the+Past+-+home+page
[5] Somerset County Council, "Unlocking Somerset's Past" [Online] Available at:
http://www.somerset.gov.uk/her
[6] Northumberland County Council and Durham County Council, "Keys to the

Past" [Online] Available at: http://www.keystothepast.info

[7] English Heritage, ALGAO and the Institute of Historic Building Conservation, "The Heritage Gateway" [Online] Available at: http://www.heritagegateway.org.uk

Works Cited

Aitchison, Kenneth. 1999. *Profiling the profession: A survey of archaeological jobs in the UK*. London: Council for British Archaeology, English Heritage and the Institute of Field Archaeologists.

Aitchison, Kenneth and Rachel Edwards. 2003. *Archaeology labour market intelligence: Profiling the profession 2002/03*. Bradford: Cultural Heritage National Training Organization.

Aitchison, Kenneth and Rachel Edwards. 2008. *Discovering the archaeologists of Europe: United Kingdom, archaeology labour market intelligence: Profiling the profession 2007/08*. Reading: Institute of Field Archaeologists.

Andrews, Gill. 1991. *Management of archaeological projects*. London: English Heritage.

Bagwell, Talya. 2007. Establishing an effective outreach programme: Unlocking Somerset's historic environment. In *Informing the future of Britain's the past: Guidelines for historic environment records*, ed. Paul Gilman and Martin Newman, F.24–F.31. Swindon: English Heritage.

Bahn, Paul (ed.). 1992. *Collins dictionary of archaeology*. Glasgow: Harper Collins.

Bailey, Greg, 2008. Making a drama out of a dig. *British Archaeology* 101: 38–9.

Baker, David. 1999. *An assessment of English sites and monuments records*. Chelmsford: Association of Local Government Archaeological Officers.

Clarke, David.1968. *Analytical archaeology*. London: Methuen.

Cload, Cat. 2008 The heritage gateway project. *Conservation Bulletin* 58: 42–3.

Cload, Cat and Nigel Clubb. 2008 The heritage gateway project. *Context* 104: 23–4.

Council for British Archaeology. 2008 "Exclusive: Bonekickers Comment With No Archaeological Puns". *British Archaeology* 102: 27.

Crofts, Nick, Martin Doerr, Tony Gill, Stephen Stead and Matthew Stiff (ed.). 2005. *Definition of the CIDOC conceptual reference model*. Paris: ICOM/CIDOC Special Interest Group.

DCMS (Department for Culture Media and Sport). 2008. *Draft heritage protection bill.* London: The Stationery Office.

de Moulins, Dominique, 2004. Archaeological science data and the SMR/HER. *Historic Environment Record News* 3: 8–11, www.heritagegateway.org.uk/NR/rdonlyres/45C2FF6D-3407-4BF0-9975-2A94B032BA23/0/hern_03.pdf (accessed July 23 2008).

Durham County Council and Northumberland County Council. n.d. *Keys to the past* www.keystothepast.info.

Dyson-Bruce, Lynn. 2004. Is there a Point in the Polygon?. *Historic Environment Record News* 3: 3–7, www.heritagegateway.org.uk/NR/rdonlyres/45C2FF6D-3407-4BF0-9975-2A94B032BA23/0/hern_03.pdf.

English Heritage. 2004. *Heritage counts 2004.* London: English Heritage.

—. 2005a. *Discovering the past, shaping the future: Research strategy 2005–2010.* London: English Heritage.

—. 2005b. *English heritage research agenda: An introduction to the themes and programmes.* London: English Heritage.

—. 2008. *Heritage at risk.* London: English Heritage.

—. n.d. PastScape. www.english-heritage.org.uk/pastscape.

English Heritage and the Association of Local Government Archaeological Officers. 2005. *Unlocking our past: Guidelines from English Heritage's national monuments record and the Association of Local Government Archaeological Officers for historic Environment records on applying for grants from the Heritage Lottery Fund (HLF).* Swindon: English Heritage.

English Heritage, the Association of Local Government Archaeological Officers: England and the Institute of Historic Building Conservation. n.d. Heritage Gateway. www.heritagegateway.org.uk.

Fairclough, Graham, George Lambrick and David Hopkins. 2002. Historic landscape characterization in England and a Hampshire case study". In *Europe's cultural landscape: Archaeologists and the management of change*, eds. Graham Fairclough and Stephen Rippon, 69–80. Brussels: Europae Archaeologiae Consilium.

Fox, Claire. 2004. Identity crisis, whose heritage is it anyway? Monumental folly. *Civic Focus* 47: 9.

Garmonsway, George Norman. trans., 1972. *The Anglo Saxon chronicle.* London: Everyman's Library.

Gilman, Paul and Martin Newman (eds.). 2007. *Informing the future of Britain's the past: Guidelines for historic environment records.* Swindon: English Heritage.

Gould, Shane. 2004. Analysing and recording historic buildings *Context*

84: 23–30, www.ihbc.org.uk/context_archive/84/gould/record.html.

—. 2005. Analysis and recording of historic buildings within the English planning framework: An assessment of current practice. *The Archaeologist* 55: 12–13.

Haig, Richard. 2003. Virtual heritage – Making virtual reality work. *Historic Environment Record News* 2: 5–6, www.heritagegateway.org.uk/NR/rdonlyres/3FFD4F04–9A06–4076–A171–19BD9E17B15D/0/hern_02.pdf.

Heritage Lottery Fund. 1999. *Unlocking Britain's past: A strategic framework for support from the Heritage Lottery Fund for sites and monument records.* London: Heritage Lottery Fund.

Hinton, Peter and Michael Dawson. 2008a. Convergence in the historic environment. *Context* 104: 10–11.

Hinton, Peter and Michael Dawson. 2008b. Convergence in the historic environment: Seminar. *The Archaeologist* 68: 53–54.

Hodder, Ian. 1998. *The archaeological process: An introduction.* Oxford: Blackwell.

Holtorf, Cornelius. 2007. *Archaeology is a brand! The meaning of archaeology in contemporary popular culture.* Oxford: Archaeopress.

Horton, Mark. 2008. Don't mess with me, I'm an archaeologist. *Rescue News* 105: 7.

International Council of Museums (ICOM). 2008. The CIDOC Conceptual Reference Model. http://cidoc.ics.forth.gr.

Jones, Andrew. 2002. *Archaeological theory and scientific practice.* Cambridge: Cambridge University Press.

Lee, Edmund. 2006. *Management of research projects in the historic environment: The MoRPHE project managers guide,* Swindon: English Heritage.

Matthews, Christopher, N. 2004. Public significance and imagined archaeologists: Authoring the pasts in context" *International Journal of Historical Archaeology* 8(1): 1–25.

MORI. 2000. *Attitudes towards the heritage: Research study conducted for English Heritage, April–July 2000.* London: MORI.

Munjeri, Dawson. 2003. *Intangible heritage in Africa: Could it be "Much-ado-about nothing"?* ICOMOS 14th General Assembly and Scientific Symposium. www.international.icomos.org/victoriafalls2003/munjeri_eng.htm.

Newland, Cassie, Greg Bailey, John Schofield and Anna Nilsson. 2007. "Sic transit Gloria Mundi". *British Archaeology* 92: 16–21.

Newman, Martin. 2001. *The sites and monuments records data audit programme – A review.* Swindon: English Heritage.

—. 2002. *The SMR content and computing survey 2002,* Swindon: English Heritage.

—. 2005. What a difference a year makes: Recent developments in historic environment records. *The Archaeologist* 57: 15.

—. 2007. Not surfing but drowning: Historic environment data on the Internet, addressing intellectual barriers to access. In *Contemporary and historical archaeology in theory: Papers from the 2003 and 2004 CHAT Conferences,* ed. Laura McAtackney, Matthew Palus and Angela Piccini, 67–74. Oxford: Arcahaeopress. BAR S1677.

—. forthcoming. Curation and conceptualization: Archaeological theory and curatorial archaeology, strange bed fellows?. *Assemblage* www.assemblage.group.shef.ac.uk.

Orton, Clive. 1980. *Mathematics in archaeology.* London: Collins Archaeology.

Page, Robin. 2007. Where the action was: Recording music clubs and venues. *Conservation Bulletin* 56: 36–37.

Renfew, Colin. 1987 *Archaeology and language: The puzzle of the Indo-European origins.* London: Pimlico.

Royal Commission on the Ancient and Historical Monuments of Scotland, n.d. Canmore. www.rcahms.gov.uk/search.html.

Royal Commission on the Ancient and Historical Monuments of Scotland and Historic Scotland. n.d.. PASTMAP.
www.rcahms.gov.uk/search.html.

Royal Commission on the Ancient and Historical Monuments of Wales. n.d. Coflein. www.coflein.gov.uk.

Schofield, John (A.J.). 2000. Never mind the relevance? Popular culture for archaeologists. In *Matter, materiality and modern dulture,* ed. Paul Graves-Brown,131–150. London: Routledge.

—. 2006. Rethinking heritage management. *British Archaeology* 89: 11.

Simpson, John and Edmund Weiner (eds.). 1991. *The compact Oxford English Dictionary.* Oxford: Oxford University Press.

Smith, Laurajane. 1993. Towards a theoretical overview for heritage management. *Archaeological Review from Cambridge* 12(1): 55–75 .

—. 1994. Heritage management as postprocessual archaeology. *Antiquity* 68: 300–309.

—. 2004. *Archaeological theory and the politics of cultural heritage.* Abingdon: Routledge.

—. 2006. *Uses of heritage.* Abingdon: Routledge.

Smith, Laurajane and Emma Waterton. forthcoming. Introduction. In *Taking archaeology out of heritage,* ed. Emma Waterton and Laurajane Smith. Newcastle-upon-Tyne: Cambridge Scholars Publishing.

Somerset County Council. n.d. Unlocking Somerset's Past. www.somerset.gov.uk/her.

Stoll, Robert. 1961. *Introduction to set theory and logic.* San Francisco: W.H. Freeman.

Tapper, Bryn. 2006. *England's historic seascapes, historic seascape characterization (HSC): National HSC method statement.* Truro: Cornwall County Council for English Heritage.

Taylor, Timothy. 2007. Screening biases: Archaeology, television and the banal. In *Archaeology and the media,* ed. Timothy Clack and Marcus Britain, 187–200. Walnut Creek, CA: Left Coast Press.

UNESCO. 1972. *Convention concerning the protection of the cultural and natural heritage.*

Whitehouse, Sue. 2008. Historic environment records: What next? *Context* 104: 39–41.

Waterton, Emma and Laurajane Smith. forthcoming. There is no such thing as heritage. In *Taking archaeology out of heritage,* ed. Emma Waterton and Laurajane Smith. Newcastle-upon-Tyne: Cambridge Scholars Publishing.

CHAPTER TEN

WHERE THE VALUE LIES:
THE IMPORTANCE OF MATERIALITY
TO THE IMMATERIAL ASPECTS OF HERITAGE

JOHN CARMAN

Introduction

Archaeology—once purely the province of students of the most ancient human societies, and generally perceived as focusing upon the deep past—is today understood as a wider study, "an approach, a set of methods, ideas and perspectives which are used to investigate the past through its material remains" (Bailey et al. 2009, 2). Indeed for some, archaeology is not about the past at all, but instead can be seen as the science of studying material culture. As such, archaeologists are concerned for all classes of material, and in all its forms. There is as much interest in studying an abandoned twentieth century Council flat (Buchli and Lucas 2001), a twentieth century protest camp, nuclear test facilities (Schofield et al. 2006) or road islands (roundabouts) and supermarkets (Graves-Brown 2007) as a Neolithic flint scatter or an Egyptian Old Kingdom tomb. The corollary is that there is as much interest in studying material from the distant past as in studying those objects that come from our own age. But archaeologists are interested in much more than "things"—the physical objects, materials and remains themselves. They are interested in the ideas, thoughts and social relationships in which these objects are embedded and which they represent—both in the past and in the present. Indeed, there is a very specific interest in the "life cycle" of such material amongst archaeologists, even as purely physical objects (see for example Schiffer 1972), and this interest brings even the most ancient object into the present (Schiffer 1987; Gosden and Marshall 1999; Holtorf 2002).

Archaeologists, then, study material culture from the past, but are equally interested in it as a part of our present. In doing so, archaeology is a discipline concerned with the very nature of material culture—both as "material" and as that elusive phenomenon called "culture". No other discipline combines such interests. This is an argument for retaining archaeology as a key contributor to the study of heritage and its understanding—and here, "heritage" is always to be understood not as a gift from the past but as a creation of the present. This paper will seek to make the argument for the involvement of archaeology in heritage by approaching it from apparently contradictory, but nevertheless linked, directions: that heritage is inevitably more intangible a phenomenon than tangible, and yet that its intangibility needs to attach to something tangible in order to exist at all. In doing so, this chapter will address the intangibility of the tangible and the tangibility of the intangible.

Castles of Stone

There is perhaps no more tangible heritage object than the castle of brick or stone. Castles are a widespread type of structure: they are found all over the world, built of all kinds of materials. They generally fall within the category of "heritage" because few cultures build or use castles any more and they have an abundant capacity for survival: they tend to be fairly robust structures.

Figure 10.1: Sedan Fortress, France

The great fortress at Sedan in north-eastern France dates from the thirteenth century, and it was developed to meet new challenges and new technologies of siege warfare from then until the twentieth century (Figure 10.1). At its height—in the sixteenth and seventeenth centuries—it was nearly treble its present size and was for a long part of its history the largest fortress in Europe. It never fell to siege or assault, and played a part in every major war in Western Europe from the fifteenth to the twentieth centuries: only the advent of long-range artillery and air-power made it obsolete as a site of defence. It is remembered particularly for the great battle that was fought around it in 1870, as part of the Franco-Prussian conflict of that year, the last of the so-called Wars of German Unification. The battle at Sedan ranks sufficiently high in local, and indeed French national, memory to have an entire room devoted to it in the museum contained within the fortress. Sedan is located within France and represents the final victory of that war of German over French troops, and yet the event is celebrated in a monument in the town square, in other monuments elsewhere and especially in the nearby military cemetery with a large obelisk.

These monuments do not mark French success, as do many military monuments, but instead the valour of French soldiers and the suffering of both soldiers and civilians at the hands of the invader. The current obelisk at Sedan is not the original that was first raised in the 1890s: it is a replacement raised after the Second World War when again Sedan fell to German forces. In 1941, the original was destroyed and replaced with a German monument in suitable neo-classical (even brutalist) style overtly celebrating a German victory on what was then seen (at least by the German high command) as German soil. The increasingly dilapidated condition of the Nazi monument testifies to the attitude now taken towards it by the Sedan authorities.

All these objects—the fortress, the French and German memorials, and other sites in the area that recall the battle—are tangible objects that are also solid and robust: but this is, of course, not the significance they carry. Their status as "historic monuments" or as "heritage" lies instead in the ideas they represent, which are alternative ideas about a past event that in itself is now unrecoverable in any physical sense and therefore quite intangible. At Sedan, to the intangibility of past action is added the intangibility of ideas about that past action—of valour in defeat, of claims to territory, of long-term rivalry between France and Germany. Those rival ideas themselves—in an era of European integration (or at least cooperation)—now find their place as part of the past: this is intangibility squared, as ideas about ideas also become part of the shared past.

Inevitable Intangibility

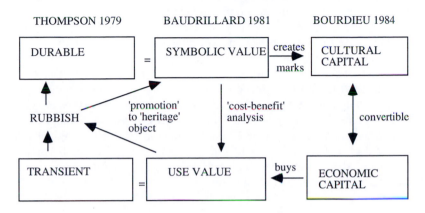

Figure 10.2: A model of heritage

The idea that there is less that is "tangible" about heritage than there is "intangible" is not new. Heritage, to put it simply, is something (or a group of somethings) "promoted" out of the everyday to a special cognitive realm where we think about it differently. The origin for this model (discussed in more detail in Carman 2002, 167–175; 2005c, 51–53) lies in Michael Thompson's *Rubbish Theory* (1979). This offers a mechanism for this "promotion" process out of one cognitive category of material to another, via his third category of rubbish, which is material we choose to treat as if it is not there. For Thompson, material is "real" but what makes things what they are is not their physical form but the ideas we have about them. The same applies in Jean Baudrillard's (1981) distinction between the realm of use and exchange values and of symbolic values: any object is merely an object, but it becomes what it represents because of the way we treat it and think about it. Accordingly, a simple gold finger-ring carrying a solitaire diamond as decoration given by a lover to his beloved on promise of marriage becomes a different object— an "engagement ring", carrying the particular association of the couple's relationship and requiring the performance of specific rituals in its presence (the expression of a desire to view it, admiration and praise, the offer of congratulations). These ideas map rather well onto Pierre Bourdieu's (1984) consideration of the interchangeability of, and people's differential access to, economic and cultural capital. Here, "cultural capital" defines one's status in the world and the ability to operate in particular social milieus, and also indicates one's ability to distinguish objects of cultural worth. The exchange of objects of cultural worth for economic value, or the ability to pay for expensive education, provides mechanisms by which the economic and cultural realms may interact.

Heritage is therefore inevitably a realm of ideas rather than a collection of things. Any object can become a heritage object: it has nothing to do with the physical attributes of the object, but rather what we hold to be important about it. This is the same point that Cornelius Holtorf and Tim Schadla-Hall (2000) have made regarding "aura" and "authenticity", that what we think about objects depends upon the contemporary context: the "authentic replica" or "authentic reproduction" can really exist and can be valued as much—and sometimes more—than an "authentic original". An object does not have to be old—or even pretend to be—to be granted "heritage" status; and it does not have to be really what it purports to be: fictional objects can be granted it too.

Figure 10.3: Whiteworks

The novelist Arthur Conan Doyle used Whiteworks on Dartmoor in southwest England as the model for his great Grimpen Mire in the Sherlock Holmes novel *The Hound of the Baskervilles* (Conan Doyle 1902) (Figure 10.3). It was the site of lead mining from the seventeenth to early nineteenth centuries and, as a consequence, the area is a dangerously wet and marshy area with water-filled depressions and pits now overlain by deceptively solid-looking plantlife. Despite its interest as a site of industrial heritage, it is as the Grimpen Mire that the place is frequently visited today: to the extent that one of the houses on the edge of the area carries a sign saying in very strong language that it is nothing to do with *The Hound of the Baskervilles* or, indeed, anything else Sherlockian, and please leave its inhabitants alone! Here, a fictional reference gives heritage status to a real location, but one which is not the real place visitors seek.

What this ultimately means is that not only can the category of heritage include any object, it can include anything at all—not only the physical but also the ideational: and, as Michael Thompson (1979, 56) neatly puts it, it is not that "things are … ideas, but that ideas are things".

Intangible Objects

The point about heritage objects—what makes them heritage, rather than anything else—is that they represent intangible qualities we value. But heritage does not only consist of objects: it consists of memories of objects and of memories of activities. Douglas and Isherwood (1979, 37) refer to collective (corporate) saving as having an "otherworldly morality" because it extends the life of the collective beyond that of its individual members. Collectives—such as military regiments, for instance—do indeed have existences beyond that of their individual members. In the British army, it became traditional to consider the regiment as immortal, and individual soldiers traded their own finite lives for the immortality of the unit: in this way, however short or long their life with that unit, they too partook of that immortality. This is one reason why old soldiers (and young ones) become so upset when reorganizations of the armed services lead to the disappearance of their regiment: their claim on the future has been removed from them. In fact, the usual procedure is for the regimental tradition to attach itself to a smaller unit in a new formation, at company or platoon level.

However, institutional descent need not be so direct to be recognized. At Cropredy Bridge in Oxfordshire (Figure 10.4), a stone tablet was placed in the 1930s at the site of a battle that took place in the 1640s. This object was created to stand for the memory of the event that was that battle: the intangible past event recalled only as intangible memory by the creation of a modern physical object. Each year at the spot, a re-enactment of the battle takes place by enthusiasts, some groups of whom claim an institutional descent from original participants by naming their "regiments" after those who fought on the day. Some of these regiments leave tokens—wreaths of flowers, perhaps—in memory of their fallen "comrades" of three hundred years previously. This process—of placing the tablet, of re-enactment, of leaving tributes in remembrance—represents the reversal of the normal process of preserving objects from the past to represent intangible qualities. Here, instead, the intangible is represented by the creation of new objects.

Figure 10.4: Memorial at Cropredy Bridge

Battlefields themselves are also heritage objects. Oudenaarde in Belgium was the site of a great battle in the early eighteenth century. It is a typical battlefield landscape and, apart from a low mound which is all that remains of what was once a castle, it is a very empty and uninteresting piece of real estate. What battlefield preservation is aimed at—a point made strongly by a number of commentators, and especially Foard (2001)—is the memory of the now unrecoverable event rather than the material evidence of the event that may be present in that space: that these places matter as the place where a historic event took place, rather than as archaeological sites. Hence one reason, I think, for the general lack of discussion of the ontology of such places in the literature (although on this see Carman 2005b) is that what they represent are not the places themselves or the objects they contain, but instead serve to evoke in the mind a past event. This is partly about remembrance and memorialization, but also about imagination and a kind of "fictionalizing" of the past by requiring the use of imagination alone as the mode of interpreting the event: this is because so little remains except the shape of the space, and sometimes not even that.

Battlefield memorials are an interesting category of object in their own right (Carman 2003; Carman and Carman 2006, 184–206). Like the example from Cropredy, they mostly post-date the event by some time. There was a medieval preference for building churches on battlefields soon after the event, but this practice was abandoned by the sixteenth century and the raising of other kinds of memorials is a practice of later centuries still (Borg 1991). What they mark is no longer present and was of course only fleeting in any case. They also mark different kinds of things that are not present. A great church built at the town now called Batalha celebrates the Portuguese victory of Aljubarotta fought several kilometres away and out of sight. A smaller monument at Tewkesbury marks that battle, but is now as likely to be used as a convenient location to park a bicycle. Both of these monuments commemorate the event particularly.

Other monuments commemorate persons present at the battle they mark. Individual monuments may commemorate the death of individuals, such as that at Roliça in Portugal, in memory of Colonel Lake who fell in battle there in 1808. Groups may equally be remembered, such as the large numbers of mercenaries who died at in the battle of Stoke Field (1487) and marked by the stone in the nearby churchyard. Similarly, those who were present may be recalled, as for the Irish who fought for France at Fontenoy (1745) or those who fought for the allies at Corunna (1809). Alternatively, the presence of a prominent individual may be marked, such as by the obelisk raised to King Louis XV of France, not on the battlefield of Fontenoy (1745) but at Cysoing, some two kilometres away, where he spent the nights before and after the conflict. All of these persons have of course gone: all are now deceased, and no visible evidence remains of them at the place where they are commemorated.

Figure 10.5: Portuguese Tomb of the Unknown Soldier

Remembrance of the dead is a specific category of commemoration. The Portuguese Tomb of the Unknown Soldier, commemorating World War One in particular, is located in the great church at Batalha, which itself commemorates war from six centuries earlier (Figure 10.5). More modest memorials to the dead of World War One can be found in the streets of St Albans, England, the site of a battle five centuries earlier. These memorials to the dead of modern conflicts sit away from the locations of that conflict, remembering not only people who are gone but also the distant events that took them.

Heritage sites, objects and places thus represent not things but the memory of things. The things they act to remember are always things that are gone: events, activities, people collectively or individually. They carry ideas and associations and values that are not concrete and cannot be measured or assessed in concrete terms: the physical description of a place, object or site is not a statement of its value or meaning. Beyond the memory of things, some represent the memory of the memory of things. All these fall into the category of the "intangible". When we talk about heritage, then, we are inevitably in a realm of the intangible: the idea of there being a "tangible" heritage, which is somehow distinct from an "intangible" one, is a shibboleth and a myth we need to move away from.

Paradoxically, the recognition of those intangible qualities as crucial to the category of "heritage" by official agencies also invites us to consider the role of those who engage with materiality in a new light. The next section will highlight how recent discussions of "heritage value" have sought to turn intangible qualities into tangible form.

New Heritage Values

We live in what has been termed the "Audit Society" (Power 1997), in which we are required to place a measurable value upon all things. The corollary, however, is that only those things that are measurable can be measured. It follows, then, that only those attributes the value of which is measurable are considered valuable. At the service of such ill-defined but contextually relative terms as "effectiveness", "efficiency" and "accountability" we find ourselves bound to offer tangible and measurable justifications for the preservation and custodianship of cultural heritage.

Recent initiatives in valuing cultural heritage reflect these aspects of the Audit Society. In 2005, English Heritage and other agencies commissioned a report from an environmental economics consultancy on *Valuation of the Historic Environment* (eftec 2005). Its opening statement is "Heritage assets are economic goods" because—like other economic goods—they provide "flows of wellbeing" (eftec 2005, 7). Rather than being concerned with activities, projects and programmes as its full title suggests it should, the report actually concerns itself with how one might assess the value of such "heritage assets". In January 2006, the Accounting Standards Board (ASB) for England and Wales published a "consultation document" on accounting for such "heritage assets" (ASB 2006), which would require a full financial valuation of such objects to be included in an institution's balance sheet as assets. Despite arguments against such a move on a number of grounds—some ethical, some practical, some grounded in accounting technicalities, and some a mixture of two or more of these—the ASB has since published its statement of how to account for such objects in financial terms

In a parallel development, the Heritage Lottery Fund commissioned the think-tank DEMOS to help them reconsider the evaluation of heritage projects, especially in light of new ideas about "public value" (DEMOS 2005). This was followed up by a conference early in 2006 where ideas about the concept of "public value" were explored (Clark 2006) (Figure 10.6). The concept of "public value" was presented to us as a measure of "what the public value" and as the space of interaction between three types of value. The first is so-called *"intrinsic"* value, which represents the meanings and associations carried by the cultural heritage: in other words, its academic research potential, and its symbolic and associational values. The second is so-called *"instrumental"* value, which represents the kinds of benefits that accrue to a community or to society in general from maintaining or using a site or monument: these could be in terms of tourist potential, or economic regeneration; in other words, its amenity value. The third is so-called *"institutional"* value, which derives from the activities of the organization responsible for managing or using the site or monument or place: these were defined in terms of *"how* organizations relate to their publics [and includes] creating trust and mutual respect between citizens ... and providing a context for sociability and the enjoyment of shared experiences" (Hewison and Holden 2006, 15, emphasis in original). While it was recognized that "instrumental" and "institutional" values would represent tangible returns that can be measured, albeit with some difficulty, it was generally agreed that the measurement of "intrinsic" cultural value was inherently more problematic. The general feeling was that this was the province of heritage professionals such as art and architectural historians, and archaeologists.

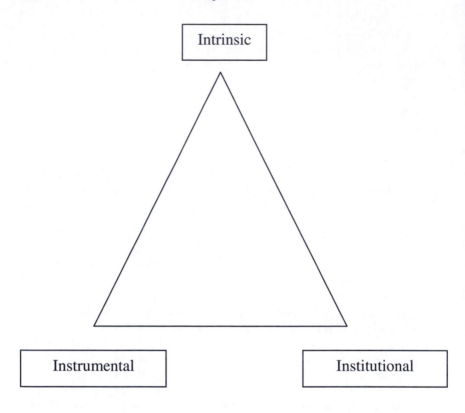

Figure 10.6: The "public value" triangle (Source: Hewison and Holden 2006, 15)

Both these attempts at valuation—in financial terms (ASB 2006) and in terms of "Public Value" (Clark 2006)—represent efforts at turning the value of the cultural heritage into tangible, measurable terms. For the ASB this takes the form of a straightforward accounting exercise. The "Public Value" schema incorporates other forms of valuation, but essentially reduces heritage to a purely utilitarian object, relegating its "cultural" values to the (largely immeasurable) "intrinsic" category.

The Role of Archaeology

By contrast with the ASB and "Public Value", the usual approaches to valuation of the archaeological resource serve the interests of archaeology as a discipline and as a field of activity. As Tim Darvill (2005, 39) has put it, measures of archaeological importance are an "interest group methodology applicable to specific elements of the resource, in order to allow some kind of ranking or discrimination". These can be contrasted with the more generally-held "value schemes" of wider society, which, he argues, are constructed of almost perfectly opposite elements, but with which they are linked to professional schemes of value in a hermeneutic circle (Darvill 2005, 37–9). Any accounting or financial scheme similarly serves the interests of institutional accountability in order to allow comparison between the relative effectiveness of different bodies responsible for stewardship of the heritage. It, too, is an "interest group methodology" in Darvill's terms—serving the interests of the accounting and audit community. And, despite its name and rhetoric, the scheme of Public Value proposed by DEMOS and others is equally unrelated to the relationship of actual people to their pasts. The one group not considered here are indeed real people: intrinsic, instrumental and institutional values are all kinds of abstracted, bureaucratic measures, detached from any sense of personal or group affinity to object or place. Yet the great lesson of surveys of public attitudes to the heritage (for example, English Heritage 2000) is precisely that sense of "belonging" which is central to the whole idea of having a heritage. Paradoxically this was an aspect strongly emphasized at the *Capturing the Public Value of Heritage* conference (Clark 2006), but remains excluded from the practice of policy—either public or disciplinary—as opposed to statements of intent (see for instance English Heritage 2000; DCMS 2001)

The experience of archaeologists, however, indicates an alternative way forward. Bill Boyd and his colleagues in Australia identified the processes by which professional interest in sites engendered the development of local interests and values built around a site's various attributes and different constituencies (Boyd et al. 2005, 98–107). They show how local Aboriginal interests mostly focussed upon sites representing Indigenous and traditional attitudes to land and environment, or to the history of their engagement with incoming colonizers. European Australians also recognized such claims and sometimes the spiritual dimension these indicate. Others, however, were more concerned with current social and economic uses—as tourist sites, recreational space, or thoroughfares—although not all of these necessarily conflicted with Aboriginal conceptions: the attitude of skateboarders to a rock-art site, for instance, could be seen as another example of the site's significance to a particular subculture (Boyd et al. 2005, 107), and indeed a close alliance was thereby forged between these otherwise quite different groups. It was by raising questions about such places from an archaeological and ethnographic perspective that values were ascribed that marked their importance to inhabitants of the locality and beyond.

The same set of processes was evident at the Hilton of Cadboll site in Scotland (Jones 2004). Here, excavation of the lower portion of an inscribed Pictish stone and its reconstruction ignited controversy over the ownership and placement of the reunited object, which was claimed both by the national museum in Edinburgh and the locality. Investigation of the contexts within which contemporary meanings for the stone are created identified a complex set of interlocking values. Academic and intellectual values included those of archaeology, art history, folklore and oral history (Jones 2004, 27–33). In parallel to these, there was a more symbolic sense of its identity, as a living part of the community, and as an object "born" into the locality (Jones 2004, 33–7). As such, it at once belongs to the community, is part of it and also constitutive of it: "as well as being conceived of as a living member of the community, the monument is also simultaneously an icon for the [community] as a whole" (Jones 2004, 37). This extends into the monument's role in the construction of a sense of place, and indeed of re-forging a "lost" sense of community cohesion (Jones 2004, 39) that can be "healed" (at least symbolically) by reuniting the two original pieces of the monument.

These are ideas about "cognitive ownership", defined by Boyd and his colleagues (2005, 93) as "a deliberately provocative term designed to focus attention on the diversity of socially-constructed values which may be identified for any cultural place [and] refers to the interest in or association with a site claimed ... by any person or group", specifically emphasizing the diversity of such associations that may co-exist simultaneously or change over time. Such notions inevitably relate closely to what has been called elsewhere "social value". This is a measure of "collective attachment to place", and places where this is evident have been conveniently defined—again by work in Australia (Johnston 1992, 7)—as those which "provide a sense of connection with the past, tie the past affectionately to the present, provide an essential reference point in a community's identity or sense of itself, help give a disempowered group back its history, and provide a sense of collective attachment to place". Such places "loom large in the daily comings and goings of life" and are "places where people gather" (Johnston 1992: 7).

Sites such as Hilton of Cadboll (Jones 2004) and those cited by Boyd and his colleagues (2005) clearly fall within this category. It is clear that the kinds of values that are ascribed to such places are multiple and can be conflicting, but at the same time, none necessarily prevent the ascription of other values to the same object at the same time. Accordingly, intellectual and academic values can sit alongside popular, economic, recreational and tourist values. This means that "cognitive ownership" may allow each claimant to a resource full access to it without interference from or interfering with access by others. By giving full reign to such cognitive claims, each can take from the resource without placing any restraint upon similar taking by others. It is not so much of a stretch from here to the exercise of a voluntary physical restraint on actual use of the resource so as not to deny it to others; in other words, a value-based conservation programme that is not entirely reliant upon bureaucratic structures, systems of reporting to public agencies and the measurement of tangible returns (Carman 2005a).

Conclusion

The significance of these examples is not that this sense of "cognitive ownership" automatically exists and only needs to be recognized (*contra* Clark 2006). Instead, the message of Hilton of Cadboll and of Boyd's work in Australia is that the active interest shown by students of culture serves to *create* new values that are then ascribed *by others* to the material under study. These examples of "community" projects serve to emphasize the link between valuing the archaeological past and a feeling of "ownership" of that past. It is this aspect of the relations between people and objects from the past that is lacking in current initiatives, be they professional archaeological or accounting schemes, or schemes of "public value". The paradox is that it is not those who have been talking and writing about schemes of archaeological value who have been able to provide a model that will counter the impact of "the audit society" on our work. Instead, it is among those who conduct community archaeology projects that we find what we seek. What we have failed to do is to translate the language of that work into the language of our own.

What is clear is that archaeology creates real value—not just archaeological value, but other values too—by virtue of engendering interest in the focus of our work. Such newly created values—whether they relate to the uses to which a place may be put, or the sense of community it creates, or the unexpected links and alliances that emerge between diverse groups within and between communities (such as Aboriginal elders and teenage skateboarders)—are all equally valid and relevant to heritage conservation. The point of this for the argument of this chapter is that it is *archaeologists* who are creating these values—and that the values so created inevitably attach to material objects. While the value of heritage is always intangible, it is to tangible objects that they attach,

and the people best suited to deal with this tangible material are
archaeologists.

Works Cited

Accounting Standards Board. 2006. *Heritage assets: Can accounting do
    better?* Accounting Standards Board Discussion Paper. London:
    Accounting Standards Board.
Bailey, Greg, Cassie Newland, Anna Nilsson, John Schofield, Steve Davis
    and Adrian Myers. 2009. Transit, transition: excavating J641 VUJ.
    Cambridge Archaeological Journal 19 (1): 1–27
Baudrillard, Jean. 1981. *For a critique of the political economy of the sign.*
    Trans. C. Levin. St. Louis: Telos Press.
Bourdieu, Pierre. 1984. *Distinction: A social critique of the judgment of
    taste.* London: RKP.
Borg, Alan. 1991. *War Memorials: From antiquity to the present.* London:
    Leo Cooper.
Boyd, William .E., Maria M. Cotter, Jane Gardiner and Gai Taylor. 2005.
    "Rigidity and a changing order … disorder, degeneracy and daemonic
    repetition": Fluidity of cultural values and cultural heritage
    management. In *Heritage of value, archaeology of renown: Reshaping
    archaeological assessment and significance*, ed. Clay Mathers, Tim
    Darvill and Barbara Little, 43–57. Gainesville: University Press of
    Florida.
Buchli, Victor and Gavin Lucas. 2001. *Archaeologies of the contemporary
    past.* London: Routledge.
Carman, John. 2002. *Archaeology and heritage: An introduction.* London
    and New York: Continuum.
—. 2003. Legacies of war in creating a common European identity.
    International Journal of Heritage Studies 9 (2): 135–150.
—. 2005a. *Against cultural property: Archaeology, heritage and
    ownership.* London: Duckworth.
—. 2005b. Battlefields as cultural resources. *Post-Medieval Archaeology*
    39 (2): 215–223
—. 2005c. Good citizens and sound economics: The trajectory of
    archaeology in Britain from "heritage" to "resource". In *Heritage of
    value, archaeology of renown: Reshaping archaeological assessment
    and significance*, ed. Christopher Mathers, Tim Darvill and Barbara
    Little, 43–57. Gainesville: University Press of Florida.
Carman, John and Patricia Carman. 2006. *Bloody meadows: Investigating
    landscapes of battle.* Stroud: Sutton.

Clark, Kate ed. 2006. *Capturing the public value of heritage: The proceedings of the London conference 25–26 January 2006*. London: English Heritage

Conan Doyle, Sir Arthur. 1902. *The hound of the Baskervilles*. London: George Newnes.

Darvill, Tim. 2005. "Sorted for ease and whiz"? Approaching value and importance in archaeological resource management. In *Heritage of value, archaeology of renown: Reshaping archaeological assessment and significance*, ed. Christopher Mathers, Tim Darvill. and Barbara Little, 21–42. Gainesville: University Press of Florida.

DEMOS 2005. *Challenge and change: HLF and cultural value. A report to the Heritage Lottery Fund*. London: Heritage Lottery Fund.

DCMS. 2001. *The historic environment: A force for our future*. London: DCMS.

Douglas, Mary and Baron Isherwood. 1979. *The world of Goods: Towards an anthropology of consumption*. London: Allen Lane.

eftec 2005. *Valuation of the historic environment: The scope for using results of valuation studies in the appraisal and assessment of heritage-related projects and programmes*. eftec, London.

English Heritage. 2000. *The power of place: The future of the historic environment*. London: English Heritage

Foard, Glenn. 2001. The archaeology of attack: battles and sieges of the English Civil War. In *Fields of conflict: Progress and prospects in battlefield archaeology, proceedings of a conference held in the Department of Archaeology, University of Glasgow, April 2000*, ed. Philip Freeman and Tony Pollard, 87–104. Oxford: Archaeopress.

Gosden, Chris and Yvonne Marshall.1999. The cultural biography of objects. *World Archaeology* 31 (2): 169–178

Graves-Brown, Paul. 2007. Concrete islands in *Contemporary and historical archaeology in theory: Papers from the 2003 and 2004 CHAT conferences*, ed. Laura McAtackney, Matthew Palus and Angela Piccini, 75–82. Oxford: Archaeopress.

Hewison, Robert and John Holden. 2006. Public value as a framework for analysing the value of heritage: The ideas. In *Capturing the public value of heritage: The proceedings of the London conference 25–26 January 2006*, ed. Kate Clark, 14–18. London: English Heritage.

Holtorf, Cornelius. 2002. Notes on the life of a pot sherd. *Journal of Material Culture* 7 (1): 49–71.

Holtorf, Cornelius and Tim Schadla-Hall. 2000. Age as artefact. *European Journal of Archaeology* 2 (2): 229–248

Jones, Siân. 2004. *Early medieval sculpture and the production of meaning, value and place:Tthe case of Hilton of Cadboll.* Edinburgh: Historic Scotland.

Johnston, Chris. 1992. *What is social value? A discussion paper.* Australian Heritage Commission Technical Publication 3. Canberra: Australian Government Publishing Services.

Power, Michael. 1997. *The audit society: Rituals of verification.* Oxford: Oxford University Press

Schiffer, Michael. B. 1972. Archaeological context and systemic context. *American Antiquity* 37, 156–165.

—. 1987. *Formation processes of the archaeological record.* Albuquerque: University of New Mexico Press.

Schofield, John, Colleen Beck and Harold Drollinger. 2006. Alternative archaeologies of the Cold War: The preliminary results of fieldwork at the Greenham and and Nevada Peace Camps. In *Landscapes under pressure: Their and practice of cultural heritage research and preservation,* ed. Ludomir Lozny, 149–62. New York: Springer.

Thompson, Michael. 1979. *Rubbish theory: The creation and destruction of value.* Oxford: Clarendon.

CHAPTER ELEVEN

UNPICKING ARCHAEOLOGY AND HERITAGE: CAN UNDERSTANDING TERRITORIES AND COMMUNITY HELP?

JONATHAN KENNY

Introduction

In the United Kingdom, the phrase "community archaeology" is commonly used to suggest public engagement with a set of physical and intellectual activities that encompass archaeology. A desire to encourage public engagement with the historic environment has been expressed at a governmental and institutional level, reflected in publications such as English Heritage's *Power of Place* (2000). Such statements are supported by the financing of many local history and archaeology projects by millennium funding and, more recently, through Heritage Lottery Fund (HLF) schemes. I am currently employed as a community archaeologist, supported by the HLF, in York and this experience forms the basis of the positions developed in this chapter.

Since the 1970s, archaeological activity in the UK has been dominated by "professionals" working in developer-led archaeology or teaching and carrying out research in academia. To imbue their professional activity with social value, those who practice archaeology rely in part on the idea of heritage to sustain it. It has been suggested by Waterton and Smith (this volume) that heritage, as a socially constructed phenomenon, should not be associated with the practice of archaeology. However, the practice of archaeology is itself socially constructed and ultimately cannot be untangled from the various social constructs that constitute heritage.

To understand the relationship between archaeology and heritage, this chapter uses the practice of "community archaeology" in the UK as a lens through which we can view these phenomena in action. The particular lens provided by community archaeology focuses on relationships between professional and non-professional actors, and I will use the work of Allen (1995) and Samuel (1994) to model these relations in a spatial manner. It is the intention of this chapter to characterize "top down" and "bottom up" approaches to community archaeology in the UK, though it is not my intention to reify one at the expense of the other. The most important point is that they are carried out in the face of the linkage between heritage and archaeology in a manner that reflects the nature of archaeology, heritage and, indeed, community as social constructs. The core argument of this chapter, then, is that we cannot extract archaeology from heritage. Instead, we need to unpick the relationships between archaeology, heritage and community, understand the idea of social constructions and then use this work to make us more reflective when working with communities.

Defining Heritage

To begin this chapter, I highlight three approaches to "heritage": "heritage" the idea, "heritage" as shared culture and "heritage" as property. Although they are considered separately, these three kinds of heritage are interrelated through the expression of ideas and culture in physical artefacts or buildings. By the ownership of these artefacts and buildings, either individually or in common, the heritage of ideas and shared culture are given physical embodiment.

For Nick Merriman (1991), heritage highlights opposing understandings of communal and individual "ownership". On one hand, there is "culture (represented by artefacts and buildings) and landscape that are cared for by the community and passed on to the future to serve people's need for a sense of identity and belonging". On the other is "the manipulation (or even invention) and exploitation of the past for commercial ends" (Merriman 1991, 8). This focus on heritage as a socially constructed phenomenon was encapsulated in David Lowenthal's book *The Past is a Foreign Country* published in 1985. Lowenthal noted that representations of heritage are an essential part of identity and that without an understanding of the past nothing would be familiar and the present would make no sense. Yet he also saw heritage as a burden that cripples innovation when the past is understood as a social "given". Lowenthal also discussed the possibility that the social construction of "heritage" allows for multiple meanings. This challenges the understanding of heritage as static, introducing a flexible approach that allows for continual reinvention of the past to suit the present. Lowenthal argues for a more inclusive way forward in understanding heritage:

> What reassurance can be gained from vestiges of a past so prone to vicissitude? What virtue has a "heritage" whose permanence is chimerical? The answer is that a fixed past is not what we really need, or at any rate not all we need. We require a "heritage" with which we continually interact, one which fuses past with present. This "heritage" is not only necessary but inescapable; we cannot now avoid feeling that the past is to some extent our own creation. If today's insights can be seen as integral to the meaning of the past, rather than subversive of its truth, we may breathe new life into it (Lowenthal 1985, 410).

Lowenthal raised the possibility that the "heritage industry" could hold back change, but he also sought an alternative heritage. He also highlighted a definition of heritage that could be enabling and enriching for people. Other commentators such as Robert Hewison (1987) and Patrick Wright (1985) preferred to emphasize the problems of heritage when presented and perceived as a social "given", which the public receive in an unquestioning and obedient manner. Both authors have reflected on the rise of the "heritage industry" in Britain, criticizing it as a cultural response to the collapse of British power and as having a penchant for wrapping itself in the flag of nationalism. In his book *The Heritage Industry* (1987), Hewison declared that this appropriation of the past for political ends represented the end of history itself. Likewise, Patrick Wright commented in *On Living in the Old Country* (1985) that "heritage" was linked to a common sense notion where society is constantly comparing itself to an idealized past.

This turn against heritage was termed "heritage baiting" by Raphael Samuel in his book *Theatres of Memory* (1994). He commented on the negative image given by "heritage baiters" to conservation officers at local authorities and within English Heritage and noted the accusation that heritage managers and developers sought to turn the country into "a gigantic museum, mummifying the present as well as the past" (Samuel 1994, 260). Samuel identified Hewison, Wright and Cannadine as the main "heritage baiters". He called Hewison's book (1987) the "squib that ignited 'heritage baiting'" and Wright's book (1985) a more substantial exercise in "heritage baiting" (Samuel 1994, 261). Lastly, Samuel identified historian Cannadine as a "heritage baiter" quoting his words on BBC Radio 3 on 5th January 1993, when he talked about "this heritage junk" that "represents a bunker mentality imprisoning the county in a time warp".

In his summing up of the "heritage baiting" movement, Samuel returned to two main problems. One was the way that an argument from those who considered themselves radical sounded very conservative. It sounded, says Samuel, like the right-wing critics of new history taught in schools in the late 60s and early 70s. "Heritage", say the heritage baiters "takes the mind out of history, offering a Cook's tour or package-holiday view of the past as a substitute for the real thing" (Samuel 1994, 265). The second problem that Samuel had with the "heritage baiters" is basic snobbery. The charge that "heritage" presentation is "vulgar" speaks for itself. Heritage presentation is often bracketed with theme parks or Disneyland; its association with entertainment is a cause of offence (Samuel 1994, 265–71). Samuel countered the "heritage baiters" by looking for energy and strength in heritage. To do so, he looked at the Mary Rose heritage presentation in Portsmouth, a warship from Henry VIII's fleet that sank in the Solent and was recovered in the 1970s and 80s by a combination of academics, divers, engineers and fundraisers. Here was Samuel's energy and dynamism, including a wide variety of professionals, volunteers and those watching events on the television.

Samuel also highlighted activity like family history that involves people in using historic documents for their own research agenda. Archaeological projects like the excavation of the Spitalfields church crypt bring forward individual histories at a community level rather than grand historical narratives. Samuel was particularly interested in the potential that archaeology brings to the energy and strength of heritage. His views seem to have been borne out by an increase in interest in archaeology on television in the 1990s, an increase that has continued to this day. This style of heritage is presented as a problem solving activity that has conflicting possibilities that invite people into the debate. The role of the expert has changed from a fount of all truths to a source of advice that may help in solving the problem. English Heritage and local authorities fund a number of regional services for metal detectorists identifying metal objects and recording their finds. Most metal detectorists work today as enthusiastic amateur archaeologists; the treasure hunters have long since lost patience and put their equipment in the attic. This interest has expanded still further with interest in getting involved with all kinds of archaeological activity at a community level.

Historical re-enactment societies (a regular sight at museum and heritage presentations) also feature in Samuel's argument. Some are professional actors paid by the heritage presentation where they appear, but most are independent groups. These societies consist of people who interact with particular interpretations of the past and interpret it for themselves, based in part on their own experimentation. They use academic research for their own ends, interacting with heritage. Such groups are no longer a small set of enthusiasts, but a wide variety of groups specialising in historical periods ranging from the Iron Age to the recent past.

Prominent in the debate about "heritage" has been the work of Barbara Bender who is particularly interested in the ways in which heritage sites, such as Stonehenge, become contested landscapes (Bender 1992, 1998). Bender is far more interested in the moments when heritage becomes contested between interest groups. She is interested in the social interactions with heritage (ideas and physical representations) that allows the static to be contested. Bender considered the ways in which traditional heritage conservation in the late 1990s restricted access to Stonehenge, a particular monument in a particular landscape. This conservation, she argued, sought to stabilize the idea of Stonehenge as a symbol of nationhood and an enduring monument to the past (Bender 1998, 151). Bender described a more complex set of social actors and values, "a multitude of voices and landscapes" that through time "mobilize different histories, differently empowered, fragmented, but explicable within the historical particularity of British social and economic relations, and a larger global economy" (Bender 1998, 131). The Stonehenge case study focused on the "Free Festivals" of the 1980s, which challenged the flagging of authority and nationalism with which Stonehenge was vested. The conflict hit a peak at the "Battle of the Bean Field" in 1985, when "New Age" travellers were violently evicted from the vicinity.

In Bender's work, we see heritage as dynamic and contested. Yet how does this relate to the static, exclusive and unchanging heritage identified by the "heritage baiters" (Hewison (1987), Wright (1985) and Cannadine (1989)? When we observe people interacting with sites and monuments as representations of heritage in different contexts we can see that these physical representations of the past are vested with multiple meanings (Kenny 2002). These multiple meanings are used and reused by people in their identity negotiations on an irregular basis, brought to the fore only by specific events in the life of an individual or community. This idea of heritage, then, is also contestable in the most unexpected ways. Understood like this, we can see Samuel's "theatre of memory" as a stage on which individual and group identity can be formed, reaffirmed and renegotiated. Seen in this light, heritage can at times be imbued with energy, particularly at a community level. Yet this same heritage also tends to the static, and is often used to ossify "commonsense" truths that may be divisive and exclude members of communities.

Relating Archaeology to Heritage

The practice of archaeology is one of the physical and intellectual ways through which people gain insight into past cultures and add to our individual and communal narratives of the past. Archaeology as a practice and archaeologists as practitioners also take a degree of responsibility for the research, presentation and care of many of the sites and monuments that they practice on. The very actions that we undertake as archaeologists are also actions in heritage, either reaffirming "common sense" truths about the past or contesting them. The sites and monuments that archaeologists excavate or conserve are physical representations of heritage defined above. In which case archaeologists cannot extract themselves from the social world in which they live and work. To gain insight into the way in which archaeology is bound to heritage we can look more closely at community archaeology.

What is Community Archaeology?

Anglophone archaeology has, in the post-war period, been increasingly concerned with the relationship between the public and archaeology (McGimsey 1972; Merriman 2004). The discussion of "public archaeology" has been dominated by debates about the best ways for professionals and academics to present archaeology to the public. After all, without a public sense of value for archaeology, what is the point in doing it, and who will pay for it to be done? In this debate, the practice of archaeology has been bound to broader social constructs, especially heritage. With this attachment to a complex heritage defined above, archaeology makes a Faustian pact with a socially constructed concept that includes in its make-up divisive and exclusionary concepts and assumption based on things such as nationalism (Kohl and Fawcett 1995), racism (Arnold and Haßmann 1995) and class (Smith 2009).

Community archaeology can be understood as a sub-set of public archaeology, in that it relates to the ways in which the public can participate in activities normally reserved for, and protected by, academic or professional archaeology. Where community archaeology is practiced there is a (often limited) taking of control by the public. In some cases, the archaeological activity is driven by the public who have a particular interest. This can be understood as a "bottom up" approach to community archaeology and is either supported by the professional or academic or seen as a threat. It is more often the case, particularly in traditional public archaeology, for the professional or academic to offer limited interaction or control of archaeological practice in a more top down manner. Examples of bottom-up and top-down community archaeology approaches have sprung up in a number of different contexts worldwide. Communities in the UK, encouraged by the media in many cases, have begun seeking deeper understanding of narratives of the past in their own families or in local landscapes (Samuel 1994; Holtorf 2007). Professional heritage managers, museums professionals and archaeologists have responded through a number of schemes and projects (see for instance, chapters in Merriman 2004).

In a similar manner, but encompassing different identity issues, many Indigenous peoples around the world have sought, or now seek, to control the landscapes, and sites and places in them, that both colonial and postcolonial powers have attempted to alienate (see, for instance, chapters in Birkhead et al. 1992; Davidson, et al. 1995; Swindler et al. 1997). Academic archaeological research projects have recognized the importance of interacting with local cultures and communities and have developed their own models of community archaeology.

There is a long tradition of people from local communities interacting with the archaeology on their door steps. Reusing special places in the landscape is often observed by archaeologists. For example, Richard Bradley (1987) describes the reuse of monuments through time at Yeavering in northern England, while Henry Cleere (1989) draws our attention to *tombaroli* in Italy or *huaqueros* in Central and South America as examples of local communities who have seen remains from the past as a source of income in the present. In the UK, early antiquarian archaeologists used local labour to carry out excavations. The same antiquarian movement led to the formation of both national and local interest societies, many of which survive today.

This interest in the past solidified in the 1940s and 50s, at which time it became common place for people to work as volunteers for local eminent archaeologists. This was true in York, where Peter Whenham carried out many excavations in the city using volunteers and school groups in the 1950s and 60s. In York, this led to the formation of an independent archaeology group called the York Excavation Group, which had the confidence and skills to carry out many excavations without professional or academic supervision and operated in the city as part of the "rescue" movement in the face of extensive development (Addyman 1973). The 1970s saw the steady development of professional archaeology, both in academic circles and in the field, squeezing out many of the independent groups. As this process of professional development was fed by the protection of heritage, built into planning law or guidance, opportunities for the public to investigate the landscape in which they lived became restricted. The opportunity to participate in archaeology in the UK was kept alive, however, within academic archaeology through training digs. Training excavations have in the past been used by university departments to carry out research and to train students in archaeological field methods. Many such field schools have welcomed paying customers from all walks of life, but in the main they do not draw in people from local communities.

Concern about the relationship between archaeological excavation projects and the communities in which they are located has been a driving force for a particular kind of community archaeology exemplified by projects at Çatalhöyük in Turkey described by Ian Hodder (2006) and Quseir in Egypt led by Stephanie Moser and described by Gemma Tully (2007). Tully (2007) has reviewed a number of community archaeology projects to identify key components in circumstances where there is a significant cultural difference between the archaeological team and local communities. Tully defines the role of community archaeology as a top down activity, nominating the following sequence of steps or "activities" originally defined by Moser et al. in 2002:

- Communication with local community
- Employment, training and volunteering amongst local people
- Public Presentation
- Interviews and oral history work with local people
- Educational resources
- Photographic and video archive
- Community controlled merchandising

In some ways, community archaeology in the UK developed along the same lines as these steps. It was controlled by professionals or academics who invited the public to participate in some way with their archaeology and the narratives that they told. Growing pressure on those who manage "heritage resources" (often archaeologists) by agendas of social inclusion and public accountability drove some of this, reinforcing the "top down" model of community archaeology. Although archaeologists have to make considerable changes to the way that they work to accommodate the aspirations of communities, they still have control of the work. When pressure to encourage inclusion is applied, it is easer to deliver this "top down" and is certainly easier to demonstrate results and demonstrate accountability.

Interest in archaeology amongst the varied communities that constitute "the public" in the UK has always existed, reflected in the popularity of visiting sites and participating as volunteers in the post-war years. Professionalisation and the processual approach to academic archaeology in the 1960s and 70s saw a reduction in opportunities for participation but an increase in the desire for archaeologists to explain their work through other media. Interest in archaeology has since expanded again in the wake of popular archaeology and history on television, printed media and the Internet (Holtorf 2007). This interest in archaeology may not of course equate to an interest in "heritage". The role of the archaeologist as a developer of narrative, and as a resource of evidence for the public to use in narrative development makes it almost impossible to extract archaeology from heritage. As soon as the interpretation process begins, the archaeologist begins to work in the field of heritage; it is the narrative nature of the archaeological process that intertwines archaeology and heritage. The narratives that archaeologists create can be read in many different ways by people engaging with their constructions of their heritage. The results are not always what the archaeologist anticipates, especially when heritage is contested, but the intertwining of the two is nevertheless made. This process of intertwining can also build back from heritage to the archaeologist as they respond to the ways that their narratives are used. Ultimately, because the archaeologist and the person constructing their own sense of identity and heritage are using evidence to build narratives they are both intertwined in a social process.

The growing interest in archaeology fuelled an already developed local and family history network that was grounded in the antiquarian concept of local studies. Such groups are generally composed of people interested in hearing talks of local interest and often support smaller groups of people who actively undertake research. Local history groups and societies were also encouraged by millennium-funded projects and, more recently, participation in local planning policies, such as village design statements. In the last decade, local history groups have expanded, and some have developed interests in activities such as archaeology that they have seen portrayed on their TV screens by series such as *Time Team, Meet the Ancestors, Trench Detectives, Surviving the Iron Age, Coast* and many specific programmes on sites such as Pompeii.

Recent Development in York

In York, communities were encouraged by an interest in their own
landscape, success in studying local history, an expansion in historical
and archaeological TV programmes and planning issues (village design
statements), which have triggered an interest in more people to locating
community "value" in the local historic landscape. Groups around York
have sought support and advice to carry out their own research using
archaeology. Because the community groups around York are well
organized and confident in their ability to interact with local services
and organizations, they have been able to take the lead with a good deal
of support from interested organizations in creating a community
archaeology project. This involvement from local communities from the
start has led to a more "bottom up" style of community archaeology. In
the case of York, the demand for help was met by an HLF funded
project that supplied a Community Archaeologist, based at York
Archaeological Trust. The Greater York Community Archaeology
Project offers advice, training, equipment and outreach to develop local
skills to answer local community's questions.

"Top down" community archaeology invites members of the local
community to participate in an established archaeological project, such
as Hungate in York or Dig Manchester. At Hungate a large scale
development of flats in a part of the City that has not been widely
studied archaeologically has included community archaeology
involvement. Local people are invited to work onsite which is also used
to offer activities for the York Youth Offending Team. At DIG
Manchester, the University of Manchester Archaeological Unit based at
the museum, ran a number of excavations, usually of nineteenth century
sites, aimed at specifically including local people in a number of ways.
The "top down" approach, wherever it takes place, meets all or most of
Tully's key components.

The "top down" community archaeology project is supervised and
run by professional archaeologists. When the professional fails to
recognize that archaeology cannot sit objectively outside local politics,
they can find themselves fuelling divisive factors in the community. The
archaeologist can quickly find themselves on one side or the other in a
debate over contested heritage, sometimes on the side that is trying to
overturn the accepted and static heritage position on other occasions
representing the status quo. This unintentional opening up of local rifts
was observed by Sian Jones (2005) in her work with a community in
Scotland as a fragment of the Hilton of Cadboll cross slab was
excavated. Jones observed a rift between those who felt that the cross

slab should join another piece at the national museum in Edinburgh and those who thought it should remain in the local area. The rift opened up a number of other divisions in the apparently quiet community concerning who belonged and who did not belong to that community. The archaeologists were entangled in a process of exclusion and appropriation of heritage that they might not have been able to avoid, but could have understood better from the start.

"Bottom up" community archaeology is driven by local interests, making it just as vulnerable to divisive factors. The archaeologist is involved at the invitation of the local community and has to take into account the ambitions and hopes of the local community. In such situations, it is vital that the incomer is able to be self reflexive, realizing that they are not sitting outside the community as some kind of objective observer but play a role in the acting out of community dynamics as assumptions about the local heritage are consolidated, challenged or both. The "bottom up" approach makes it easier to develop local links that the professionals and academics do not always have time to achieve in the normal course of their activities.

Many of the community projects around York have developed their own interests and have raised funds, usually through the HLF, to carry out projects. These projects have often included the employment of professional archaeologists to carry out specific tasks. A local archaeological unit (Onsite Archaeology) was employed through HLF funds to supervise community excavations at villages just outside York (Dunnington and Copmanthorpe, South Ainsty Archaeological Society). In nearby Cawood, the community, with the support of English Heritage, have taken on the management of a scheduled ancient monument at the Bishop's Palace and associated castle Garth, and at the same time have raised funds—most significantly from the now defunct Local Heritage Initiative (LHI)—to survey the site. They now use the support of local community archaeologists and both staff and students at the University of York to carry out test pitting to answer questions raised by the survey.

The "bottom up" approach to community archaeology throws up communities of interest that are not necessarily defined by geographic location. These may develop around specific landscape features that pass through many geographic locations, such as the River Foss in York, which passes through or near a number of geographically located groups, but is also researched by two groups with a specific interest its past. The interests of community groups are not always aligned with professional or academic research interests, and they also carry out research where the professionals are unlikely to tread. Professional archaeology in the UK is almost exclusively led by the planning and development structure in the country. Academic research projects may, and do, light upon particular communities, but they are often driven by different research agendas to those of local communities.

Whether it is "top down" or "bottom up", community archaeology is built around a relationship between professionals and non-professionals. Both are practicing archaeology, and by interpreting that archaeology they are creating conceptual narratives for their heritage. The relationship between the archaeologists and the non-professionals adds yet another layer to the playing out of heritage through the practice of archaeology.

Locating Community Archaeology in a Professional Territory

The description above of community archaeology suggests a positive but also divisive relationship with professional and academic archaeology. This relationship is important in understanding the location of community archaeology in archaeology itself and heritage. A useful way of bringing a spatial element to the relationship can be found through applying the work of Liz Allen (1995), drawing on the work of Abbott (1988), to study the development of the role of the practice nurse in the health service. Allen devised a model of professional territory to understand the way in which a group of health workers were able to undertake tasks and roles that where previously the domain of other professionals to carve out their own territory.

Archaeology has created its own professional territory. The archaeological territory is defined by specific activities that mark out or proclaim the performance of these activities as "professional" or "academic". The work of those within the archaeological professional territory is given value by skills that have been developed through education, training and experience, even an ability to speak and understand a particular professional vocabulary. Archaeologists and their territory are also protected by institutions and employment practices, universities or the Institute for Archaeologists (IfA). The professional territory is also defined by responsibility for material resources, a kind of professional ownership of specific equipment, sites and monuments.

Community archaeology does the same kind of work as the practice nurses did; it splits the practice of archaeology into component tasks and identifies those tasks that can be undertaken by the amateur. The amateur has gone on to take over certain tasks from the professional, usually with the collaboration of the professional. Some groups have become skilled in the use of geophysics; others carry out extensive fieldwalking surveys. In some cases, volunteers take over roles around excavations such as finds washing activities. Activities that are not highly valued by the majority of the profession are the first parts of a territory to be appropriated. This is the normal way, as described by Allen, in which one group takes on the work of others, but it also demonstrates the position of the community as the inferior partner in the process. Long established amateur archaeology groups such as that in Pontefract, Yorkshire, have shown that they can take on most of the tasks performed by the professional, but for most groups the process of carving out a part of the professional territory is less developed.

The processes of asking questions about the local landscape are the usual starting point for community groups, and this is an important first step. Penetration into the professional territory can often end at this early stage, especially if a professional is employed to do the work. However, data gathering can be a positive step into professional territory that can be achieved with support and confidence building. This is one of the central roles of the community archaeologist employed in York. Learning to understand work that has already been done by reading archaeological reports, carrying out landscape surveys, geophysical surveys, and undertaking field walking are all big strides into the professional territory of the archaeologist. It is clear that the further the public step into the professional territory, the more conflict they may generate. Data can be used to develop narratives that the professional might not agree with. Carrying out work may be seen as taking work away from the professional, especially in "top down" situations where volunteers are welcomed on site.

Developing confidence to undertake tasks in the professional territory of the archaeologist can be intimidating. This is the nature of professional territories; they are protected, for example, by specialist language that is used as a marker of that territory. The right to speak or hold an opinion on a particular topic, a category entitlement, is a fundamental part of interaction between people. It takes a lot of confidence building for someone to feel a category entitlement to speak as if one has a place in a particular professional territory. Only a few community members gain the confidence to feel a sense of category entitlement to speak as an archaeologist, which reflects the task that they are undertaking. A person who does not feel category entitlement feels

intimidated. It is this intimidation, felt by the person on the outside of
the professional territory (and usually unintentional), that the
community archaeologist who resides within the professional territory
works to unpick and decipher for the interested and enthusiastic public.
If we can locate community archaeology in the territory of the
professional, can we also locate it in the concepts of socially constructed
heritage and archaeology?

Locating Community Archaeology in Socially
Constructed Heritage

The idea of social construction was first applied in the 1960s by
Berger and Luckmann (1966) and has been used to understand many
social phenomena since. The concept of the social construction of
cultural truths was used in the early 1980s by Eric Hobsbawm and
Terence Ranger (1983) to understand the construction of tradition—the
process of creating heritage and then setting it in stone through cultural
actions and symbols. If we consider that the many facets of heritage
reside in a conceptual space in which people can play out any number of
their perceptions of the world, as suggested by Samuel (1994), it is
possible to locate community archaeology in relation to heritage.
Samuel suggests that heritage and representations of the past form a
stage on which individuals, who make up communities, can play out
their sense of self identity. Community archaeology as a process of
undertaking a series of physical activities in the landscape becomes a set
of actions taking place on Samuel's stage. Indeed, it is possible to
understand the construction of heritage as building blocks on the stage
of a "theatre of memory" as ideas, social processes and material things.

Material things such as monuments, landscapes and places can be
understood as real props on the stage of the theatre of memory. The
ways in which people use these props can be investigated as they talk
about their sense of visual identity (Kenny 2002). On the stage of the
Theatre of Memory people are constantly negotiating, and sometimes
rapidly renegotiating, their relationship to ideas through the building
blocks that go together to construct their sense of self and community.
These building blocks include aspects of heritage, although Lowenthal
(1998) has argued that heritage elements are likely to set certain social
constructions in stone and make them immutable. However, as I have
shown elsewhere, it is possible to research ways in which people can
use the same heritage monuments to articulate different senses of
identity (2002). This is achieved by focussing on different aspects of a

building or other monument, allowing people to change their position or narrative much more quickly than Lowenthal suggests, depending on the context in which they are placed.

The material aspects of heritage lend themselves to people within communities because they are physical and can be discovered, touched and observed, allowing people to negotiate a sense of self as they explain their observations. Of course the same physical nature of material heritage also tends to accentuate static, often ossifying, commonsense truths that may be divisive and exclude members of communities as well as binding them. The thought process, which should be part of the work of the archaeologist, needs to be applied to the interpretation and narrative building associated with material heritage allowing for reflection and potential contestation of heritage.

Socially Constructed Archaeology

The definition of "heritage" that I have adopted above has inherent problems for people and communities when interacting with heritage. Heritage is bound to truths that are social constructions, which lead us to forget to contest them unless circumstances change. It is all too easy to follow the stereotyped, and sometimes divisive, view of our heritage without understanding the many meanings that may be available to us when understanding the past. Perhaps we should try to extract the material from it and conceptually add it to archaeology instead. After all, archaeology is an academic subject, in part, at least, a science that can remain objective. This is a rather too simplistic view to take of archaeology, however. Indeed, the subject has taken a reflexive turn, illustrated by the works Michael Shanks and Christopher Tilley (1987), and should be understood as a social construct itself. Drawing on the concepts of science studies beginning with Thomas Kuhn's work on the nature of science and how it works as part of society (1962), later followed by Michael Mulkay's work *Science and Sociology of Knowledge* (1979), we can see that the processes and activities that go together to become archaeology are influenced by the way that society works in the same manner as heritage. If we see archaeology as an activity, we can still see it as one played out in the conceptual space or theatre as heritage.

On the stage of the theatre of memory, archaeology and its activities are the bringers of materiality. It is possible to transfer the actions that constitute archaeology from the conceptual space that is a professional territory onto the stage. Whilst acting on the stage, everyone is participating in the social construction of archaeology within the academic and professional territory. On the bigger stage of the theatre of memory there are many more actors than we find in the safe confines of the professional territory. Here, we find the public in all its forms, helping to construct an archaeology that may or may not be appreciated by the professional archaeologist.

Cornelius Holtorf (2007) outlines some of the "building blocks" used in the construction of archaeologists as adventurers, detectives, makers of revelations and carers for all things ancient. These "building blocks" exist outside the archaeologist's territory on the bigger stage of the theatre of memory. Holtorf observed the prominence of public perceptions of the archaeologist as adventurer, as detective, as making profound revelations and taking care of ancient sites and finds. It seems likely that it is these constructions of the archaeologist that attract many of those who participate in community archaeology. These constructions reify the archaeologist and increase the attraction for the public in interacting with professionals and academics on the same stage. Naturally, the same reification can also put the archaeologist on a pedestal making them seem unapproachable. Either situation has its problems, in both cases resulting in disappointment if the archaeologist fails to live up to the image.

The simple physicality of many archaeological practices gives people who make up communities activities that they can do whilst acting on the stage. If allowed to participate in archaeology, people can then reflect, along with the professional archaeologist, on the interpretations they are making. They may be influenced by the stereotyped nature of heritage as suggested by Hewison (1987), Wright (1985) and Cannadine (1989), but they also have the opportunity to seek out the contested nature of heritage (Bender 1998) drawn from their own experience of archaeology. Like any community activity, this can be divisive within the community, for example the rifts observed by Jones (2005) at Hilton of Cadbol, and does not always make community archaeology an easy ride, so is it worth trying to separate archaeology from heritage?

Extracting One from the Other

Despite the socially constructed nature of archaeology, it does not seem vested with the same divisive powers as heritage. Archaeology is a set of professional and academic practices that can certainly generate stereotyped responses to certain evidence. Heritage, however, has at its heart issues of identity that when stereotyped as commonsense truths carry elements of social exclusion that can be socially damaging and divisive. In reality, the world is not so simple as to allow us to extract the one from the other. Conceptually, heritage and archaeology are detached but often conflated as the archaeologist generally researches aspects of heritage and then feeds back into the narratives that drive heritage.

On the stage of the theatre of memory, it is difficult to see heritage and archaeology as separate. The processes of social construction that encompass both archaeology and heritage are so closely intertwined that separation becomes difficult. As with the understanding of the process of science (Mulkay 1979), we cannot separate those processes from the social world in which they sit. In effect, the stage on which archaeology and heritage play themselves out is an integral part of a whole range of social processes that operate there. It is possible to unpick the relationships, reflect on and understand them in specific contexts, but having one process, archaeology, sit objectively exempt from the difficulties brought by the other is likely to be unattainable.

It might be possible to separate heritage and archaeology if we see them in the more simplified world of the professional territory. Archaeology, as we have seen, presents a set of activities, physical and intellectual, that may be, and often have been tucked away behind a professional territorial boundary. However, can heritage as a concept claim its own territory? Heritage has its own physical embodiment, the sites and monuments that socially constructed heritage deems worthy of protection. Heritage also has its own set of institutions, such as museums, which contain artefacts and the activities bound up in preserving, interpreting, visiting and educating.

Therefore heritage has its own professional territory, made up of a number of related professions, arguably older than that of archaeology. However, do the stereotyped understandings of heritage reside in the professional territory of the heritage professional any more than the archaeologist? Some interpretations of heritage are suggested by heritage and archaeology professionals but many others are played out of the stage of the "theatre of memory", a place available to all outside the direct control of either profession. By applying the concept of professional territory, it is possible to simplify the relationship of archaeology and heritage, making them sit separately but still interacting on the same stage with a concept that we can understand as the "idea of heritage". In this way, the "idea of heritage", along with its tendency to create stereotyped truths and the potential for contesting these truths, is available to archaeologists and heritage professionals as well as the rest of society.

So can either the heritage profession or archaeology exist independently of the idea heritage? If we contain our arguments within professional territories we simplify matters to argue that the "idea of heritage" can be extracted from archaeology and the heritage profession. But reality is that archaeology and the heritage professions are played out on a bigger conceptual stage than this. On this stage, we have the "idea of heritage" used and arranged by all who make up our communities to negotiate their senses of self and others. This is where heritage poses difficulties if it is allowed to exist without reflexive questioning. This reflexive questioning often emerges from members of communities who find themselves disenfranchised by the dominant "idea of heritage". The practices of archaeology, history and the heritage profession also have a responsibility to themselves and society to avoid ossifying certain social constructions as commonsense truths without allowing for the possibility of contestation.

The responsibility for professionals and academics to introduce reflexivity into their narratives of the past is especially important if communities are invited or walk into the academic and professional territories. The nature of professions leads to the reification of practitioners and a sense of inadequacy amongst those outside the professional territory. The statements made by professionals are difficult for the outsider to disagree with when they are invited guests within the professional domain. Naturally, this responsibility makes more conceptual work for the professional and takes them into direct work on areas of contention that they may never have anticipated. It also means devoting more time and resources to supporting and encouraging communities to work with their own past, enjoying the benefits, but also showing them that the past is not an ossified representation of certain heritage constructs, but a changing and exciting way of understanding the world around us.

Conclusion

This chapter suggests that it is probably impossible to separate archaeology from the "idea of heritage" unless a very specific model is used to represent them such as the concept of professional territory. The "idea of heritage" has a tendency towards setting certain ideas in stone as commonsense truths, but is also given a sense of dynamism by continual questioning of these truths. If it is possible for professional and academic models of archaeology and heritage to exist within professional territories, they also have to interact with the rest of society and the "idea of heritage" in the wider world, on what Samuel (1994) has described as the theatre of memory. This association with the "idea of heritage" imbues professional and academic practice with social "value", so there is no alternative for practitioners other than to interact on Samuel's stage.

If archaeology and the "idea of heritage" are inextricably bound through social construction, or archaeology and professional heritage need the "idea of heritage" to establish their value in society, it is difficult to see one existing without the other. Given these relationships it becomes incumbent on archaeologists to give people, especially community groups who want to participate, access to things inside their "professional territory" if they wish to continue to have "value" in society. In addition to giving the public access to some of the professional secrets guarded by archaeology, still more needs to be done to understand the complexities of heritage as an idea that influences social processes in a complex world of identity, ownership, time, boundaries, legitimisation, order and social value.

Works Cited

Abbott, Andrew. 1988. *The system of professions: An essay on the division of expert labour.* Chicago: University of Chicago Press.

Addyman, Peter. 1973. *Rescue archaeology in York.* Billingham: Teesside Museum and Art Galleries Service.

Allen, Elizabeth A. P. 1995. Developing an occupational territory: The professionalisation of practice nursing; a study of professionalisation processes in practice nursing using two qualitative case studies. PhD diss., University of York.

Arnold, Bettina and Henning Haßmann. 1995. Archaeology in Nazi Germany: The legacy of the Faustian bargain. In *Nationalism, politics and the practice of archaeology*, ed. Philip L. Kohl and Clare Fawcett, 70–81. Cambridge: Cambridge University Press.

Bender, Barbara. 1992. Theorizing landscapes, and the prehistoric landscapes of Stonehenge. *Man: The Journal of the Royal Anthropological Institute* 27(4). 735–755.

—. 1998. *Stonehenge: Making space.* Oxford: Berg.

Berger, Peter and Thomas Luckmann. 1966. *The social construction of reality: A treatise in the sociology of knowledge.* Garden City, NY: Anchor Books.

Birkhead, Jim, Terry Delacy and Laurajane Smith eds. 1992. *Aboriginal involvement in parks and protected areas.* Canberra: Aboriginal Studies Press.

Bradley, Richard. 1987. Time regained: The creation of continuity. *Journal of the British Archaeological Association* 140: 1–17.

Cannadine, David. 1989. *The pleasures of the past.* London: Collins.

Cleere, Henry. 1989. Introduction: the rationale of archaeological heritage management. In *Archaeological heritage management in the modern world*, ed. Henry Cleere, 1–19. London: Unwin Hyman.

Davidson, Iain, Christine Lovelle-Jones, and Robyne Bancroft. 1995. *Archaeologists and Aboriginies working together.* Armidale: University of New England Press.

English Heritage (Collective authorship). 2000. *Power of place: The future of the historic environment.* London: English Heritage.

Hewison, Robert. 1987. *The heritage industry, Britain in a climate of decline.* London: Methuen.

Hobsbawm, Eric and Terence Ranger, eds 1983. *The invention of tradition.* Cambridge: Cambridge University Press.

Hodder, Ian. 2006. *Çatalhöyük: The leopard's tale.* London: Thames & Hudson, London.

Holtorf, Cornelius. 2007. *Archaeology is a brand! The meaning of archaeology in contemporary popular culture.* Oxford: Archaeopress.

Jones, Siân. 2005. "That stone was born here and that's where it belongs": Hilton of Cadboll and the negotiation of identity, ownership and belonging". In *Able minds and practised hands: Scotland's early medieval sculpture in the 21st century*, ed. Sally M. Foster and Morag Cross, 37–53. Edinburgh: Society for Medieval Archaeology.

Kenny, Jonathan. 2002. Visual repertoire, focusing activity and the "value of heritage": Using the "mental library of views" to evoke local place-identity, Britain and Europe. PhD diss., Lancaster University.

Kohl, Philip L. and Clare Fawcett, eds. 1995. *Nationalism, politics, and the practice of archaeology.* Cambridge: Cambridge University Press.

Kuhn, Thomas S. 1962. *The structure of scientific revolutions.* Chicago: University of Chicago Press.

Lowenthal, David. 1985. *The past is a foreign country.* Cambridge: Cambridge University Press.

—. 1998. *The heritage crusade and the spoils of history.* Cambridge: Cambridge University Press.

McGimsey, Charles R. 1972. *Public archaeology.* New York: New York Seminar Press.

Merriman, Nick. 1991. *Beyond the glass case: The past, the heritage and the public in Britain*. Leicester: Leicester University Press.

—. 2004. Introduction: Diversity and dissonance in public archaeology. In *Public archaeology*, ed. Nick Merriman, 1–17. Abingdon: Routledge.

Moser, Stephanie, Darren Glazier, James E. Philips, Lamya Nassr el Nemr, Mohammed Saleh Mousa, Rascha Nasr Aiesh, Susan Richardson, Andrew Conner and Michael Seymour. 2002. Transforming archaeology through practice: strategies for collaborative practice in the Community Archaeology Project at Quseir, Egypt. *World Archaeology* 34 (2): 220–248.

Mulkay, Michael. 1979. *Science and the sociology of knowledge*. London: Allen and Unwin.

Samuel, Raphael. 1994. *Theatres of memory: Past and present in contemporary culture*. London: Verso.

Shanks, Michael and Christopher Tilley. 1987. *Reconstructing archaeology: Theory and practice (New studies in archaeology)*. Abingdon: Routledge.

Smith, Laurajane. 2009. Deference and humility: The social values of the country house. In *Valuing historic environments,* ed. Lisanne Gibson and John Pendlebury, 33–50. Abingdon: Ashgate.

Swindler, Nina, Kurt E. Dongoske, Roger Anyon and Alan S Downer. ed. 1997. *Native Americans and archaeologists: Stepping stones to common ground*. London: Altamira Press.

Tully, Gemma. 2007. Community archaeology: General methods and standards of practice. *Public Archaeology* 6 (3): 155–187.

Waterton, Emma and Laurajane Smith. forthcoming. There is no such thing as heritage. In *Taking archaeology out of heritage,* ed. Emma Waterton and Laurajane Smith. Newcastle-upon-Tyne: Cambridge Scholars Publishing.

Wright, Patrick. 1985. *On living in the old country*. London: Verso.

An Interview With Janet Hopton (Poppleton History Society)*

Tell us a bit about the Poppleton community project.

JH: We began as a pilot project for community archaeology, and I can
never remember the date exactly, but it was somewhere around 1997. The
York Archaeological Forum (YAF)[1], with archaeologist A as the chair at
the time, was keen to involve the community in some way. They were
interested in studying the York landscape and York's hinterland. They
decided it would be a good thing to look at the Hinterland and include us
because we had a very lively history society, which had begun in 1989. A
pilot project to study the hinterland in Poppleton was commenced. In a
sense, that is where the community archaeology movement in York began.
We did field walking in different areas of the village, which archaeologist
B led on a lot of Sunday afternoons. We looked at the church and the
churchyard, our moated site and various other things and gradually as we
were going along the YAF said it would be good to have a community
archaeologist. At the time, archaeologist B was the only archaeologist for
the city and the work he did with us was extra. I think there was a general
feeling at YAF that it would be great to have a dedicated community
archaeologist in York, and lottery funding was looked at. After due
process, it ended up with the YAF getting a lottery fund grant through
YAT applying, who became the line manager for the community
archaeologist. We have been going for about five years. The community
has achieved a lot, and I would say our relationships with archaeologists
are very good. The arrangement is that there is a project management
board, and an advisory group. We are a very good example of how
archaeologists have been working very closely with communities.

There are very few dedicated community archaeologists across the
country and everybody does it a little bit differently, but you do need a
dedicated person and the idea is he/she is the facilitator—they don't do it
for you, they teach the groups how to do things. We have training sessions
in which we can learn how to fieldwalk, how to sort things, how to do

---

* Interviewers: Steve Watson and Laurajane Smith

geophysics and they make the equipment accessible and give advice. Certainly all the archaeologists have always been very willing to help. The current archaeological chair of the YAF is looking at ways archaeology students can be involved as well in helping community groups. I mean, you could not really have greater cooperation.

Is it because archaeologists have been involved from the very start?

JH: Well, it could be. I mean it evolved from their idea to study the hinterland. New local groups have been formed, often a mixture of history and archaeology, and the Time Line Group, which acts as an umbrella organization for them. This is the interesting thing, archaeologists have welcomed the Time Line groups. For some archaeologists, it was perhaps diluting the more archaeological aspects, and I am sure some of them think you must not go too far.

How do you mean diluting?

JH: When I first went to the YAF meetings, they were very much archaeology focused, but once community archaeology became more established, there has been a lot on community archaeology being discussed in this group. Which is fine, but I think for people, or archaeologists, who want to compare notes on pure archaeology, they do not want to be bogged down with a lot of the meeting time spent on this— community archaeology is only one part. I really, though, have had no bad experiences with archaeologists. They have all been more than helpful.

Your group was one of the first to form itself, and it formed specifically around a conservation issue, is that right?

JH: First, there was the history group. Then the preservation action group started, also in 1989. They were not the same—they were kept quite separate. The history society was purely to look at the history of the local area. We had been talking about starting one for years but a development threat in 1989 galvanized us into action. We felt that if we had a history society we could use that as part of our action, you know, a bit political perhaps. I mean, if you are fighting development you have to…we had an archaeologist support us there, and a local historian, but it is useful to have a local history society as well and it went from strength to strength.

How was archaeology used in that process in the development of the historical society and preservation group?

JH: Not at all. The preservation group lobbied Harrogate Borough Council to speed up with designating a Conservation Area that would include the Manor Farm area and give it the necessary protection.

What role did archaeology or archaeologists play in the development of events in Poppleton that led to the conservation of the Manor Farm area?

JH: We had used archaeology in the action group in the sense that we had to pester English Heritage about their proposal to reassess the ancient monument. We got support from archaeologist C about the importance of the area in archaeological terms. The ancient monument designation only initially covered the moated site. It did not cover other important areas. Archaeologist C was crucial for saying, "this is important too", and he sent us one or two photos. Things like that. We had the help of archaeologists, and a historian, we used professionals in protecting the area.

Was that a conscious thing on your part, to add some gravitas to your cause?

JH: Oh yes and we needed it. We were losing the battle. We were very distant from the county councillors who cover North Yorkshire, which is vast. They were very helpful in the end, but it needed people like archaeologist C to get involved.

And you think because of that you, throughout this process, that you have always shared the same priorities with the archaeologists?

JH: Totally. When we started we had an array of about four or five archaeologists, and we had one of these identification sessions, and 70-odd people turned up, and they talked about different things and showed great enthusiasm, they have always been very helpful and supportive—responding if we needed help rather than saying what they wanted to do.

We are also interested in the relationship between archaeology and heritage. From your point of view, do you have a sense of what heritage is? Is it the same as archaeology?

JH: I have thought about this carefully. I think this is a very confusing area and I have thought that for some time. I mean before I got involved in archaeology I always thought that archaeology was under the ground. Gradually I have realized, especially with the training program that happens through community archaeology, that archaeology is now considered something different, much wider, but I still don't think it is the same as heritage. Archaeology is under the ground obviously, and its landscapes, but it also covers things like archives, textiles, stained glass and extant buildings, not just those that are ruinous, but standing structures. Heritage, well, a lot of that is heritage, so archaeology is part of heritage, very definitely, but heritage embraces even wider things.

My idea of what heritage is: First, there are buildings, structures, open spaces and landscapes. Obviously, this overlaps with archaeology. However, heritage also includes traditions, for example the Mystery Plays in York. I was Lord Mayor for a while, and there are two traditions that the Sheriff has: testing the ales in August (the Sheriff's Assize of Ale) and the Sheriffs Riding. This happens just before Christmas, in which the Sheriff and his army go to the four gates of the city, starting at Micklegate, and they read a proclamation which says that beggars, prostitutes, evil doers can come into the city for Christmas. Traditions like that are part of our heritage. More recent events are now being remembered and are becoming traditions, such as Remembrance Sunday, which is now a national tradition.

There is another group of things like ceremonial roles and institutions, like civic office, the Lord Mayor and the Sheriff, and our Honorary Aldermen and the Guilds—that is heritage, too. There are legacies, also. The Quaker legacy is part of what makes York—it gives it its flavour—and then railways and chocolate—I do not know how you define that. Then there are people that have made an impact, people like Joseph Rowntree and the influence he had. You can go back to Constantine as part of our heritage...Guy Fawkes, Dick Turpin, I don't know where you stop with heritage, but all these things make the heritage of this city and there'll be other things, too.

When you describe it like that it seems to leave archaeology behind...

JH: Well, it does. Archaeology is just one element, even when it is at its widest definition. The other thing about heritage is that these are all things from the past, but we are also creating heritage all the time as well, we are creating the future's heritage. Heritage is what we have inherited from the past, which gives it the wider scope to include all of those things that I have just said and also that it is a continuous process.

There are some things perhaps that people would prefer not to see remain as one's heritage, so I think heritage is something we have to make decisions about and we make value judgements about. Heritage is what we value from the past, then, and that, you see, links in with questions about who should manage heritage, communities or professional heritage managers or both? That links very closely. You obviously need professional heritage managers, but you need communities because they are the ones who can tell you what is valuable to them, hence the importance of Local Lists.

When you are talking about the future of heritage, the other thing I thought about was the York Design Awards and we say this is heritage of the future. We have to make sure heritage of the future is good, and there is obviously a value judgement there. I think heritage is so much wider than archaeology. Archaeology is part of it, of course. Certainly local input is very important. You see this so much in planning, things come up to be demolished by a developer and you get people saying what is to be demolished is of importance. So, this is where the community comes in.

Notes

[1] The YAF was comprised of the York and North Yorkshire archaeologists and archaeologists from the University of York, the private sector and public sector.

Further Reading

Hodges, Andrew and Steve Watson. 2000. Community-based heritage management: A case study and agenda for research, *International Journal of Heritage Studies* 6 (3): 231–243.

NOTES ON CONTRIBUTORS

Dr John Carman is a University Research Fellow and Senior Lecturer in Heritage Valuation in the Institute of Archaeology and Antiquity, University of Birmingham. His research interests in heritage focus upon theorizing issues of the values given to archaeological material and issues of ownership. He is the author of *Valuing Ancient Things: Archaeology and Law* (Leicester University Press 1996), *Archaeology and Heritage: An Introduction* (Continuum 2002) and *Against Cultural Property: Archaeology, Heritage and Ownership* (Duckworth 2005), and co-editor of *Interpreting Archaeology: Finding Meaning in the Past* (Routledge 1995), *Managing Archaeology* (Routledge 1995), *World Heritage: Global Challenges, Local Solutions* (Archaeopress 2007) and *Heritage Studies: Methods and Approaches* (Routledge 2009). He is currently working on the co-authored *Archaeological Practice in Great Britain: A Heritage Handbook* with John Schofield and Paul Belford (One World Archaeology), and a co-edited volume with Robin Skeates and Carol McDavid (OUP).

Dr Keith Emerick is an Inspector of Ancient Monuments with English Heritage, based in the York office. He is also convenor of the Ancient Monument Inspectors group and was a member of the English Heritage "Conservation Principles" steering group. Keith researched part-time for a PhD at the University of York on the subject of conservation philosophy, with particular emphasis on the role of the heritage professional from the Ministry of Works to the present.

Dr Kalliopi Fouseki holds a BA in Archaeology from the University of Athens. After completing an MA in Cultural Heritage Studies at University College London, she conducted a PhD focusing on the management of in-situ archaeological museums. She has worked at the New Acropolis Museum (Athens), the archaeological museum of Ancient Olympia and the Museum of London. She also worked as a post-doctoral researcher on the *1807 Commemorated* project at the University of York. Currently she is working as a New Audience Advocate at the Science Museum of London.

Don Henson is Head of Education and Outreach at the Council for British Archaeology. He moved into heritage education, working in museums and galleries, after spending his earlier career researching the uses and manufacture of stone tools in the Neolithic and Early Bronze Age. His current interests include early medieval history and archaeology, landscape studies, the role of the past in the present, public engagement with the past, and the portrayal of archaeology and the past in film and television. He is also Chair of the World Archaeological Congress Public Education Committee and the Committee for Audio-Visual Education in Archaeology. His publications include *Archaeology in the English National Curriculum* (CBA 1997), *The English Elite in 1066: Gone but not forgotten* (Anglo-Saxon Books 2001), *Education and the Historic Environment* (Routledge 2004, co-editor) and *The Origins of the Anglo-Saxons* (Anglo-Saxon Books 2006). He also likes Japanese food and real ale!

Dr Jonathan Kenny began his career in social housing, working with communities in Plymouth, Poole and Cambridge. In 1995, Jonathan obtained his degree at the University of York and went on to gain a Masters in Archaeological Heritage Management in 1996. Jonathan then crossed the Pennines to begin his PhD at Lancaster University, on a case studentship funded by the ESRC and English Heritage. Here, he studied the role of standing heritage in the local, national and European identity negotiation process. On completion in 2001, Jonathan returned to work at the University of York with the Archaeology Data Service as a European projects officer and, after short spells with Internet Archaeology and the Parks & Gardens Access UK project, became Community Archaeologist for the Greater York Community Archaeology Project based at York Archaeological Trust in late 2006.

Dr Marjolijn S. M. Kok is senior researcher in landscape and heritage at the AAC/projectenbureau of the University of Amsterdam, where she also finished a PhD in offering sites in the wet low, low-lying parts of the landscape from the pre-and protohistoric period in the Western Netherlands. With Heleen van Londen, she co-authored the content of four e-learning modules on European heritage management within the Leonardo da Vinci programme "E-learning European Heritage." Her interests include archaeological theory and its practice, and gender/identity and heritage. She is a member of the research group "Heritage and Cultural Landscapes" at the Amsterdam Archaeological Centre.

Martin Newman is the Datasets Development Manager at the National Monuments Record, where he is responsible for the curation of information on heritage items in a range of English Heritage databases and GIS. Previously he was responsible for the Lead Role for supporting local Historic Environment Records. He is an Archaeological Sciences (BSc) graduate from Bradford University and a member of the Institute for Archaeologists. His publications include joint editorship of *Informing the Future of the Past* (2007), a co-authored chapter in *Archaeological Resource Management in the UK: An Introduction* (Hunter and Ralston 2006) and contributions to conference monographs originating from Computer Applications and Quantitative Methods in Archaeology (CAA) and Contemporary History and Archaeology in Theory (CHAT).

Dr Laurajane Smith is Reader of Heritage Studies at the University of York. From 2010, she will be based at the Australian National University, Canberra. Her research interests include the re-theorisation of ideas of heritage, the interplay between class and heritage, multiculturalism and heritage representation, heritage public policy and community heritage. She is author of *Archaeological Theory and the Politics of Cultural Heritage* (2004); *Uses of Heritage* (2006); co-author (with Emma Waterton) of *Heritage, Communities and Archaeology*; and editor of *Cultural Heritage: Critical Concepts in Media and Cultural Studies* (2007), and co-editor of *Intangible Heritage* (2009); *Issues in Management Archaeology* (1996); *Women in Archaeology: A Feminist Critique* (1993) and *Aboriginal Involvement in Parks and Protected Areas* (1992). She is also editor of the *International Journal of Heritage Studies.*

Dr Emma Waterton holds an RCUK Academic Fellowship in Heritage and Public History at the Research Institute for the Humanities, Keele University. Her research interests centre on examining the discursive constructions of "heritage" embedded in public policy, with emphasis on how dominant conceptualisations may be drawn upon and utilised to privilege the cultural and social experiences of particular social groups, while actively marginalising others. Further interests include considering community involvement in the management of heritage, exploring the divisions implied between tangible and intangible heritage, and understanding the role played by visual media. Publications include the co-authored volume (with Laurajane Smith) *Heritage, Communities and Archaeology* (Duckworth 2009) and the co-edited volume (with Steve Watson) *Culture, Heritage and Representations* (Ashgate forthcoming).